Ultimate Luxury
HOME PLANS COLLECTION

MW00442089

150 Timeless Designs

Award Winning Luxury Estate Homes from 1794 to 8088 square feet.

A DESIGNS DIRECT PUBLISHING BOOK

Presented by

Sater Design™ COLLECTION

Sater Design Collection, Inc.
The Center at the Springs
25241 Elementary Way, Suite 102, Bonita Springs, FL 34135

Dan F. Sater II - CEO and Author

Dan F. Sater II - Editor-in-Chief

Alma Mezzell - Senior Editor

Dana Lee Gibson - Art Director/Production Manager

Contributing Illustrators
Sean DiVincenzo/Lone Wolf Drafting & Design
CG Render Visualization Studio, Inc.
Concept Visualization · Digital Rendering
Marc Zsabo · Dave Jenkins

Contributing Photographers
C.J. Walker, Larry Taylor, M.E. Parker, Doug Thompson, Kim Sargent
Michael Lowry, Jerry Willis, Richard Leo Johnson, Herb Booth
Oscar Thompson, Tom Harper, Everett & Soule, Dan Forer, Naples Kenny,
Joseph Lapeyra, Bruce Schaeffer, Stein Photography, Giovanni Photography
Danielle Sater

Printed by: Toppan Printing Co., China
First Printing: September 2014
10 9 8 7 6 5 4 3 2 1

Contents

Custom Luxury Homes

We have had great success at marketing our pre-drawn luxury home plans. We are constantly surprised at the number of consumers that are unaware that we are first and foremost a custom design firm. With over thirty-five years experience and over 500 residential design awards, the Sater Group is one of the pre-eminent luxury residential design firms in the world. We have literally designed thousands of homes for clients all over the globe.

The following pictures are just a small sampling of some of those custom homes. We are able to create any home in any style and in any setting. Whether it's a modern pueblo, timeless Mediterranean or Old Florida Cottage we can create your desired look.

Please view these custom luxury homes and many others at our SaterGroup.com website. Feel free to call us for more information on how we can create your new custom dream home!

See this plan and more online at: www.saterdesign.com

See this plan and more online at: www.saterdesign.com

~ Any plan can be customized to meet your needs, find out how by calling 800-718-7526. ~

Alamosa

Dramatic rooflines, ornamented windows and a boldly articulated entry combine to create a striking façade. Inside, a barrel-vaulted foyer opens to spectacular views through to the cupola area to the grand solana. Soaring coffered and curved beamed ceilings and pre-classical marble columns define the varied spaces of the public realm. A two-sided fireplace warms the formal rooms as well as the secluded study.

A view-oriented design, windows line the rear perimeter of the home creating a seamless connection with the outdoors. Retreating glass walls open the leisure room to the solana and lanai, creating a flexible space for every occasion. The gourmet-caliber kitchen enjoys wide-open views of the casual living areas, defined not by walls, but stone floors and coffered ceilings.

Away from the public rooms, the entire left wing of the home is dedicated to the private master retreat. A private garden, spacious walk-in closet, morning kitchen and access to the lanai create a spa-like retreat. On the upper level, a winding balcony hall connects a loft arena, wet bar, exercise room and media room with a spacious guest suite.

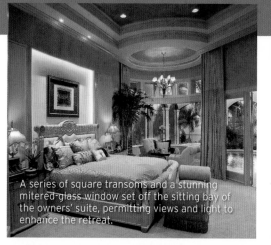

A series of square transoms and a stunning mitered-glass window set off the sitting bay of the owners' suite, permitting views and light to enhance the retreat.

Dramatic dining with barrel vaulted ceiling and recessed, built-in server.

Stone floors and coffered ceilings define the wide-open spaces of the casual living area. An arching doorway secludes a convenient butler's pantry that links the food-preparation area to a wet bar and wine cellar.

Photographed home may have been modified from the original construction documents.

Decorative pillars and columns demonstrate the influence of the ancient Greeks in this magnificent master bath, while a luxurious whirlpool tub offers a very modern indulgence.

Carved Crema Maya stone columns articulate the boundaries of the formal dining room, enhanced by a barrel-vaulted ceiling. The cupola shelters a sitting space in front of the two-story fireplace, while ornate floriated capitals repeat the classical patterns of the surround and frieze.

Laden in stone, the plein air solana extends the livability of the leisure room and includes a corner fireplace and an alfresco kitchen.

The pampering guest bedroom features a full-bath, walk-in closet and glass doors that open to the side courtyard.

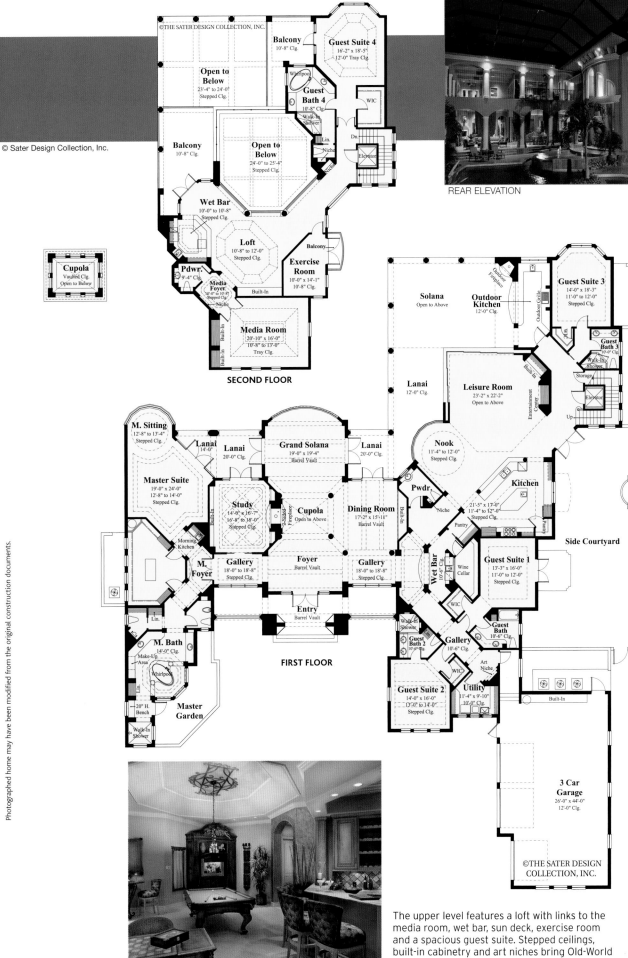

SECOND FLOOR

Balcony
10'-8" Clg.

Guest Suite 4
16'-2" x 18'-5"
12'-0" Tray Clg.

Open to Below
23'-4" to 24'-0"
Stepped Clg.

Guest Bath 4
10'-8" Clg.
Walk-In Shower

WIC

Balcony
10'-8" Clg.

Open to Below
24'-0" to 25'-4"
Stepped Clg.

Niche

Dn.

Elevator

Wet Bar
10'-0" to 10'-8"
Stepped Clg.

Loft
10'-8" x 12'-0"
Stepped Clg.

Balcony

Exercise Room
10'-0" x 14'-1"
10'-8" Clg.

Pdwr.
9'-4" Clg.

Media Foyer
10'-0" to 10'-8"
Stepped Clg.
Niche

Built-In

Media Room
20'-10" x 16'-0"
10'-8" to 13'-0"
Tray Clg.

Built-In

Cupola
Vaulted Clg.
Open to Below

REAR ELEVATION

FIRST FLOOR

M. Sitting
12'-8" to 13'-4"
Stepped Clg.

Lanai
14'-0"

Lanai
20'-0" Clg.

Grand Solana
19'-0" x 19'-4"
Barrel Vault

Lanai
20'-0" Clg.

Master Suite
19'-0" x 24'-0"
12'-8" to 14'-0"
Stepped Clg.

Study
14'-2" x 16'-7"
16'-8" to 18'-0"
Stepped Clg.

Cupola
Open to Above

Dining Room
17'-2" x 15'-11"
Barrel Vault

Pwdr.

Niche

Nook
11'-4" x 12'-0"
Stepped Clg.

Solana
Open to Above

Outdoor Fireplace

Outdoor Kitchen
12'-0" Clg.

Outdoor Grille

Guest Suite 3
14'-0" x 18'-3"
11'-0" to 12'-0"
Stepped Clg.

Lanai
12'-0" Clg.

Leisure Room
23'-2" x 22'-2"
Open to Above

Entertainment Center

Guest Bath 3
10'-0" Clg.
Walk-In Shower

Storage

Elevator

Up

Kitchen
21'-5" x 17'-0"
11'-4" to 12'-0"
Stepped Clg.

Morning Kitchen

M. Foyer

Gallery
18'-0" to 18'-8"
Stepped Clg.

Foyer
Barrel Vault

Gallery
18'-0" to 18'-8"
Stepped Clg.

Wet Bar
10'-6" Clg.

Wine Cellar

Pantry

Pantry

Guest Suite 1
13'-3" x 16'-0"
11'-0" to 12'-0"
Stepped Clg.

WIC

Side Courtyard

Entry
Barrel Vault

Walk-In Shower

Guest Bath 2
10'-6" Clg.

Gallery
10'-6" Clg.

Guest Bath
10'-6" Clg.

M. Bath
14'-0" Clg.

Make-Up Area

Whirlpool

Lin.

Master Garden

20" H. Bench

Walk-In Shower

Guest Suite 2
14'-0" x 16'-0"
13'-0" to 14'-0"
Stepped Clg.

WIC

Art Niche

Utility
11'-4" x 9'-10"
10'-0" Clg.

Built-In

3 Car Garage
26'-0" x 44'-0"
12'-0" Clg.

SPECIFICATIONS:

Bedrooms: **5**

Full Baths: **5**

Half Baths: **2**

Width: **118' 0"**

Depth: **147' 10"**

1ST Floor: **6122** *sf*

2ND Floor: **1966** *sf*

Total Living: **8088** *sf*

Foundation: **Slab**

Exterior Wall: **8" Block**

PLAN PRICING:

Vellum & PDF - **$8088**

CAD - **$13750**

PLAN NUMBER:

6940

PLAN NAME:

Alamosa

The upper level features a loft with links to the media room, wet bar, sun deck, exercise room and a spacious guest suite. Stepped ceilings, built-in cabinetry and art niches bring Old-World craftsmanship to the modern spaces.

Fiorentino

The graceful curves of rotundas, dramatically changing roof pitches and architectural enhancements like half columns, corbels, and an arbor delight the eye with their gentle movement. Guests know they've arrived as they step up to the entry terrace and are embraced by the home's elegant entry. The gentle curve of the elegant staircase that sweeps upward in a rotunda, the curved windows in the living room and breakfast nook, and the graceful arc of a wet bar and wine room heighten the visual appeal of this plan. Large windows look longingly onto a loggia, where sunlight and shadow play hide and seek between columns. The home hugs this outdoor space, offering different perspectives and experiences from each room. Architectural lighting at night creates an alluring ambience that beckons to be indulged, to be experienced. A media room is the ultimate retreat for the owners of the home and the guests enjoying the privacy of two second floor guest suites. Seclusion is found in the loft overlooking the dining room and the deck above the loggia-an ideal vantage point for stargazing. The master suite sets the stage for serene interlude, beginning with the elevated garden tub that looks through three arched windows onto a privacy garden and culminating in the bedroom's sitting area overlooking the loggia-meant to be enjoyed with a refreshing beverage from the suite's morning kitchen.

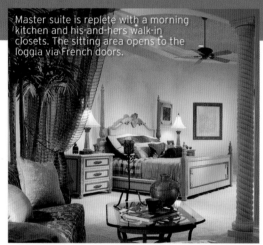

Master suite is replete with a morning kitchen and his-and-hers walk-in closets. The sitting area opens to the loggia via French doors.

Featuring a corner fireplace, built-in entertainment center, exposed beam ceiling and retreating glass walls that open to the loggia.

Ample space for a professional-grade hooded range, double sinks and spacious dual pantries.

Photographed home may have been modified from the original construction documents.

This Italianate-style rotunda staircase, with its sleek balustrade, vertical windows, mile-high exposed-beam ceiling and smooth curves and arches appears to break the bonds of earth and disappear into the heavens.

Bright and airy breakfast nook with mitered glass overlooks loggia and pool beyond.

The loft overlooking the living room and dining room with built-in server in the background.

Rich accents in wood bring an aura of Old-World grace and sophistication to a private study adjacent to the formal living room.

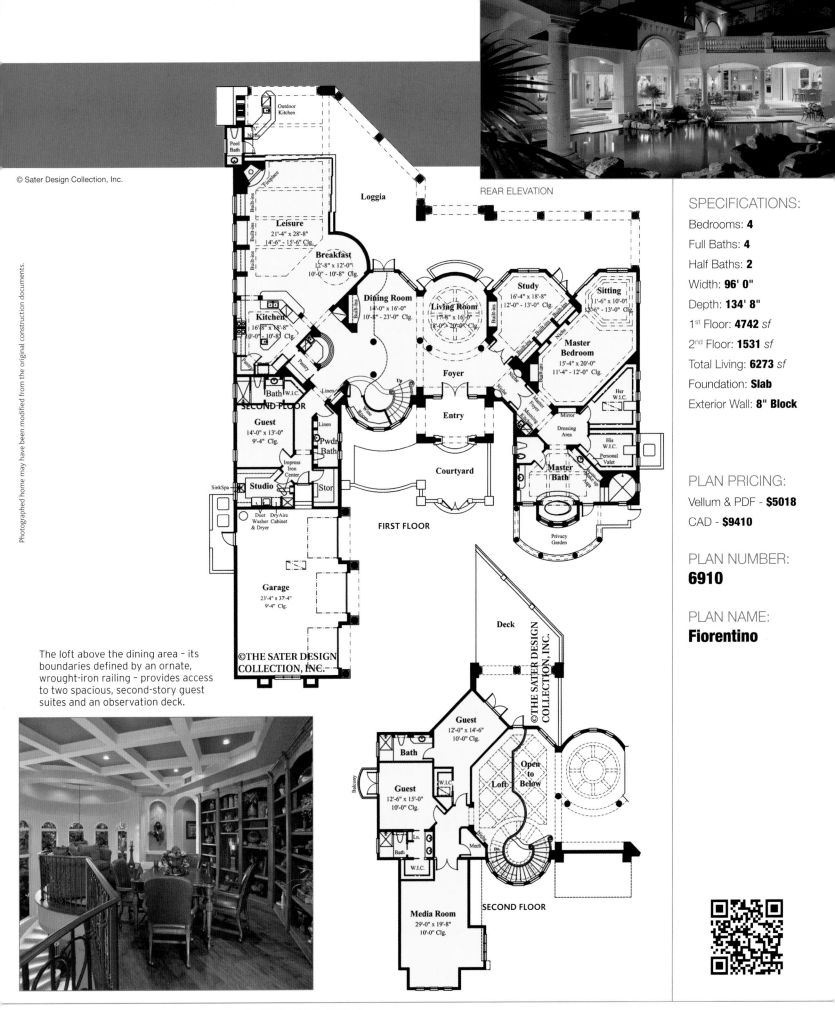

© Sater Design Collection, Inc.

REAR ELEVATION

Leisure
21'-4" x 28'-8"
14'-6" - 15'-6" Clg.

Breakfast
12'-8" x 12'-0"
10'-0" - 10'-8" Clg.

Loggia

Dining Room
14'-0" x 16'-0"
10'-8" - 23'-0" Clg.

Living Room
17'-8" x 16'-0"
18'-0" - 20'-0" Clg.

Study
16'-4" x 18'-8"
12'-0" - 13'-0" Clg.

Sitting
11'-6" x 10'-0"
12'-6" - 13'-0" Clg.

Kitchen
16'-8" x 18'-8"
10'-0" - 10'-8" Clg.

Master Bedroom
15'-4" x 20'-0"
11'-4" - 12'-0" Clg.

Foyer

Her W.I.C.

SECOND FLOOR

Bath W.I.C.

Guest
14'-0" x 13'-0"
9'-4" Clg.

Linen

Pwdr Bath

Entry

Mirror

Dressing Area

His W.I.C.

Personal Valet

Impress Iron Center

Courtyard

Master Bath

SinkSpa

Studio

Stor

Duct Dry Air
Washer Cabinet
& Dryer

FIRST FLOOR

Privacy Garden

Garage
23'-4" x 37'-4"
9'-4" Clg.

©THE SATER DESIGN COLLECTION, INC.

The loft above the dining area – its boundaries defined by an ornate, wrought-iron railing – provides access to two spacious, second-story guest suites and an observation deck.

Deck

Guest
12'-0" x 14'-6"
10'-0" Clg.

©THE SATER DESIGN COLLECTION, INC.

Bath

Guest
12'-6" x 15'-0"
10'-0" Clg.

W.I.C.

Balcony

Loft

Open to Below

Ln.

Bath

Niche

Mech

W.I.C.

Media Room
29'-0" x 19'-8"
10'-0" Clg.

SECOND FLOOR

SPECIFICATIONS:

Bedrooms: **4**

Full Baths: **4**

Half Baths: **2**

Width: **96' 0"**

Depth: **134' 8"**

1st Floor: **4742** sf

2nd Floor: **1531** sf

Total Living: **6273** sf

Foundation: **Slab**

Exterior Wall: **8" Block**

PLAN PRICING:

Vellum & PDF - **$5018**

CAD - **$9410**

PLAN NUMBER:

6910

PLAN NAME:

Fiorentino

Padova

The home exemplifies casual elegance whether from it's inviting porte-cochere, to it's round turreted stair tower, or to it's open view oriented living spaces. No space in this home disappoints. Crafted in a transitional Spanish-Mediterranean flair, the Padova's barrel tiled hip rooflines with cast stone accents, makes a stunning statement of luxury.

The grand two story foyer and living room is sure to make a lasting impression. The overlooking loft can be used for a quiet reading library or fun entertaining. This is accessed by a stunning circular staircase that overlooks the barel vaulted dining room.

Rounding out the second floor is a theater room, guest suite, viewing deck and bunk room for visiting grandchildren.

Just as the Padova's formal areas impress, the informal areas bring relaxation to it's owners and guests alike. The gourmet kitchen with walk-in pantry and pass-thru bar are ideally located in the middle of both spaces. Perfect for entertaining large groups or family.

The master suite is both roomy and intimate and includes a bay windowed sitting area and stepped tray ceiling.

Study with rich wood built-in bookshelves and stepped ceiling.

The kitchen features a walk-in pantry, island counter and raised serving counter.

The beautiful carved limestone fireplace surround is the centerpiece of the home's living room. A floor to ceiling curved glass wall of segmented windows brings the outdoors in.

The home's rear area is as dramatic as the front. Outdoor kitchen is great for entertaining.

Wrought Iron railings overlooking the dining room and stair vestibule below. The elegant circular stairway is highlighted by the unique inverted dome ceiling above.

The striking wrought iron entry doors and surround set the stage for the barrel vaulted foyer and two-story living room beyond, which is accented by a carved stone fireplace.

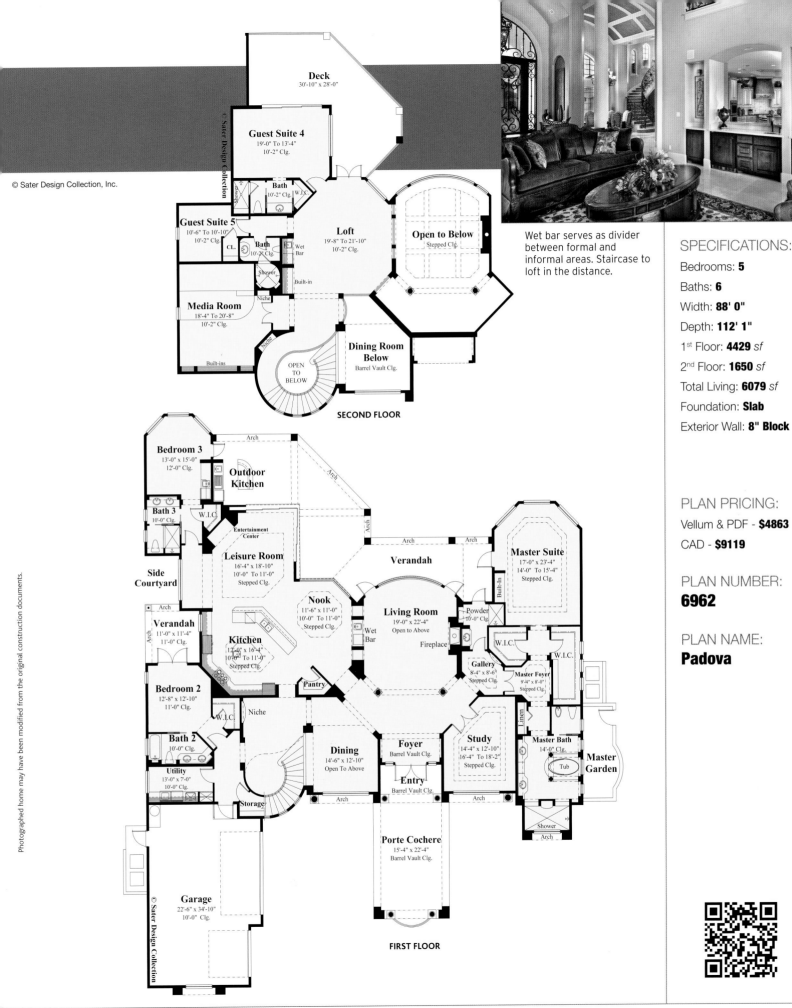

© Sater Design Collection, Inc.

SECOND FLOOR

Deck
30'-10" x 28'-0"

Guest Suite 4
19'-0" To 13'-4"
10'-2" Clg.

Bath
10'-2" Clg.

W.I.C.

Guest Suite 5
10'-6" To 10'-10"
10'-2" Clg.

Bath
10'-2" Clg.

Loft
19'-8" To 21'-10"
10'-2" Clg.

Wet Bar

Built-in

Open to Below
Stepped Clg.

Shower

Niche

Media Room
18'-4" To 20'-8"
10'-2" Clg.

Built-ins

OPEN TO BELOW

Dining Room Below
Barrel Vault Clg.

Wet bar serves as divider between formal and informal areas. Staircase to loft in the distance.

FIRST FLOOR

Bedroom 3
13'-0" x 15'-0"
12'-0" Clg.

Arch

Outdoor Kitchen

W.I.C.

Bath 3
10'-0" Clg.

Entertainment Center

Leisure Room
16'-4" x 18'-10"
10'-0" To 11'-0"
Stepped Clg.

Side Courtyard

Verandah
11'-0" x 11'-4"
11'-0" Clg.

Arch

Kitchen
12'-0" x 16'-4"
10'-0" To 11'-0"
Stepped Clg.

Nook
11'-6" x 11'-0"
10'-0" To 11'-0"
Stepped Clg.

Living Room
19'-0" x 22'-4"
Open to Above

Wet Bar

Fireplace

Verandah

Master Suite
17'-0" x 23'-4"
14'-0" To 15'-4"
Stepped Clg.

Built-In

Powder
10'-0" Clg.

W.I.C.

W.I.C.

Master Foyer
9'-4" x 8'-0"
Stepped Clg.

Gallery
8'-4" x 8'-6"
Stepped Clg.

Pantry

Bedroom 2
12'-8" x 12'-10"
11'-0" Clg.

W.I.C.

Niche

Bath 2
10'-0" Clg.

Utility
13'-0" x 7'-0"
10'-0" Clg.

Storage

Dining
14'-6" x 12'-10"
Open To Above

Foyer
Barrel Vault Clg.

Study
14'-4" x 12'-10"
16'-4" To 18'-2"
Stepped Clg.

Linen

Master Bath
14'-0" Clg.

Tub

Master Garden

Entry
Barrel Vault Clg.

Shower

Arch

Porte Cochere
15'-4" x 22'-4"
Barrel Vault Clg.

Garage
22'-6" x 34'-10"
10'-0" Clg.

© Sater Design Collection

SPECIFICATIONS:

Bedrooms: **5**

Baths: **6**

Width: **88' 0"**

Depth: **112' 1"**

1st Floor: **4429** sf

2nd Floor: **1650** sf

Total Living: **6079** sf

Foundation: **Slab**

Exterior Wall: **8" Block**

PLAN PRICING:

Vellum & PDF - **$4863**

CAD - **$9119**

PLAN NUMBER:
6962

PLAN NAME:
Padova

Prima Porta

Mediterranean elements of pastoral wood and wrought iron create an Old-World atmosphere that is juxtaposed with state-of-the-art appliances and new-world amenities.

The entry portico is the first expression of the Mediterranean atmosphere that infuses the interior, with a quoin surround of the main entry and repeating arches throughout. Once inside, in addition to recurring arches, stepped ceilings accented with wood beams are also found in many rooms.

Entertaining on any scale is accomplished with minimal effort with a spacious, gourmet kitchen, an additional outdoor kitchen, luxurious dining room, convenient butler's pantry, two fireplaces and an elegant wet bar. Outdoor spaces coax inhabitants and guests alike, out to enjoy the solana and expansive covered lanai. Guests invited to spend the night will be perfectly at home in three guest suites complete with full baths and walk-in closets.

An opulent master retreat begins with a magnificent foyer and continues with a spacious bedroom and walk-in closet with a built-in island. The owners' lavish bath features dual vanities, a curved walk-in shower, make up counter, bench and a centrally located tub.

Convenient built-ins anticipate the needs of residents throughout the home with custom shelving, a variety of storage spaces, elegant art niches and a desk located off of the kitchen.

This gourmet kitchen is awash in elegant appointments and state-of-the-art amenities. Contrast is provided by Mediterranean-inspired details including the wood-beamed ceiling.

A wood-beamed, stepped ceiling joins the fireplace in emanating inviting warmth. Arch forms surround the fireplace, with a display niche on both sides and an arched mirror atop the intricate mantel.

Serene tranquility calls from every room of the house, beckoning for enjoyment of the covered lanai, cozy sitting areas, outdoor fireplace, pool and spa. A breath of fresh air is only a step away, as most rooms throughout feature French doors and retreating glass walls to access the lanai.

Elegance abounds in this spacious, elongated master suite, reflected in an arched bed niche, built-in shelves, a stepped ceiling and French doors to the lanai.

The sumptuous spa tub is the centerpiece of this unmistakably indulgent master bath crowned with a stepped ceiling, accented with moldings.

The leisure room is open to the kitchen with a convenient eating bar dividing the space. This arrangement allows interaction and both rooms to enjoy breezes from the lanai. The deep, wood-beamed ceiling detail is echoed from the kitchen.

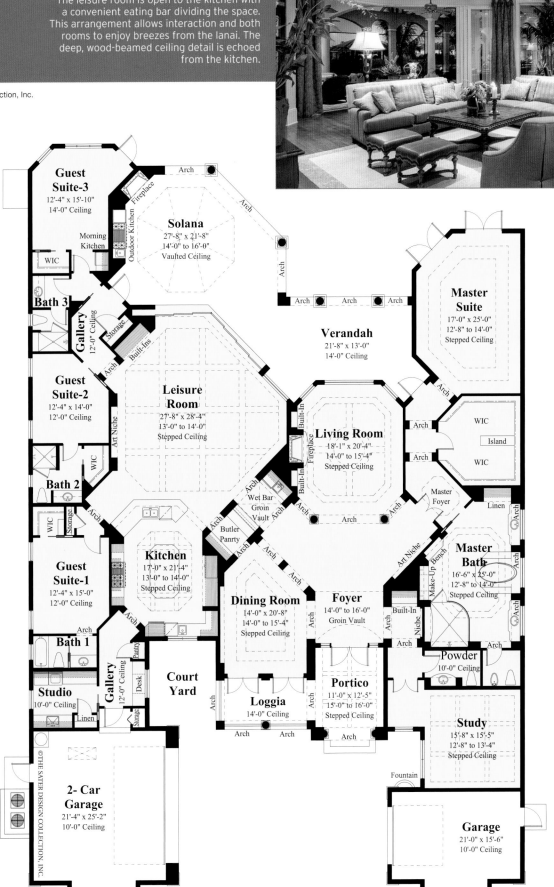

Guest Suite-3
12'-4" x 15'-10"
14'-0" Ceiling

Morning Kitchen

WIC

Bath 3

Gallery 12'-0" Ceiling

Guest Suite-2
12'-4" x 14'-0"
12'-0" Ceiling

Art Niche

WIC

Bath 2

WIC

Storage

Guest Suite-1
12'-4" x 15'-0"
12'-0" Ceiling

Bath 1

Gallery 12'-0" Ceiling

Desk

Studio
10'-0" Ceiling

Linen

Storage

2- Car Garage
21'-4" x 25'-2"
10'-0" Ceiling

Outdoor Kitchen

Fireplace

Arch

Solana
27'-8" x 21'-8"
14'-0" to 16'-0"
Vaulted Ceiling

Arch

Arch

Built-Ins

Storage

Leisure Room
27'-8" x 28'-4"
13'-0" to 14'-0"
Stepped Ceiling

Kitchen
17'-0" x 21'-4"
13'-0" to 14'-0"
Stepped Ceiling

Pantry

Butler Pantry

Wet Bar Groin Vault

Court Yard

Dining Room
14'-0" x 20'-8"
14'-0" to 15'-4"
Stepped Ceiling

Loggia
14'-0" Ceiling

Arch Arch

Arch Arch Arch

Verandah
21'-8" x 13'-0"
14'-0" Ceiling

Built-In

Fireplace

Built-In

Living Room
18'-1" x 20'-4"
14'-0" to 15'-4"
Stepped Ceiling

Arch Arch

Foyer
14'-0" to 16'-0"
Groin Vault

Portico
11'-0" x 12'-5"
15'-0" to 16'-0"
Stepped Ceiling

Arch

Master Suite
17'-0" x 25'-0"
12'-8" to 14'-0"
Stepped Ceiling

Arch

WIC

Island

WIC

Arch

Master Foyer

Linen

Make-Up Bench

Art Niche

Master Bath
16'-6" x 25'-0"
12'-8" to 14'-0"
Stepped Ceiling

Built-In

Niche

Arch

Arch

Powder
10'-0" Ceiling

Study
15'-8" x 15'-5"
12'-8" to 13'-4"
Stepped Ceiling

Fountain

Garage
21'-0" x 15'-6"
10'-0" Ceiling

SPECIFICATIONS:

Bedrooms: **4**

Baths: **4½**

Width: **80' 0"**

Depth: **118' 0"**

1st Floor: **5224** sf

Total Living: **5224** sf

Foundation: **Slab**

Exterior Wall: **8" Block**

PLAN PRICING:

Vellum & PDF - **$4179**

CAD - **$7836**

PLAN NUMBER:

6955

PLAN NAME:

Prima Porta

Gabriella

This Mediterranean inspired estate home reflects the best in elegant yet casual living. It's turreted and varied tiled rooflines recall Old World imagery. One is greeted by the home's combined great room and dining room upon entering. This room's soaring coffered ceiling space with pocketing sliders that open onto the home's outdoor veranda brings in plenty of natural light. A pleasant surprise is the overlooking Juliet's balcony from the loft above. Looking out upon the veranda and its outdoor fireplace and kitchen area is the home's well appointed kitchen.

The master wing with it's spacious master suite that incorporates a morning kitchen, as well as sitting room that overlooks the veranda and outdoors. The master bath features his and her closets and vanities, island whirlpool tub and walk-in shower.

The main level is rounded out with home office or optional 6th bedroom, powder bath, utility room and a detached guest cabana suite.

Upstairs is an expansive loft with three adjoining bedrooms each with it's own bath. Perfect for children or guests.

It is easy to see why Sater Design's "Gabriella" home plan is a family favorite.

Tray ceilings and bed niche accentuates the master suite. The sitting area is accessed through the stone columned archway and affords panoramic views of the pool and beyond.

The wet bar is conveniently located between the dining room and kitchen for ease of entertaining.

The granite countered island with guest seating is the centerpiece of this gourmet kitchen, which overlooks the great room beyond.

Photographed home may have been modified from the original construction documents.

The great room is highlighted by arched built-in TV niche and bookshelves. The full-sized over mirror resonates the homes ambiance.

Outdoor living at its finest is accommodated by the spacious veranda complete with outdoor fireplace and kitchen .

Imagine being serenaded from the piano located in the loft above adjacent to the Juliet's balcony, which overlooks the two-story great room below. The large seating area overlooks the veranda via tall pocketing sliding glass doors and transom above.

Stunning island tub in the master bath. Arches lead to walk-in shower beyond.

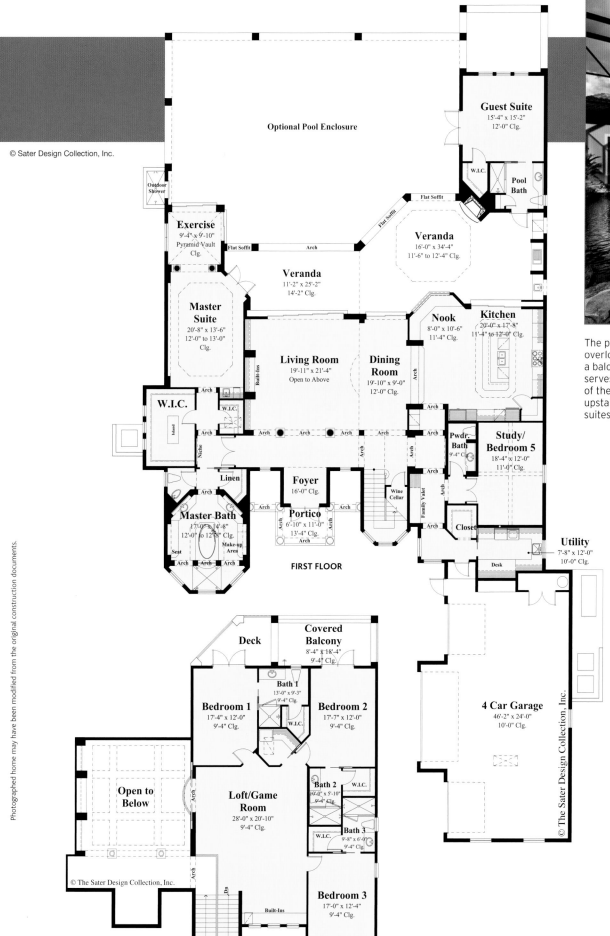

© Sater Design Collection, Inc.

Optional Pool Enclosure

Guest Suite
15'-4" x 15'-2"
12'-0" Clg.

W.I.C.

Pool Bath

Outdoor Shower

Exercise
9'-4" x 9'-10"
Pyramid Vault Clg.

Flat Soffit

Flat Soffit

Flat Soffit

Arch

Veranda
16'-0" x 34'-4"
11'-6" to 12'-4" Clg.

Veranda
11'-2" x 25'-2"
14'-2" Clg.

Master Suite
20'-8" x 13'-6"
12'-0" to 13'-0" Clg.

Nook
8'-0" x 10'-6"
11'-4" Clg.

Kitchen
20'-0" x 17'-8"
11'-4" to 12'-0" Clg.

Living Room
19'-11" x 21'-4"
Open to Above

Dining Room
19'-10" x 9'-0"
12'-0" Clg.

Built-Ins

Arch

Arch

W.I.C.

Island

Arch

Arch

Arch

Arch

Arch

Arch

Niche

Arch

Linen

Foyer
16'-0" Clg.

Wine Cellar

Family Valet

Pwdr. Bath
9'-4" Clg.

Study/ Bedroom 5
18'-4" x 12'-0"
11'-0" Clg.

Master Bath
17'-4" x 14'-8"
12'-0" to 12'-8" Clg.

Seat

Make-up Area

Portico
6'-10" x 11'-0"
13'-4" Clg.

Arch

Arch

Arch

Arch

Arch

Closet

Utility
7'-8" x 12'-0"
10'-0" Clg.

Desk

FIRST FLOOR

The pool is overlooked by a balcony that serves two of the homes upstairs guest suites.

Deck

Covered Balcony
8'-4" x 18'-4"
9'-4" Clg.

Bath 1
13'-0" x 9'-3"
9'-4" Clg.

Bedroom 1
17'-4" x 12'-0"
9'-4" Clg.

Bedroom 2
17'-7" x 12'-0"
9'-4" Clg.

W.I.C.

4 Car Garage
46'-2" x 24'-0"
10'-0" Clg.

Open to Below

Loft/Game Room
28'-0" x 20'-10"
9'-4" Clg.

Arch

Bath 2
10'-0" x 5'-10"
9'-4" Clg.

W.I.C.

Bath 3
9'-8" x 6'-0"
9'-4" Clg.

W.I.C.

© The Sater Design Collection, Inc.

Arch

Dn

Built-Ins

Bedroom 3
17'-0" x 12'-4"
9'-4" Clg.

SECOND FLOOR

© The Sater Design Collection, Inc.

SPECIFICATIONS:

Bedrooms: **6**

Baths: **5½**

Width: **80' 4"**

Depth: **150' 0"**

1st Floor: **3304** *sf*

Cabana: **398** *sf*

2nd Floor: **1612** *sf*

Total Living: **5314** *sf*

Foundation: **Slab**

Exterior Wall: **8" Block**

PLAN PRICING:

Vellum & PDF - **$4251**

CAD - **$7971**

PLAN NUMBER:

6961

PLAN NAME:

Gabriella

Not available for construction in Lee or Collier Counties, Florida.

Cordillera

A desire to create a home that paid homage to Palm Beach's great Spanish-influenced villas while at the same time embracing contemporary design ideas and technologies was the inspiration behind Dan Sater's award-winning design Cordillera. The recipient of both a 2006 Aurora and FAIBD award, Cordillera incorporates modern amenities and elements such as corner-less disappearing sliding-glass walls, clubrooms, outdoor living spaces and full-house automation.

This villa-style plan opens traditionally boxed spaces to satisfying views of the landscape. The vaulted foyer opens through the front gallery to the formal core of the home: a series of three view-oriented rooms designed to encourage intimate gatherings. To the right of the home, the casual living zone incorporates a spacious leisure room that links with a nook and kitchen. Upstairs, a balcony bridge connects a game room, pub and home theater with two guest suites.

Aurora Awards
The 2006 Aurora Awards Winner
Custom Home Over $3,000,000

FAIBD 56th Annual Design Competition
First Place for Custom Luxury 6,500 square feet and above.

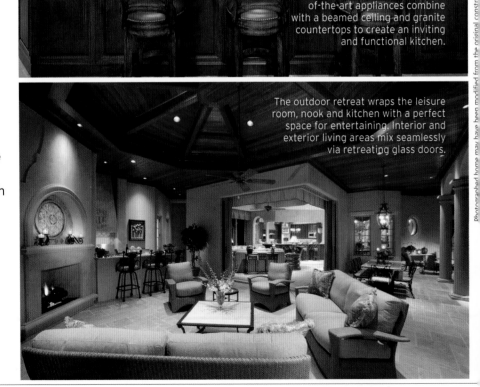

Multiple workstations and state-of-the-art appliances combine with a beamed ceiling and granite countertops to create an inviting and functional kitchen.

The outdoor retreat wraps the leisure room, nook and kitchen with a perfect space for entertaining. Interior and exterior living areas mix seamlessly via retreating glass doors.

Photographed home may have been modified from the original construction documents.

Double-paneled entry doors mirror the symmetry of the intricately carved fireplace and stone surround at the formal center of the home. A second-level balcony, with custom wrought iron detailing, overlooks the area.

Shapely columns and arches create a fluid boundary between the pool deck and solana, and shelter the outside living area from the midday sun.

Stuccoed soffits with corbel brackets accentuate Mediterranean styling.

The grand living room with stunning stone fireplace. Straight ahead of the main entry, a series of three French doors open to a spectacular pool setting, offering brilliant views both day and night.

Retreating glass doors provide a seamless connection from the leisure room to the solana, lanai and courtyard. High-end electronics integrated into the design provide surround-sound, advanced security systems and soft, subtle lighting.

The club room's media alcove allows for a full theater experience for some while others can look on while playing cards or shooting pool.

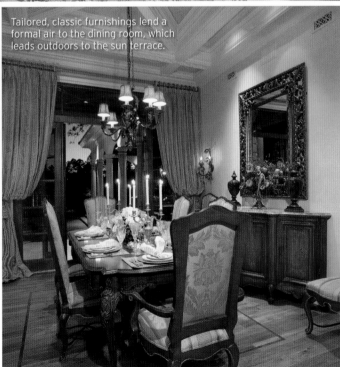

Tailored, classic furnishings lend a formal air to the dining room, which leads outdoors to the sun terrace.

Palm trees and beds of poppy-red geraniums in cut-stone planters border the freshwater lap pool, designed to extend the eye out to the lake beyond. An extensive sun terrace connects the outdoor living areas with a solana, spa and outdoor kitchen.

Framed by twin Tuscan columns, a sculpted Persian-red marble tub surround subdues the grand scale of the master bath. Past the tall muntin window and fanlight is a glimpse of the private garden.

Adjacent to the master wing, the study easily converts to a work space, reading room or home office. Double doors open to the sun terrace and pool, offering an easy transition from work to play.

Curved moldings, a coffered ceiling and a flattened arch lend dimension, depth and texture to the room, which leads outside to the sun terrace, pool and spa.

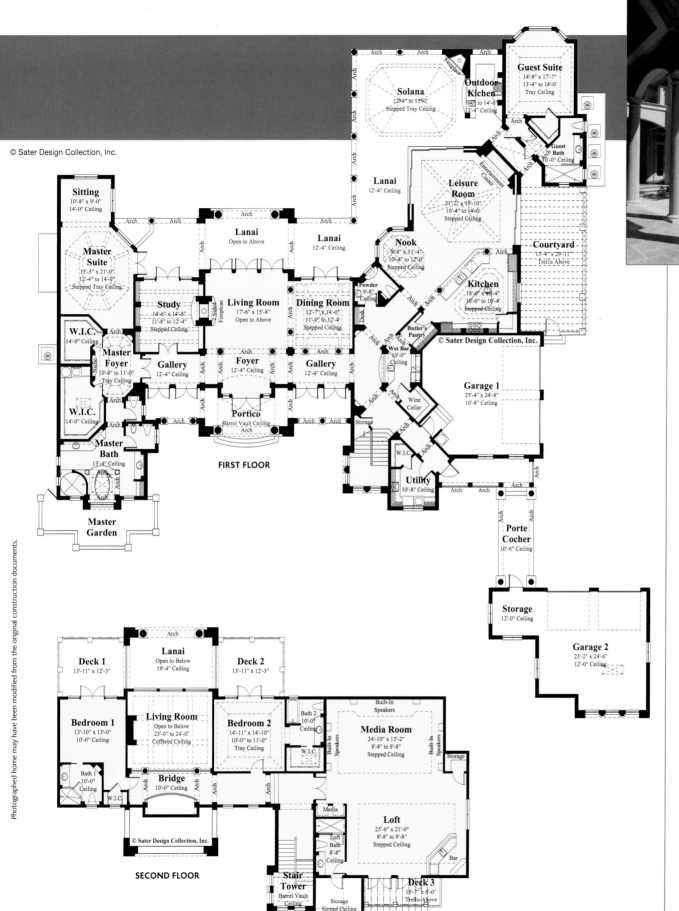

FIRST FLOOR

Sitting
10'-8" x 9'-0"
14'-0" Ceiling

Master Suite
15'-5" x 21'-0"
12'-4" to 14'-0"
Stepped Tray Ceiling

W.I.C.
14'-0" Ceiling

Master Foyer
10'-0" to 11'-0"
Tray Ceiling

W.I.C.
14'-0" Ceiling

Master Bath
13'-4" Ceiling

Master Garden

Study
14'-6" x 14'-8"
11'-8" to 12'-4"
Stepped Ceiling

Living Room
17'-6" x 15'-8"
Open to Above

Dining Room
12'-7" x 14'-0"
11'-0" to 12'-4"
Stepped Ceiling

Gallery
12'-4" Ceiling

Foyer
12'-4" Ceiling

Gallery
12'-4" Ceiling

Portico
Barrel Vault Ceiling
Arch

Lanai
Open to Above

Lanai
12'-4" Ceiling

Lanai
12'-4" Ceiling

Solana
12'-4" x 15'-0"
Stepped Tray Ceiling

Outdoor Kitchen
7'-0" to 14'-6"
12'-4" Ceiling

Guest Suite
14'-8" x 17'-7"
13'-4" to 14'-0"
Tray Ceiling

Guest Bath
10'-0" Ceiling

Leisure Room
21'-2" x 19'-0"
10'-4" to 14'-0"
Stepped Ceiling

Nook
9'-8" x 11'-4"
10'-4" to 12'-0"
Stepped Ceiling

Kitchen
18'-0" x 10'-4"
10'-0" to 10'-4"
Stepped Ceiling

Powder
9'-8" Ceiling

Butler's Pantry

Wet Bar
10'-0" Ceiling

Wine Cellar

Courtyard
13'-4" x 29'-11"
Trellis Above

Garage 1
25'-4" x 24'-8"
10'-8" Ceiling

Utility
10'-8" Ceiling

Storage

W.I.C.

Porte Cocher
10'-6" Ceiling

Storage
12'-0" Ceiling

Garage 2
23'-2" x 24'-6"
12'-0" Ceiling

© Sater Design Collection, Inc.

SECOND FLOOR

Deck 1
13'-11" x 12'-3"

Bedroom 1
13'-10" x 13'-0"
10'-0" Ceiling

Bath 1
10'-0" Ceiling

Living Room
Open to Below
23'-0" to 24'-0"
Coffered Ceiling

Lanai
Open to Below
19'-4" Ceiling

Deck 2
13'-11" x 12'-3"

Bedroom 2
14'-11" x 14'-10"
10'-0" to 11'-0"
Tray Ceiling

W.I.C.

Bath 2
10'-0" Ceiling

Bridge
10'-0" Ceiling

Media Room
24'-10" x 15'-2"
8'-8" to 9'-8"
Stepped Ceiling

Built-In Speakers

Storage

Media

Loft Bath
8'-8" Ceiling

Loft
25'-6" x 21'-0"
8'-8" to 9'-8"
Stepped Ceiling

Bar

Stair Tower
Barrel Vault Ceiling

Storage
Sloped Ceiling

Deck 3
15'-7" x 6'-0"
Trellis Above

© Sater Design Collection, Inc.

A large central gable enhanced with corbels and tall pilasters anchors the space and underscores the richly textured architectural themes of the home.

SPECIFICATIONS:

Bedrooms: **4**

Baths: **5½**

Width: **126' 0"**

Depth: **141' 11"**

1st Floor: **4410** *sf*

2nd Floor: **2274** *sf*

Total Living: **6684** *sf*

Foundation: **Slab**

Exterior Wall: **2x6 Wood**

PLAN PRICING:

Vellum & PDF - **$6684**

CAD - **$11363**

PLAN NUMBER:

6953

PLAN NAME:

Cordillera

Villa Sabina

Stone arches, corbels and cornice details accentuate the façade of this Italian-inspired home, which includes a magnificent limestone-sheathed tower and cupola. The two-story foyer, living and dining rooms invite the outdoors inside through myriad windows and glass-fronted doors. Astute architectural detailing, including several unique ceiling applications, punctuates the design premise of the home.

To the right of the foyer, a stunning staircase ascends to the second-floor loft and guest suites. The kitchen, café and family room open onto an expansive verandah with retreating glass walls. The study and master retreat are adjacent to the foyer, with easy access to the verandah.

On the optional lower level, a fully equipped kitchen and family room transition to the loggia and pool area. The rear façade is a profusion of columns, arches and a balustrade-enhanced loggia, which emphasizes the connection between the interior and outside.

The centerpiece of the living room is the wall of elongated windows and corresponding arched transoms, which offer incredible lake views through an exterior arched opening.

Dual reflections of his-and-hers vanities, with their custom milled cabinetry, are captured in separate mirrors, adding depth to the room.

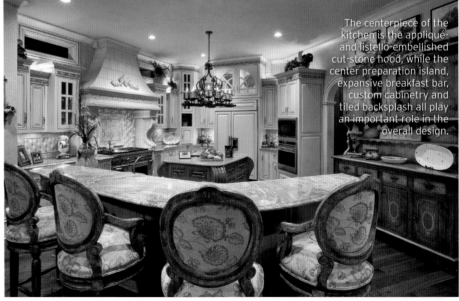

The centerpiece of the kitchen is the appliqué- and listello-embellished cut-stone hood, while the center preparation island, expansive breakfast bar, custom cabinetry and tiled backsplash all play an important role in the overall design.

Photographed home may have been modified from the original construction documents.

Tall, arched windows gradually decrease in size as the spiral staircase ascends to the second floor. Scrolled, wrought-iron grillwork adorns the banister, while a beamed appliqué-enhanced cove ceiling adds balance and depth to the space.

The luxurious master suite boasts a morning kitchen and spacious sitting room, which opens onto the covered verandah.

This spacious leisure room with arched built-ins has an open dialog with the kitchen and nook beyond.

The focal point of the gloriously appointed master bath is the elevated tub, which is enhanced by two intricately tiled steps, a pair of decorative columns and an arched stone wall.

The curved loft overlooking living room and foyer is a great spot to curl up and read that favorite book.

A pair of French doors invites guests into the masculine study. A series of custom-designed built-ins have been superbly fitted into a wall of three arched niches

A spiral staircase descends to the optional lower level, which boasts an enormous game room large enough for a variety of concurrent activities. An expansive bay-shaped wall of large paned windows reinforces the eternal connection between the indoors and outdoors.

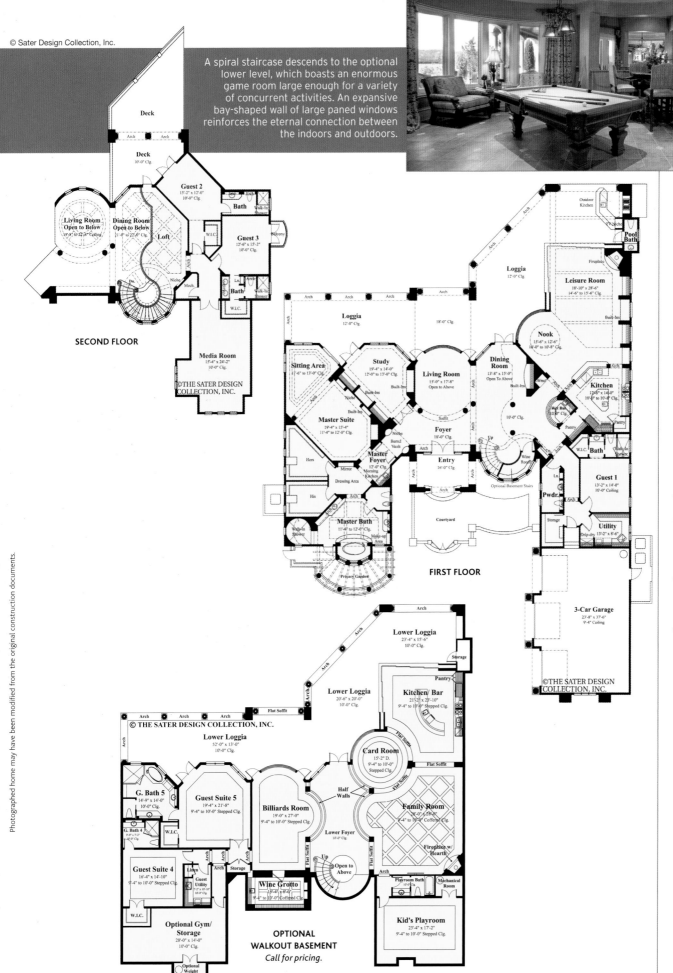

SECOND FLOOR

Deck
Arch   Arch

Deck
10'-0" Clg.

Guest 2
15'-2" x 12'-0"
10'-0" Clg.

Bath
Walk-In Shower

Living Room
Open to Below
19'-4" to 22'-6" Ceiling

Dining Room
Open to Below
21'-0" to 22'-6" Clg.

Loft

W.I.C.

Guest 3
12'-6" x 15'-2"
10'-0" Clg.
Balcony

Bath
Walk-In Shower
W.I.C.
Mech.

Media Room
15'-4" x 24'-0"
10'-0" Clg.

©THE SATER DESIGN
COLLECTION, INC.

FIRST FLOOR

Loggia
12'-0" Clg.

Loggia
12'-0" Clg.

18'-0" Clg.

Sitting Area
11'-6" x 13'-0"

Study
19'-4" x 14'-0"
12'-0" to 13'-0" Clg.

Living Room
15'-0" x 17'-8"
Open to Above

Nook
15'-6" x 12'-6"
10'-0" to 10'-8" Area

Dining Room
13'-8" x 15'-0"
Open To Above

Outdoor Kitchen

Pool Bath

Leisure Room
18'-10" x 28'-6"
14'-6" to 15'-6" Clg.

Fireplace

Master Suite
19'-4" x 15'-4"
11'-4" to 12'-0" Clg.

Foyer
18'-0" Clg.

Master Foyer
12'-0" Clg.
Morning Kitchen

Entry
16'-0" Clg.

Kitchen
12'-6" x 14'-0"
10'-0" to 10'-8" Clg.

Wet Bar

Pantry

Bath
Walk-in Shower
W.I.C.

Dressing Area

Mirror

His

Herx

Niche
Barrel Vault

Wine Room

Guest 1
13'-2" x 14'-0"
10'-0" Ceiling

Master Bath
11'-4" to 12'-0" Clg.
Make-up Area

Walk-In Shower

Courtyard

Optional Basement Stairs

Pwdr.

Storage

Utility
13'-2" x 8'-6"
Drip-dry

Privacy Garden

3-Car Garage
23'-8" x 37'-6"
9'-4" Ceiling

©THE SATER DESIGN
COLLECTION, INC.

OPTIONAL WALKOUT BASEMENT
Call for pricing.

© THE SATER DESIGN COLLECTION, INC.

Lower Loggia
23'-4" x 15'-6"
10'-0" Clg.

Storage

Lower Loggia
20'-6" x 20'-0"
10'-0" Clg.

Pantry

Kitchen/ Bar
21'-2" x 25'-10"
9'-4" to 10'-0" Stepped Clg.

Lower Loggia
52'-0" x 13'-0"
10'-0" Clg.

Card Room
15'-2" D.
9'-4" to 10'-0" Stepped Clg.

Half Walls

Flat Soffit

Family Room
28'-0" x 28'-0"
9'-4" to 10'-0" Coffered Clg.

G. Bath 5
14'-9" x 14'-0"
10'-0" Clg.

Guest Suite 5
19'-4" x 21'-8"
9'-4" to 10'-0" Stepped Clg.

Billiards Room
19'-0" x 27'-0"
9'-4" to 10'-0" Stepped Clg.

Lower Foyer
10'-0" Clg.

G. Bath 4
W.I.C.

Guest Suite 4
16'-4" x 14'-10"
9'-4" to 10'-0" Stepped Clg.

Guest Utility

Storage

Wine Grotto
9'-4" to 10'-0" Coffered Clg.

Up

Open to Above

Fireplace w/ Hearth

Playroom Bath

Mechanical Room

W.I.C.

Optional Gym/ Storage
28'-0" x 14'-0"
10'-0" Clg.

Optional Weight Storage

Kid's Playroom
23'-4" x 17'-2"
9'-4" to 10'-0" Stepped Clg.

SPECIFICATIONS:

Bedrooms: **4**

Full Baths: **4**

Half Baths: **2**

Width: **96' 0"**

Depth: **134' 8"**

1ˢᵗ Floor: **4742** *sf*

2ⁿᵈ Floor: **1531** *sf*

Total Living: **6273** *sf*

Foundation: **Slab**

Exterior Wall: **2x6 Wood**

PLAN PRICING:

Vellum & PDF - **$5018**

CAD - **$9410**

PLAN NUMBER:

8068

PLAN NAME:

Villa Sabina

Del Toro

This home celebrates the outdoors, with a floor plan that provides smart transitions between public and private realms while keeping the wide-open views in mind.

The covered entry features repeating arches that are mimicked in the bayed windows of the dining room and guest suite—even in the chimney turret. A two-story foyer opens to the living room with zero-corner pocketing glass doors, calling attention to the views beyond the pool. A fireplace with an ornate stone mantle provides warmth on chilly evenings. Just steps away are the dining room, butler's pantry and powder bath.

Both the leisure room and the pool arena

take into account the lifestyle of the modern family. The leisure room boasts built-ins for media components, books and art, pocketing glass walls for easy transitions outside, and a courtyard with fireplace and outdoor kitchen. A serving bar is all the separates this family space from the festive kitchen.

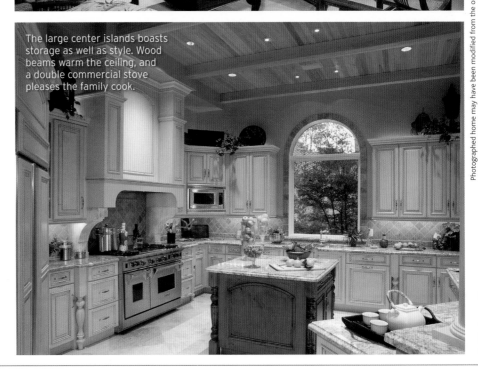

What better place to end the day than in this stunning solana, where a meal can be prepared in a secondary kitchen and enjoyed with good friends by a warm fireplace.

The large center islands boasts storage as well as style. Wood beams warm the ceiling, and a double commercial stove pleases the family cook.

Photographed home may have been modified from the original construction documents.

The leisure room boasts built-ins for media components, books and art, pocketing glass walls for easy transitions outside and a striking wood-beamed ceiling.

To one side of the foyer is a richly appointed study, with a beamed, pyramid ceiling and thoughtful built-ins tucked under arch-top bay windows.

Bayed formal dining room is adjacent to foyer and it's beautiful wrought iron entry doors.

The lanai is a work of art, incorporating steps, planters and a circular spa into the pool, and offering numerous transitions between indoor rooms and the outdoor arena.

Arching windows define the master suite sitting room and provide an exotic tropical ambience to this private owners' haven.

A private garden embraces the indulgent master bath, offering peaceful views from the spa tub and corner walk-in shower.

Mitered glass windows give the breakfast nook a view that goes on forever, making even a simple breakfast feel like a vacation.

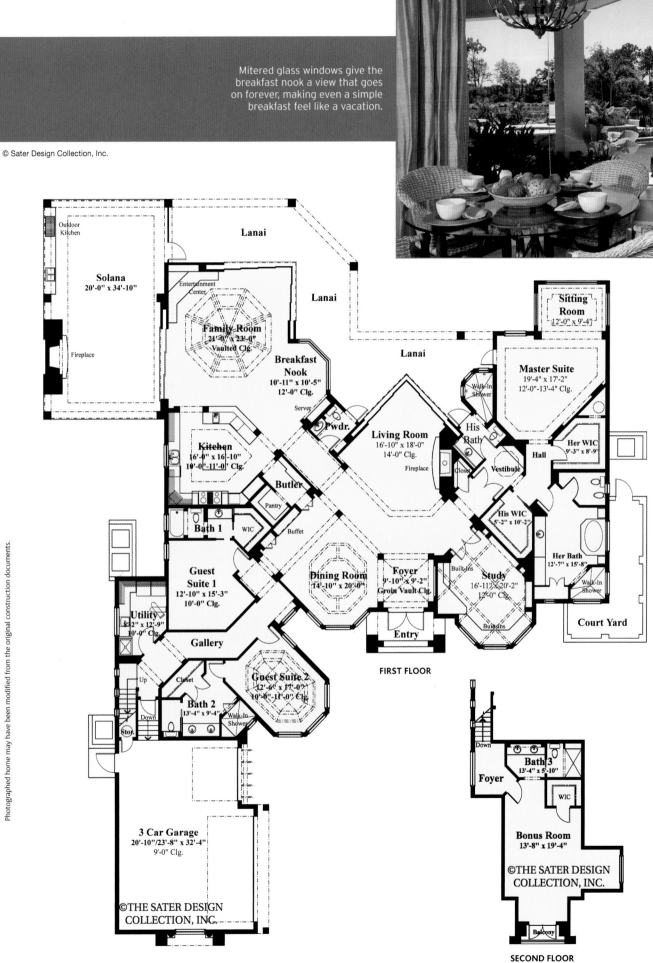

FIRST FLOOR

Solana
20'-0" x 34'-10"

Outdoor Kitchen

Lanai

Lanai

Lanai

Entertainment Center

Family Room
21'-0" x 23'-0"
Vaulted Clg.

Fireplace

Breakfast Nook
10'-11" x 10'-5"
12'-0" Clg.

Server

Kitchen
16'-0" x 16'-10"
10'-0"-11'-0" Clg.

Butler

Pantry

Buffet

Bath 1

WIC

Guest Suite 1
12'-10" x 15'-3"
10'-0" Clg.

Utility
8'-2" x 12'-9"
10'-0" Clg.

Gallery

Up

Closet

Down

Stor.

Bath 2
13'-4" x 9'-4"

Guest Suite 2
12'-6" x 17'-0"
10'-0"-11'-0" Clg.

Walk-In Shower

Pwdr.

Living Room
16'-10" x 18'-0"
14'-0" Clg.

Fireplace

Dining Room
14'-10" x 20'-0"

Foyer
9'-10" x 9'-2"
Groin Vault Clg.

Entry

His Bath

Closet

Vestibule

His WIC
5'-2" x 10'-2"

Built-Ins

Study
16'-11" x 20'-2"
12'-0" Clg.

Built-Ins

Sitting Room
12'-0" x 9'-4"

Master Suite
19'-4" x 17'-2"
12'-0"-13'-4" Clg.

Walk-In Shower

Hall

Her WIC
9'-3" x 8'-9"

Her Bath
12'-7" x 15'-8"

Walk-In Shower

Court Yard

3 Car Garage
20'-10"/23'-8" x 32'-4"
9'-0" Clg.

©THE SATER DESIGN COLLECTION, INC.

©THE SATER DESIGN COLLECTION, INC.

SECOND FLOOR

Down

Foyer

Bath 3
13'-4" x 5'-10"

WIC

Bonus Room
13'-8" x 19'-4"

Balcony

SPECIFICATIONS:

Bedrooms: **3**

Baths: **4½**

Width: **99' 9"**

Depth: **127' 3"**

1st Floor: **4645** *sf*

2nd Floor: **554** *sf*

Total Living: **5199** *sf*

Foundation: **Slab**

Exterior Wall: **8" Block**

PLAN PRICING:

Vellum & PDF - **$4159**

PLAN NUMBER:

6923

PLAN NAME:

Del Toro

Camellia Manor

The twenty-fifth anniversary of The New American Home™, the model home of the International Builders' Show, was commemorated with a traditional Plantation style fused with the latest in residential design, décor and building technologies.

A spacious and amenity-rich master suite serves the owners, while a first-level family suite is perfect for elderly parents. Two complete guest suites on the second floor create private retreats for visiting friends or children.

The core of the home hosts a magnificent living room with a two-story, lake-view bowed wall of glass as well as a breath-taking two-story fireplace. The adjacent formal dining room resides under a unique ceiling treatment, framed in wooden columns and arches. The under-stair wine cellar and a nearby butler's pantry, as well as a spacious gourmet kitchen, facilitate service of formal meals.

The kitchen boasts two islands, an eating bar and an open arrangement with the dining nook and the leisure room. The entire space is light-filled and opens to the outdoor living area through retreating walls of glass. The view-oriented outdoor living space contains a full outdoor kitchen, dining area and a living room, complete with fireplace.

An elegant study, flexible clubroom with a wet bar, craft room and a family valet at the garage entry round out the functional amenities that make life in Camellia Manor all about everyday enjoyment.

The relaxing study provides an excellent ambiance for at-home productivity with French doors to the covered lanai, a warming fireplace and stepped ceiling.

The spacious kitchen enjoys an open arrangement with the nook and leisure room and is subtly defined by a series of arches and columns lining the eating bar.

A two-story bowed window grants views not only o the pool, but also the lake beyond, while the warming fireplace creates a cozy space indoors.

The second-floor club room is a multi-functional space with an entertainment center, billiards table and wet bar.

Outdoor living spaces abound at *Camellia Manor* with the pool, spa, solana, lanai, balconies and sundeck beckoning resident outside to enjoy the alfresco amenities.

This quintessential solana includes a warming fireplace, wood-enhanced vaulted ceiling crowned with a cupola, and comfortable living room-style seating.

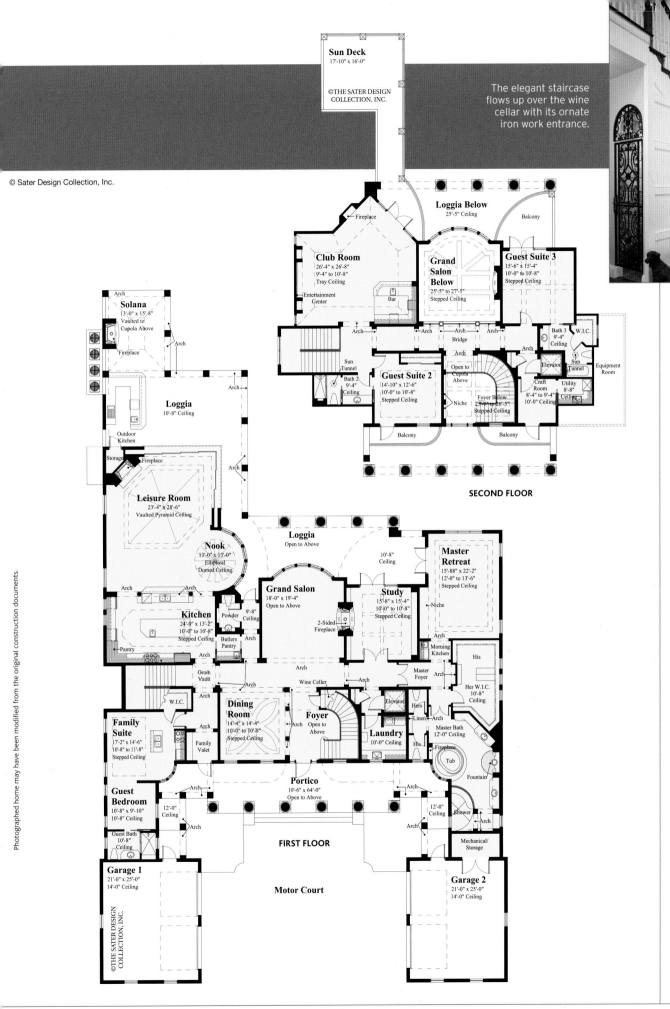

Sun Deck
17'-10" x 16'-0"

©THE SATER DESIGN
COLLECTION, INC.

© Sater Design Collection, Inc.

The elegant staircase
flows up over the wine
cellar with its ornate
iron work entrance.

Loggia Below
25'-5" Ceiling

Balcony

Fireplace

Club Room
26'-4" x 26'-8"
9'-4" to 10'-8"
Tray Ceiling

Grand Salon Below
25'-5" to 27'-5"
Stepped Ceiling

Guest Suite 3
15'-6" x 15'-4"
10'-0" to 10'-8"
Stepped Ceiling

Entertainment Center

Bar

Arch Arch Arch Arch

Bath 3
9'-4" Ceiling

W.I.C.

Bridge

Sun Tunnel

Bath 2
9'-4" Ceiling

Guest Suite 2
14'-10" x 12'-6"
10'-0" to 10'-8"
Stepped Ceiling

Arch

Open to Cupola Above

Elevator

Sun Tunnel

Equipment Room

Craft Room
8'-4" to 9'-4"
10'-0" Ceiling

Utility
8'-8" Ceiling

Niche

Foyer Below
25'-5" to 26'-5"
Stepped Ceiling

Balcony

Balcony

SECOND FLOOR

Solana
13'-0" x 15'-8"
Vaulted to Cupola Above

Arch

Fireplace

Arch

Loggia
10'-8" Ceiling

Outdoor Kitchen

Arch

Storage

Fireplace

Leisure Room
23'-4" x 28'-6"
Vaulted Pyramid Ceiling

Arch

Nook
13'-0" x 13'-0"
Elliptical Domed Ceiling

Loggia
Open to Above

10'-8" Ceiling

Master Retreat
15'-88" x 22'-2"
12'-0" to 13'-6"
Stepped Ceiling

Arch

Arch

Grand Salon
18'-0" x 19'-4"
Open to Above

Study
15'-8" x 15'-4"
10'-0" to 10'-8"
Stepped Ceiling

Niche

Kitchen
24'-0" x 13'-2"
10'-0" to 10'-8"
Stepped Ceiling

Powder

9'-8" Ceiling

2-Sided Fireplace

Morning Kitchen

His

Pantry

Butlers Pantry

Arch

Arch

Arch

Groin Vault

Wine Cellar

Arch

Master Foyer

Arch

Her W.I.C.
10'-8" Ceiling

W.I.C.

Arch

Elevator

Hers

Linen

Arch

Family Suite
17'-2" x 14'-6"
10'-8" to 11'-8"
Stepped Ceiling

Dining Room
14'-4" x 14'-4"
10'-0" to 10'-8"
Stepped Ceiling

Foyer
Open to Above

Laundry
10'-0" Ceiling

Master Bath
12'-0" Ceiling

Fireplace

Family Valet

Arch

His

Tub

Guest Bedroom
10'-8" x 9'-10"
10'-8" Ceiling

12'-0" Ceiling

Arch

Portico
10'-6" x 64'-0"
Open to Above

12'-0" Ceiling

Arch

Fountain

Guest Bath
10'-8" Ceiling

Shower

Arch

Mechanical/ Storage

Garage 1
21'-0" x 25'-0"
14'-0" Ceiling

FIRST FLOOR

Motor Court

Garage 2
21'-0" x 25'-0"
14'-0" Ceiling

©THE SATER DESIGN
COLLECTION, INC.

Photographed home may have been modified from the original construction documents.

SPECIFICATIONS:

Bedrooms: **4**

Baths: **4**

Width: **90' 0"**

Depth: **146' 4"**

1st Floor: **4830** *sf*

2nd Floor: **1895** *sf*

Total Living: **6725** *sf*

Foundation: **Slab**

Exterior Wall: **8" Block**

PLAN PRICING:

Vellum & PDF - **$6725**

CAD - **$11433**

PLAN NUMBER:
6956

PLAN NAME:
Camellia Manor

Sterling Oaks

The wide-hipped roof, classic columns and arches of the front façade proudly announce this stately residence. Under the porte-cochere, family and friends are embraced by a dramatic entry and led into the grand interior.

Past the foyer, rooms flow seamlessly from one to another, and offer generous views of the outdoors. A stunning living room takes center stage, with a soaring curved and coffered ceiling and a twenty-two-foot bowed glass wall. Nearby, the formal dining room highlights the European flair of the home.

A pass-thru wet bar connects the formal living room to the common living areas, easily serving both.

Central to the informal family area is the leisure room, kitchen and nook. All defined with stepped ceilings, this core area for family gatherings melds into one and connects to the verandah via retreating glass walls.

At the top of a staircase, the second floor offers limitless entertaining and living possibilities with a multi-purpose loft perfect for game tables and media components. Two spacious guests suites with private decks create a perfect retreat for friends and family.

The heart of the home is the leisure/kitchen/nook arena. This core for family gatherings and entertaining.

The dining room epitomizes stylish elegance with fluid arches—a graceful arched ceiling, built-in buffet with arching mirror and dramatic window.

This spacious kitchen boasts generous portions of everything from food preparation and pantry space to built-in appliances and breakfast bar seating. The ornamental hood and cabinet moldings add a Tuscan flair.

The living room's curved coffered ceiling, as grand as it is, serves merely as the stage for the star performer—a spectacular, twenty-two-foot bowed glass wall. To the right of the room, a wet bar provides cocktails while guest enjoy the view.

An entertainer's paradise! The verandah is complete with a fully equipped outdoor kitchen, spa and pool that effortlessly accommodate a party of two hundred or, if you prefer, an intimate date for two.

A second-story balcony bounded by wrought-iron balustrades extends from the rear elevation. Two stories of curved glass meet at the water's edge to create an elegant focal point on the verandah.

The master suite features a sitting area with arched windows.

The study features a dramatic arched window wall and stepped ceiling.

Relaxing master bath with Whirlpool tub, walk-in shower, and private garden beyond.

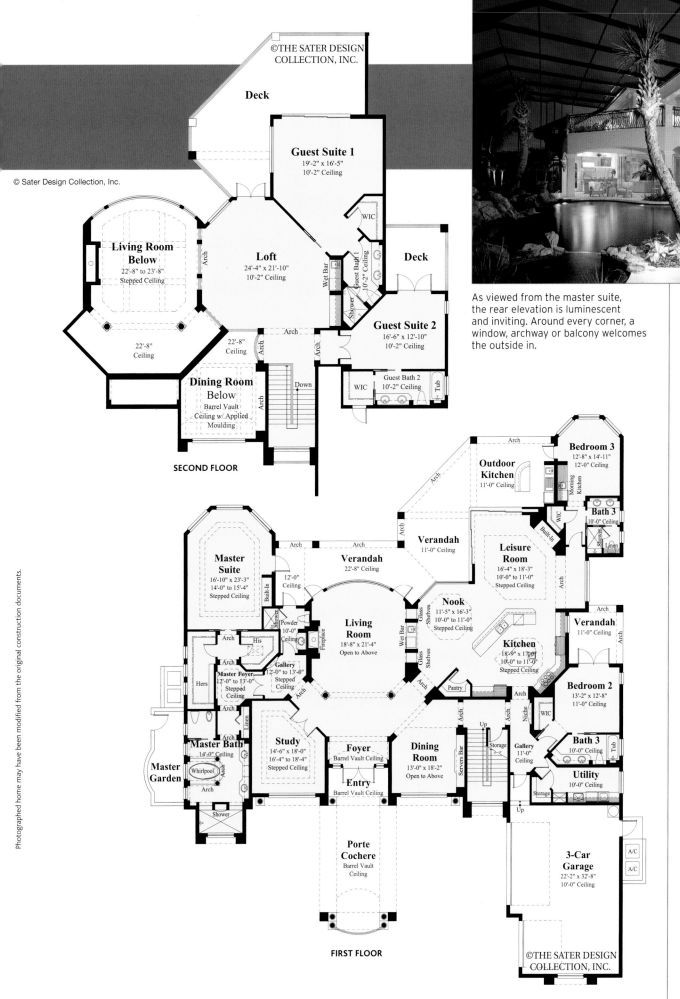

©THE SATER DESIGN COLLECTION, INC.

© Sater Design Collection, Inc.

Deck

Guest Suite 1
19'-2" x 16'-5"
10'-2" Ceiling

WIC

Living Room Below
22'-8" to 23'-8"
Stepped Ceiling

22'-8" Ceiling

Loft
24'-4" x 21'-10"
10'-2" Ceiling

Wet Bar

Guest Bath 1
10'-2" Ceiling

Shower

Deck

Guest Suite 2
16'-6" x 12'-10"
10'-2" Ceiling

Arch

22'-8" Ceiling

Dining Room Below
Barrel Vault Ceiling w/ Applied Moulding

Down

Guest Bath 2
10'-2" Ceiling

WIC

Tub

SECOND FLOOR

As viewed from the master suite, the rear elevation is luminescent and inviting. Around every corner, a window, archway or balcony welcomes the outside in.

FIRST FLOOR

Master Suite
16'-10" x 23'-3"
14'-0" to 15'-4"
Stepped Ceiling

12'-0" Ceiling

Verandah
22'-8" Ceiling

Verandah
11'-0" Ceiling

Outdoor Kitchen
11'-0" Ceiling

Bedroom 3
12'-8" x 14'-11"
12'-0" Ceiling

Morning Kitchen

WIC

Bath 3
10'-0" Ceiling

Shower

Linen

Leisure Room
16'-4" x 18'-3"
10'-0" to 11'-0"
Stepped Ceiling

Built-In

Powder
10'-0" Ceiling

Fireplace

His

Living Room
18'-8" x 21'-4"
Open to Above

Wet Bar

Glass Shelves

Nook
11'-5" x 16'-3"
10'-0" to 11'-0"
Stepped Ceiling

Glass Shelves

Kitchen
18'-9" x 17'-0"
10'-0" to 11'-0"
Stepped Ceiling

Verandah
11'-0" Ceiling

Arch

Master Foyer
12'-0" to 13'-0"
Stepped Ceiling

Gallery
12'-0" to 13'-0"
Stepped Ceiling

Pantry

Bedroom 2
13'-2" x 12'-8"
11'-0" Ceiling

WIC

Hers

Linen

Master Bath
14'-0" Ceiling

Master Garden

Whirlpool

Shower

Study
14'-6" x 18'-0"
16'-4" to 18'-4"
Stepped Ceiling

Foyer
Barrel Vault Ceiling

Entry
Barrel Vault Ceiling

Dining Room
13'-0" x 18'-2"
Open to Above

Servers Bar

Niche

Up

Gallery
11'-0" Ceiling

Bath 3
10'-0" Ceiling

Tub

Storage

Utility
10'-0" Ceiling

Storage

Up

Porte Cochere
Barrel Vault Ceiling

3-Car Garage
22'-2" x 32'-8"
10'-0" Ceiling

A/C

A/C

©THE SATER DESIGN COLLECTION, INC.

SPECIFICATIONS:

Bedrooms: **5**

Baths: **6**

Width: **88' 0"**

Depth: **110' 1"**

1st Floor: **4385** sf

2nd Floor: **1435** sf

Total Living: **5820** sf

Foundation: **Slab**

Exterior Wall: **8" Block**

PLAN PRICING:

Vellum & PDF - **$4656**

CAD - **$8730**

PLAN NUMBER:

6914

PLAN NAME:

Sterling Oaks

La Ventana

Our La Ventana home plan is an Andalusian inspired masterpiece. It's rope moulding accents give a Romanesque flair to the pointed arch entry in this detail rich Mediterranean manor house. The foyer is highlighted by a barrel vaulted ceiling and leads to the living room with floor to ceiling mitered glass and views to beyond. On the right is the formal dining room, which is open to the adjacent living room to create sense of spaciousness. Guests are welcomed to the informal areas of the house via a dramatic two-story stairway and stand behind wet bar. A walk-in wine cellar is showcased under the stairs through fixed glass.

The leisure room, kitchen and nook are beyond. This open area is perfect for relaxation and entertainment alike. The leisure room features a two story ceiling and pocketing corner-less sliding glass doors that make the space feel like part of the outdoors. Just outside the leisure room is the outdoor kitchen and a veranda that spans the entire rear of the home.

Traveling to the left of the foyer one first encounters the library/office that looks out to views in the rear. Beyond are double doors leading to the master foyer. The master suite has sitting alcove and stepped tray ceilings. The master bath has his and hers walk-in closets and vanities. It also features an island tub with walk-in shower beyond.

Upstairs is a loft that overlooks leisure room and has access to viewing porch and expansive sun deck. It also has a separate wet bar. A fourth bedroom with bath completes the second floor space of the La Ventana home plan.

Directly off of the leisure room is a veranda with an outdoor kitchen.

Wine cellar is conveniently located under stairway and its wrought iron railing.

Granite countered island kitchen is conveniently located and open to the leisure room and views beyond.

Photographed home may have been modified from the original construction documents.

The dining room with bay opens onto views while the adjacent stair lobby with wet bar leads to home's informal areas.

The dramatic two story leisure room with stone fireplace, built-ins, and pocketed sliding glass walls.

Master suite with optional sitting alcove is grand and relaxing.

Island spa and pool make for a nice addition to this home.

Upstairs loft overlooking the leisure room has great views from the lanai and deck beyond.

The living room, featuring stepped ceiling leads onto the veranda.

Spacious master bath with island tub, built-in dresser and make up all look onto private garden with fountain.

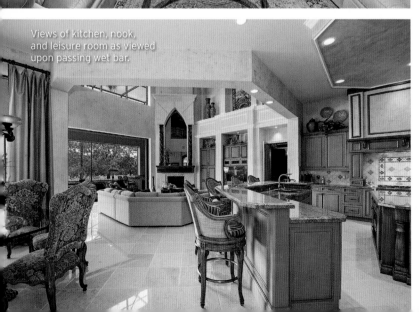

Views of kitchen, nook, and leisure room as viewed upon passing wet bar.

Study with arched built-ins overlooks veranda.

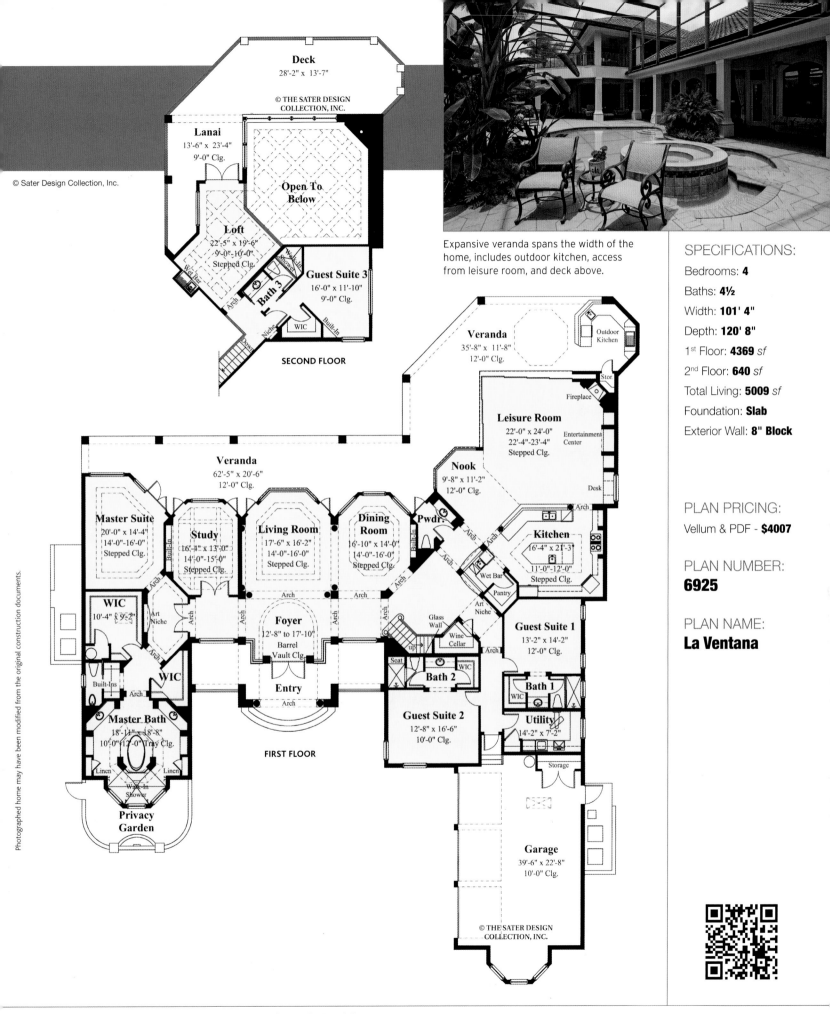

SECOND FLOOR

Deck
28'-2" x 13'-7"

© THE SATER DESIGN
COLLECTION, INC.

© Sater Design Collection, Inc.

Lanai
13'-6" x 23'-4"
9'-0" Clg.

**Open To
Below**

Loft
22'-5" x 19'-6"
9'-0"-10'-0"
Stepped Clg.

Bath 3

Wet Bar

Guest Suite 3
16'-0" x 11'-10"
9'-0" Clg.

Niche

WIC

Built-In

Down

Expansive veranda spans the width of the
home, includes outdoor kitchen, access
from leisure room, and deck above.

Veranda
35'-8" x 11'-8"
12'-0" Clg.

Outdoor
Kitchen

Stor

Fireplace

Leisure Room
22'-0" x 24'-0"
22'-4"-23'-4"
Stepped Clg.

Entertainment
Center

Desk

Nook
9'-8" x 11'-2"
12'-0" Clg.

Arch

Arch

Veranda
62'-5" x 20'-6"
12'-0" Clg.

Pwdr.

Kitchen
16'-4" x 21'-3"
11'-0"-12'-0"
Stepped Clg.

Master Suite
20'-0" x 14'-4"
14'-0"-16'-0"
Stepped Clg.

Study
16'-4" x 13'-0"
14'-0"-15'-0"
Stepped Clg.

Living Room
17'-6" x 16'-2"
14'-0"-16'-0"
Stepped Clg.

**Dining
Room**
16'-10" x 14'-0"
14'-0"-16'-0"
Stepped Clg.

Wet Bar

Pantry

Art
Niche

Guest Suite 1
13'-2" x 14'-2"
12'-0" Clg.

WIC
10'-4" x 9'-2"

Art
Niche

Glass
Wall

Wine
Cellar

up

WIC

Built-Ins

WIC

Foyer
12'-8" to 17'-10"
Barrel
Vault Clg.

Seat

Bath 2

WIC

Bath 1

WIC

Master Bath
18'-11" x 8'-8"
10'-0"-12'-0" Tray Clg.

Entry

Utility
14'-2" x 7'-2"

Linen

Linen

Walk-In
Shower

Guest Suite 2
12'-8" x 16'-6"
10'-0" Clg.

Storage

**Privacy
Garden**

FIRST FLOOR

Garage
39'-6" x 22'-8"
10'-0" Clg.

Photographed home may have been modified from the original construction documents.

© THE SATER DESIGN
COLLECTION, INC.

SPECIFICATIONS:

Bedrooms: **4**

Baths: **4½**

Width: **101' 4"**

Depth: **120' 8"**

1st Floor: **4369** sf

2nd Floor: **640** sf

Total Living: **5009** sf

Foundation: **Slab**

Exterior Wall: **8" Block**

PLAN PRICING:

Vellum & PDF - **$4007**

PLAN NUMBER:

6925

PLAN NAME:

La Ventana

Milano

All angles, curves and dramatic details, this tropical estate represents the finest in waterfront living. The dramatic porte cochere entryway at the heart of a curved driveway leads inside to a magnificent living room that appears to have no walls – its sliding glass panels disappearing to embrace the stunning lake and panoramic views. The home sprawls lengthwise, with a section angling off on one end to set apart the two main bedrooms, guest suite and garage. At the other end of the home is a fabulous master suite that includes an exercise room, an opulent his-and-hers bath, dual closets, a morning kitchen and a charming outdoor garden.

A study sits just outside the master foyer as a transition from the living room. Its unique two-story ceiling and full wet bar, combined with luxurious casual furnishings, offer a space for both relaxing and casual entertaining.

To the right of the living room, a dramatic breakfast nook with a curved glass wall floats above the swimming pool. It connects to a kitchen that is both beautiful and functional, and a family-friendly leisure room boasting striking built-ins for a fireplace, television and artwork.

The partial second level includes a fully outfitted media room a third bedroom and bath, and three loft spaces. A large observation deck completes the upper level.

Like a salon in the bow of a splendid ocean liner, the living room's ninety-degree retreating glass doors pierce the evening sky and carry the home's living room out into the brilliant colors of a tropical sunset.

Well-appointed with built-in appliances and spacious center island, this superbly designed kitchen showcases an elegant mantel vent hood supported by a pair of decorative columns.

Photographed home may have been modified from the original construction documents.

Dramatic two story leisure room with wrap around loft, balcony and coffered wood ceiling.

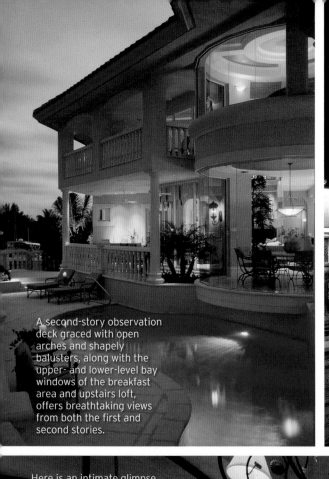

A second-story observation deck graced with open arches and shapely balusters, along with the upper- and lower-level bay windows of the breakfast area and upstairs loft, offers breathtaking views from both the first and second stories.

The master suite with its recessed niches is ideally located to soak in waterfront views beyond.

Here is an intimate glimpse of the "hers" bath in the master suite adjacent to the exercise room. This restful retreat offers a very private view of a lush master garden and boasts all of the "accoutrements" of a luxury spa.

A grand porte-cochere, with balustraded observation deck above, provides all who approach with a regal welcome.

Low-pitched roofs, stately arches and columns, elegant balustrades – these trademarks of Renaissance Revival architecture meet contemporary angled glass and stucco to create a truly unique rear elevation.

The living room's ninety-degree retreating glass doors bring the outdoors in.

SPECIFICATIONS:

Bedrooms: **5**

Baths: **7**

Width: **174' 10"**

Depth: **81' 2"**

1st Floor: **5124** *sf*

2nd Floor: **1524** *sf*

Total Living: **6648** *sf*

Foundation: **Slab**

Exterior Wall: **8" Block**

PLAN PRICING:

Vellum & PDF - **$6648**

PLAN NUMBER:

6921

PLAN NAME:

Milano

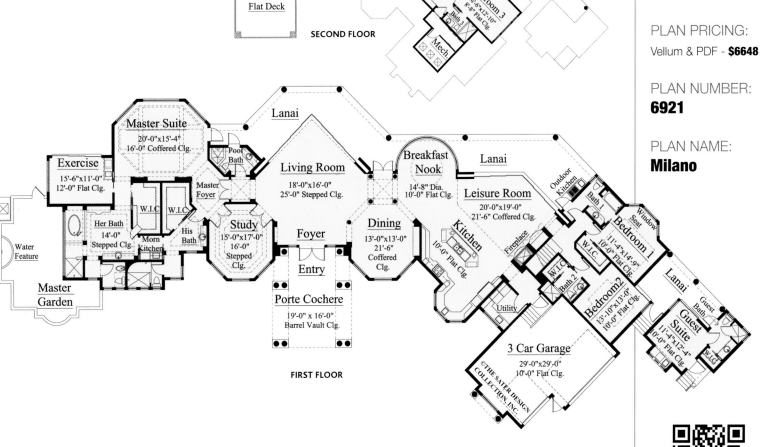

SECOND FLOOR

FIRST FLOOR

Casa Bellisima

A romantic courtyard welcomes all into this unforgettable, view-oriented design. Stone steps, scrolling wrought iron, cast-stone ornamentals, dentil molding and a magnificent cupola add captivating details to the front façade. Inside, past the barrel-vaulted foyer, the formal living room boasts a two-story coffered ceiling, fireplace, and a wall of windows and doors connecting to the outdoors. A butler's pantry, wet bar and formal dining room are situated close by. The central rotunda connects the public, formal realm with an upper-level game and guest wing, which opens to a wide deck overlooking the pool, veranda and koi pond.

Two more guest suites are found on the left side of the floor plan (where a side family entry increases the pattern of circulation through the guest wing), as is the kitchen, leisure room and nook. These open spaces are expanded by zero-corner sliding glass doors that pocket into the walls and open the common living area onto the veranda.

For added privacy, the master suite is located on the opposite wing. A three-sided fireplace warms the sitting area adjacent to the suite. Dual walk-in closets, a dressing area and a spa-like bath ensure the homeowners will always feel pampered.

Antique cypress beams hover above the food-preparation area in the kitchen, which boasts granite countertops and new-century appliances. A tumbled-stone stove hood provides an earthy element to this ultra sophisticated kitchen.

Cove lit dome ceiling positioned over circular staircase leading to home entertainment loft and upstairs guest suite.

Game room/loft is accessed via staircase and has access to large viewing deck.

The living room with its carved stone mantel is the home's centerpiece upon entering.

Gravity-defying forms define a grand, sweeping staircase that connects the main-level gallery with the game room. A sculpted edge soars above a carved vestibule leading to the wine cellar.

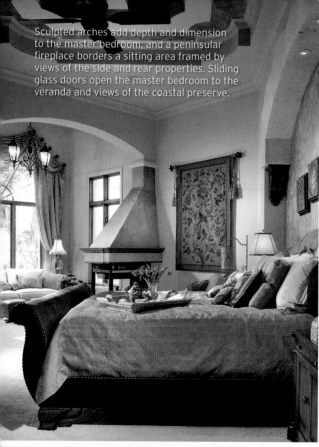

Sculpted arches add depth and dimension to the master bedroom, and a peninsular fireplace borders a sitting area framed by views of the side and rear properties. Sliding glass doors open the master bedroom to the veranda and views of the coastal preserve.

Dramatic stained glass separates the bathtub from a hidden steam room, while a private garden, two vanities and a separate make-up area complete the retreat.

Open to the leisure room and deck, the veranda features a sheltered outdoor eating area. To the left, a fireplace with a carved mahogany-and-stone surround anchors a plush sitting area.

An arcade of flattened arches spans the rear deck. The outdoor sitting area links to the leisure room through retreating glass doors.

Lancet arches signal a Venetian influence in a room designed for contemplation. Views to the front property maintain a connection with the colonial architecture of the plan and bring in a sense of the outdoors.

A massive freestanding arcade sentinels the spacious courtyard leading to the entry. Robust masonry piers and columns contrast with an intricate wrought-iron gate, which relates in a revival scheme to a pleasing sculpted fountain.

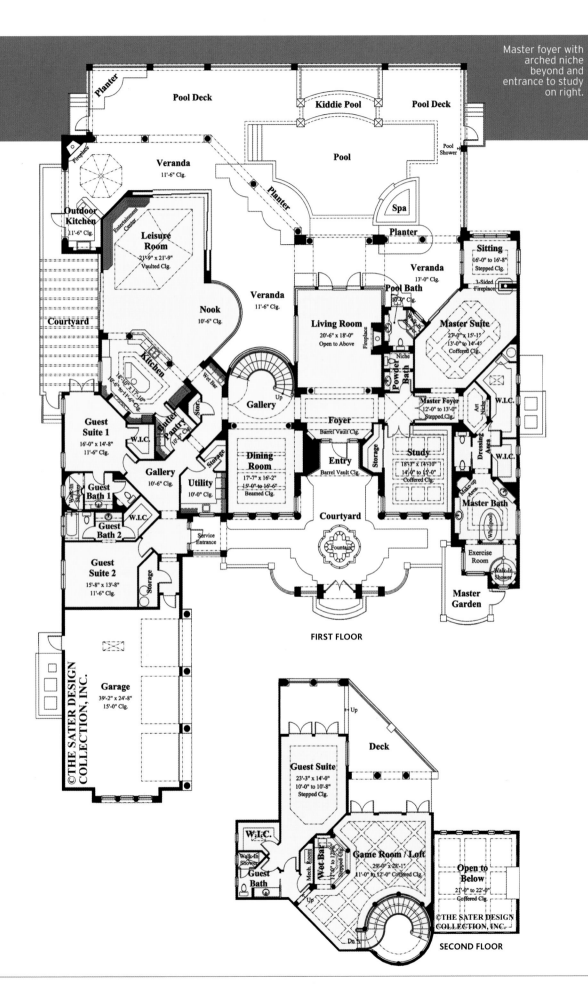

FIRST FLOOR

Planter

Pool Deck

Kiddie Pool

Pool Deck

Pool

Pool Shower

Fireplace

Veranda
11'-6" Clg.

Outdoor Kitchen
11'-6" Clg.

Leisure Room
21'-9" x 21'-9"
Vaulted Clg.

Planter

Spa

Planter

Sitting
16'-0" to 16'-8"
Stepped Clg.

3-Sided Fireplace

Veranda
13'-0" Clg.

Courtyard

Nook
10'-6" Clg.

Veranda
11'-6" Clg.

Veranda
11'-6" Clg.

Living Room
20'-6" x 18'-0"
Open to Above

Fireplace

Pool Bath
10'-3" Clg.

Master Suite
27'-0" x 15'-1"
13'-0" to 14'-4"
Coffered Clg.

Kitchen
16'-10" x 17'-10"
10'-6" to 11'-6" Clg.

Butler Pantry
10'-6" Clg.

Wet Bar

Gallery

Niche

Powder Bath

Master Foyer
12'-0" to 13'-0"
Stepped Clg.

Art Niche

W.I.C.

Guest Suite 1
16'-0" x 14'-8"
11'-6" Clg.

W.I.C.

Storage

Foyer
Barrel Vault Clg.

Storage

Dressing Area

W.I.C.

Gallery
10'-6" Clg.

Guest Bath 1

Utility
10'-0" Clg.

Dining Room
17'-7" x 16'-2"
15'-0" to 16'-6"
Beamed Clg.

Entry
Barrel Vault Clg.

Study
18'-3" x 14'-10"
14'-0" to 15'-0"
Coffered Clg.

Make-up Area

Master Bath

W.I.C.

Guest Bath 2

Courtyard

Whirlpool

Guest Suite 2
15'-8" x 13'-8"
11'-6" Clg.

Storage

Service Entrance

Fountain

Exercise Room

Walk-In Shower

Master Garden

Garage
39'-2" x 24'-8"
15'-0" Clg.

SECOND FLOOR

Up

Deck

Guest Suite
23'-3" x 14'-0"
10'-0" to 10'-8"
Stepped Clg.

W.I.C.

Walk-In Shower

Guest Bath

Wet Bar

Mech. Room

Up

Game Room / Loft
29'-0" x 28'-1"
11'-0" to 12'-0" Coffered Clg.

Open to Below
21'-0" to 22'-0"
Coffered Clg.

Dn

Master foyer with arched niche beyond and entrance to study on right.

SPECIFICATIONS:

Bedrooms: **4**

Baths: **5½**

Width: **104' 0"**

Depth: **140' 0"**

1st Floor: **5391** *sf*

2nd Floor: **1133** *sf*

Total Living: **6524** *sf*

Foundation: **Slab**

Exterior Wall: **2x6 Wood**

PLAN PRICING:

Vellum & PDF - **$5219**

CAD - **$9786**

PLAN NUMBER:
6935

PLAN NAME:
Casa Bellisima

Ristano

With many luxe design features—carved ceilings, large rooms and 21st-century electronics—the strength of this design is its unique capacity to merge indoor living areas with outer spaces through a fluid perimeter of retreating glass walls and windows. Immediately upon entry, the grand foyer leads to the formal living and dining rooms and witnesses views that extend to the veranda, pool and beyond.

To the left of the formal rooms, a wet bar and butler's pantry eases the spatial transition to the casual living space. A family-friendly zone, the kitchen flows into the generous leisure room, nook and out to the verandah. Nearby, two guest suites feature full baths and walk-in closets.

Tucked away on the other side of the home, the master wing is a truly luxurious retreat. Special features—a morning kitchen, a spa-like bath with a private garden and quiet sitting area create a sanctuary that is hard to leave. Upstairs, a spacious loft with a wet bar is a versatile space that connects two guest suites and opens to an outer deck.

An open flow defines the dining room, utilizing sleek columns and a stepped ceiling to accentuate its height.

Beautiful wet bar is strategically located between formal and informal areas of the home.

A center island with a prep sink, state-of-the-art appliances and a wraparound eating bar will please cooks of all levels.

A customized wall of niches provides space for artwork, a media center, an angled fireplace and a cozy window seat in the leisure room.

A gently curved glass window frames the living room and entry foyer, granting commanding views both inside and out.

Stone columns make a stunning framework for viewing the veranda through the floor-to-ceiling wall of curved glass in the formal living room. A step-up tray ceiling and arches provide definition to the open room, while dual art niches add a subtle touch of sophistication.

A spa-style tub encased in wood and marble floats before a glass door leading to a private garden. A walk-in shower is encased in intensely hued natural materials and a curved glass wall.

An embracing arch leads the way into a cozy sitting area that offers stirring views through a series of vertical windows. Private access to the back patios, a spectacular bathroom and a large morning kitchen complement this refined retreat.

Retreating glass walls open the leisure room to the outdoor kitchen and dining area, making entertaining outside easy and convenient. Upstairs, a spacious loft connects to the upper-level deck, a perfect place to enjoy moonlight views and fresh air.

A corbelled roofline and upper deck framed in wrought iron extend the home out and upward, while the multi-angled veranda follows the curves and corners of interior rooms and a free-form pool, providing a myriad of outdoor embracing niches.

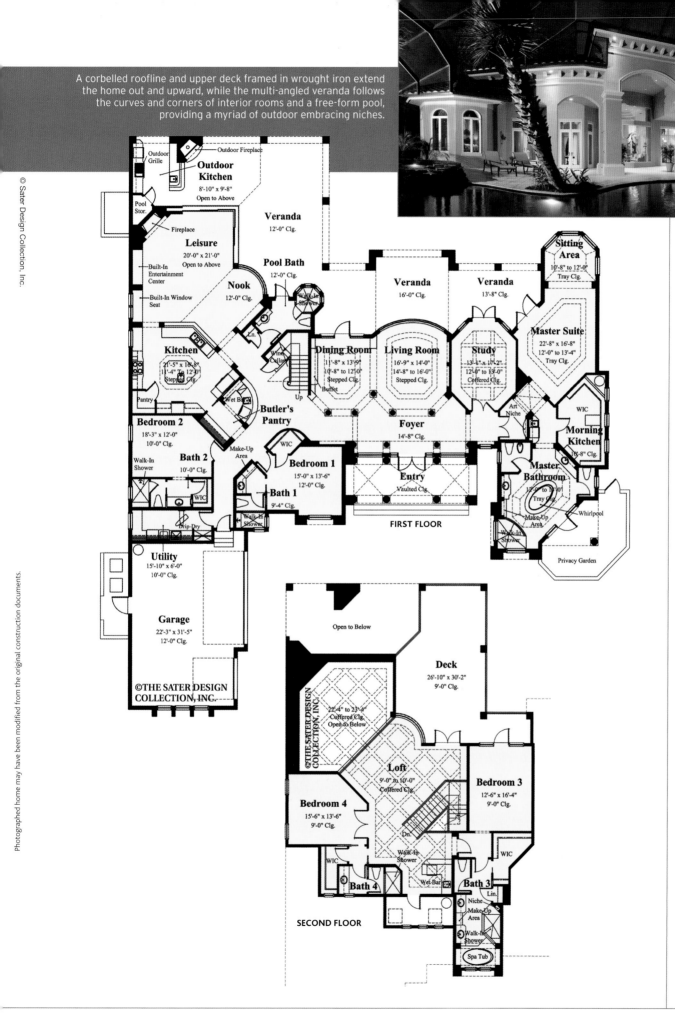

Outdoor Kitchen
8'-10" x 9'-8"
Open to Above

Pool Stor.

Fireplace

Leisure
20'-0" x 21'-0"
Open to Above

Built-In Entertainment Center
Built-In Window Seat

Veranda
12'-0" Clg.

Pool Bath
12'-0" Clg.

Nook
12'-0" Clg.

Walk-In Shower

Kitchen
21'-5" x 18'-8"
11'-4" x 12'-0"
Stepped Clg.

Pantry

Wine Cellar

Dining Room
11'-8" x 13'-9"
10'-8" to 12'-0"
Stepped Clg.

Buffet

Living Room
16'-9" x 14'-0"
14'-8" to 16'-0"
Stepped Clg.

Veranda
16'-0" Clg.

Veranda
13'-8" Clg.

Study
13'-4" x 17'-2"
12'-0" to 13'-0"
Coffered Clg.

Sitting Area
10'-8" to 12'-0"
Tray Clg.

Master Suite
22'-8" x 16'-8"
12'-0" to 13'-4"
Tray Clg.

Wet Bar

Butler's Pantry

Up

WIC

Foyer
14'-8"

Art Niche

WIC

Morning Kitchen
18'-8" Clg.

Bedroom 2
18'-3" x 12'-0"
10'-0" Clg.

Make-Up Area

Bath 2
10'-0" Clg.

Walk-In Shower

WIC

Bedroom 1
15'-0" x 13'-6"
12'-0" Clg.

Bath 1
9'-4" Clg.

Walk-In Shower

Entry
Vaulted Clg.

Master Bathroom
12'-0" x 10'-0"
Tray Clg.

Make-Up Area

Whirlpool

Walk-In Shower

Privacy Garden

Drip Dry

Utility
15'-10" x 6'-0"
10'-0" Clg.

Garage
22'-3" x 31'-5"
12'-0" Clg.

FIRST FLOOR

©THE SATER DESIGN COLLECTION, INC.

Open to Below

Deck
26'-10" x 30'-2"
9'-0" Clg.

22'-4" to 23'-4"
Coffered Clg.
Open to Below

Loft
9'-0" to 10'-0"
Coffered Clg.

Bedroom 3
12'-6" x 16'-4"
9'-0" Clg.

Bedroom 4
15'-6" x 13'-6"
9'-0" Clg.

Walk-In Shower

Dn.

WIC

WIC

Wet Bar

Bath 4

Bath 3

Niche
Make-Up Area

Lin.

Walk-In Shower

Spa Tub

SECOND FLOOR

SPECIFICATIONS:

Bedrooms: **5**

Baths: **6**

Width: **96' 0"**

Depth: **111' 0"**

1st Floor: **4186** sf

2nd Floor: **1378** sf

Total Living: **5564** sf

Foundation: **Slab**

Exterior Wall: **8" Block**

PLAN PRICING:

Vellum & PDF - **$4451**

CAD - **$8346**

PLAN NUMBER:
6939

PLAN NAME:
Ristano

Trissino

Both beautiful and functional, this home blends classical architecture design with all of the demands and desires of 21st-century living.

Sculpted masonry and a deeply recessed entry evoke the charm of a picturesque seaside villa, while circle-head windows and shapely pilasters establish an impressive street presence. A stepped ceiling provides definition for a grand foyer that opens to the central interior. Designed to deliver a sense of welcome, the home maintains an airy, outside-in disposition throughout the interior. The vaulted living room absorbs the scenery through a wall of glass framed by French doors that open to the lanai. Massive striated columns form the inner perimeters of the formal spaces and establish a natural theme that is reinforced by the use of myriad woods, polished marble and granite throughout the home.

A sleek staircase wends it way to a second-story loft that connects to the spacious poolroom.

Lanai and outdoor kitchen beyond.

REAR ELEVATION

The leisure room is well equipped for rest and relaxation, with fireplace and retreating glass walls that open to the lanai.

The vaulted living room absorbs the scenery through a wall of glass framed by French doors that open to the lanai, while the ornately carved fireplace enhances the coziness of the room.

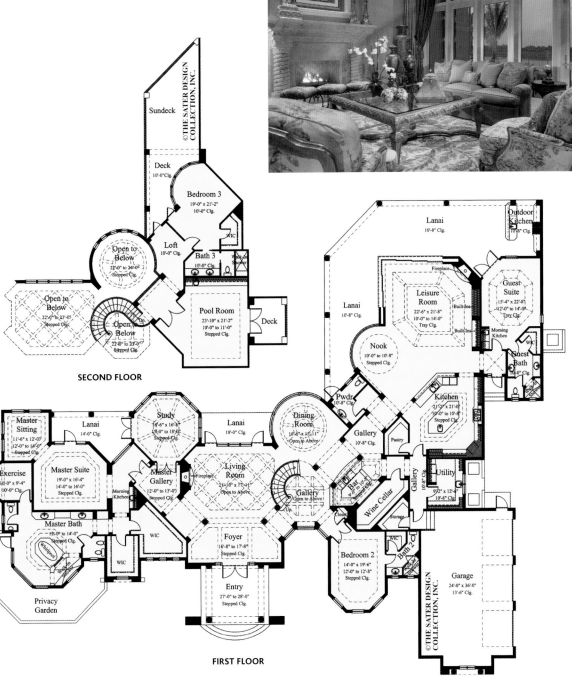

SECOND FLOOR

FIRST FLOOR

Photographed home may have been modified from the original construction documents.

SPECIFICATIONS:

Bedrooms: **4**

Baths: **4½**

Width: **142' 7"**

Depth: **118' 0"**

1st Floor: **6134** *sf*

2nd Floor: **1075** *sf*

Total Living: **7209** *sf*

Foundation: **Slab**

Exterior Wall: **8" Block**

PLAN PRICING:

Vellum & PDF - **$7209**

PLAN NUMBER:

6937

PLAN NAME:

Trissino

Ravello

An entry distinguished by a barrel-vault ceiling sets the stage for the timeless detailing found throughout Ravello. Arches, soffits and extraordinary ceiling treatments elevate the atmosphere throughout the home. An art niche is the focal point at one end of the central gallery hall, lined with arches and columns, while the luxurious master retreat's double-door entry is located at the opposite end.

Formal rooms are located front and center, with a stunning, uniquely-shaped living room greeting guests. A two-sided fireplace is shared with the private study that offers a built-in desk and custom shelving.

The formal dining room features French doors to the verandah and proximity to a wet bar with custom wine cellar. The view-oriented design offers plentiful connections to the rear outdoor living space beneath the spacious verandah, with French doors, retreating glass walls and walls of bowed glass throughout the plan.

Casual living space is also abundant, with a wide-open leisure room, kitchen and dining nook on the first floor, and a game room connecting two upper-level bedrooms. Outdoor living space includes a fireplace and a full outdoor kitchen.

Spacious master bedroom has built-in bed niche, view-oriented sitting room and verandah access.

Formal dining room has a unique stepped ceiling, rear views and access to the verandah.

In lieu of cabinetry over the kitchen's eating bar which could have potentially obstructed the extended views, a large, custom-designed furniture piece was built into an adjacent wall for additional storage.

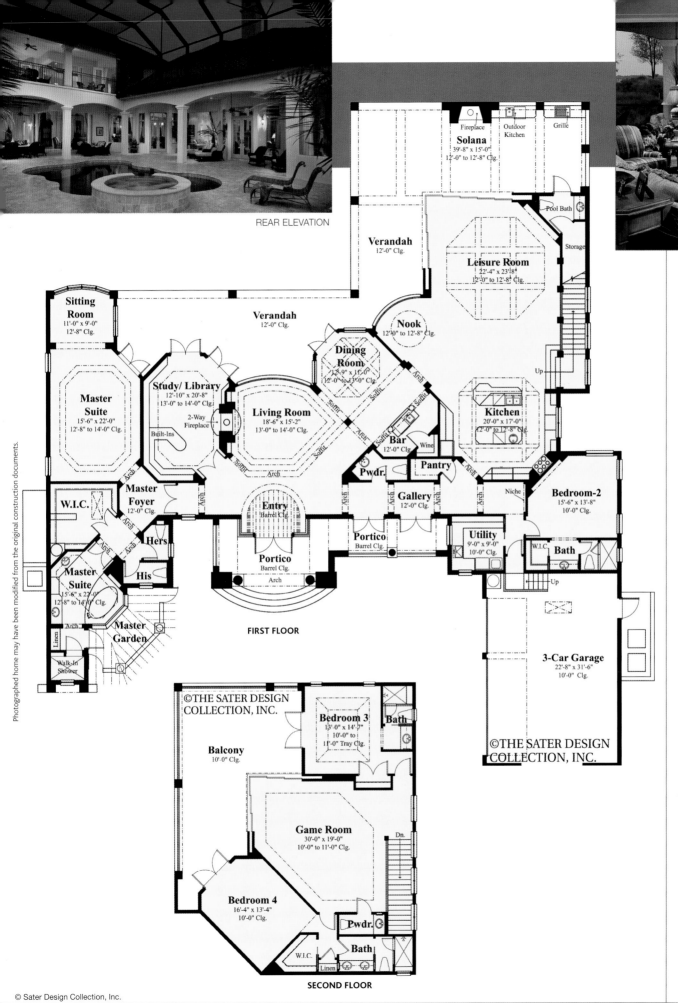

REAR ELEVATION

Solana
39'-8" x 15'-0"
12'-0" to 12'-8" Clg.

Fireplace · Outdoor Kitchen · Grille

Pool Bath

Storage

Verandah
12'-0" Clg.

Leisure Room
22'-4" x 23'-8"
12'-0" to 12'-8" Clg.

Up

Sitting Room
11'-0" x 9'-0"
12'-8" Clg.

Verandah
12'-0" Clg.

Nook
12'-10" to 12'-8" Clg.

Dining Room
13'-9" x 11'-0"
12'-0" to 13'-0" Clg.

Master Suite
15'-6" x 22'-0"
12'-8" to 14'-0" Clg.

Study/Library
12'-10" x 20'-8"
13'-0" to 14'-0" Clg.

2-Way Fireplace

Built-Ins

Living Room
18'-6" x 15'-2"
13'-0" to 14'-0" Clg.

Kitchen
20'-0" x 17'-0"
12'-0" to 12'-8" Clg.

Bar
12'-0" Clg.

Wine

Pantry

W.I.C.

Master Foyer
12'-0" Clg.

Pwdr.

Gallery
12'-0" Clg.

Niche

Bedroom-2
15'-6" x 13'-8"
10'-0" Clg.

Hers

His

Entry
Barrel Clg.

Portico
Barrel Clg.

Utility
9'-0" x 9'-0"
10'-0" Clg.

W.I.C.

Bath

Master Suite
15'-6" x 22'-0"
12'-8" to 14'-0" Clg.

Linen

Portico
Barrel Clg.

Arch

Up

Master Garden

Walk-In Shower

FIRST FLOOR

3-Car Garage
22'-8" x 31'-6"
10'-0" Clg.

Photographed home may have been modified from the original construction documents.

©THE SATER DESIGN COLLECTION, INC.

©THE SATER DESIGN COLLECTION, INC.

Balcony
10'-0" Clg.

Bedroom 3
13'-0" x 14'-7"
10'-0" to 11'-0" Tray Clg.

Bath

Game Room
30'-0" x 19'-0"
10'-0" to 11'-0" Clg.

Dn.

Bedroom 4
16'-4" x 13'-4"
10'-0" Clg.

Pwdr.

Bath

W.I.C.

Linen

SECOND FLOOR

© Sater Design Collection, Inc.

The leisure room opens up to the expansive verandah through a pair of retreating glass walls.

SPECIFICATIONS:

Bedrooms: **4**

Full Baths: **4**

Half Baths: **3**

Width: **100' 0"**

Depth: **113' 0"**

1st Floor: **4196** *sf*

2nd Floor: **1270** *sf*

Total Living: **5466** *sf*

Foundation: **Slab**

Exterior Wall: **8" Block**

PLAN PRICING:

Vellum & PDF - **$4373**

PLAN NUMBER:

6952

PLAN NAME:

Ravello

Not available for construction in Lee or Collier Counties, Florida.

Avondale

Views and more views. Each room in this impressive home – reminiscent of a country manor with its tile roof and punctuations of ledgestone, columns and iron accents – showcases the natural surroundings of the home site through expanses of fixed and moveable walls of glass.

Two ground-floor guest suites enjoy a secluded location, as does the master suite, which shares an entire wing of the home with the study. A second-floor bonus room serves as a second master suite, with a formal first-floor foyer soaring up to a vaulted ceiling, a morning kitchen, full bathroom and two balconies that amplify incoming light.

Abandoning conventional square and rectangular rooms, the floor plan opts for more interesting shapes that create a gentle undulation of the home's footprint and pockets of intimate interior and exterior spaces – a movement that is mimicked by the graceful curves of the waveless zero-edge pool.

Ceilings get extra attention with elaborate trays, barrel vaults, steps, coffers and a slumped arch ceiling with beams in the leisure room. This attention to detail is heightened by art niches, a two-sided fireplace shared by the study and formal living room, stone and marble throughout, and built-ins.

With two sets of French doors that open to a deck, guests always have the option of dining alfresco.

A barrel-vault ceiling in the formal entry and stepped ceiling in the living room, respectively, give this view from the lanai a sense of spacious elegance.

Designed with ergonomics in mind, the gourmet kitchen is comfortable and efficient. The butler's pantry is accessible from both the kitchen and the dining room.

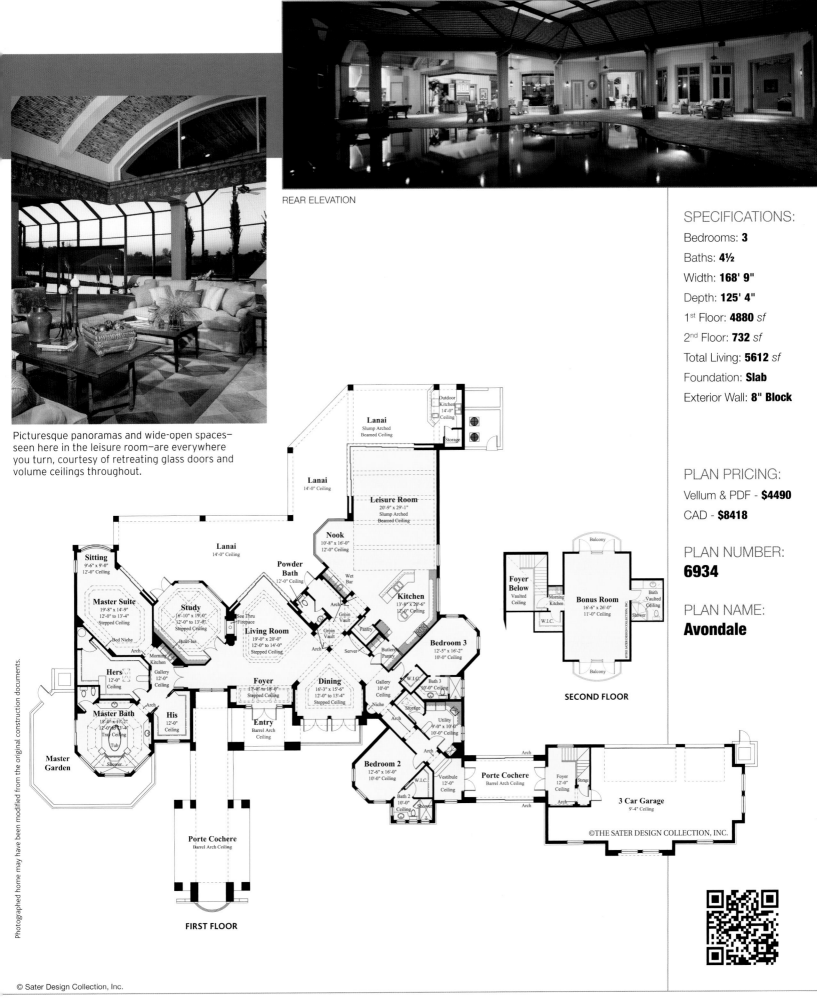

REAR ELEVATION

Picturesque panoramas and wide-open spaces—seen here in the leisure room—are everywhere you turn, courtesy of retreating glass doors and volume ceilings throughout.

SPECIFICATIONS:

Bedrooms: **3**

Baths: **4½**

Width: **168' 9"**

Depth: **125' 4"**

1st Floor: **4880** *sf*

2nd Floor: **732** *sf*

Total Living: **5612** *sf*

Foundation: **Slab**

Exterior Wall: **8" Block**

PLAN PRICING:

Vellum & PDF - **$4490**

CAD - **$8418**

PLAN NUMBER:

6934

PLAN NAME:

Avondale

FIRST FLOOR

SECOND FLOOR

©THE SATER DESIGN COLLECTION, INC.

© Sater Design Collection, Inc.

Pontedera

Mediterranean and Moorish influences come together to grant *Pontedera* its unique character and expansive graciousness, while 21st century features such as the two-story leisure room and high-tech gourmet kitchen lend balance and cutting-edge style. The dining room offers numerous entertaining options with its generous size and a beautiful niche designed to house a custom, built-in buffet and dramatic mirror. Tall arched windows with forward views provide soothing natural light and a lovely frame for tropical sunsets. Entertainment options are expended outdoors where the solana hosts a full kitchen, complete with built-in grille and serving counter. Accessed through zero-corner pocket sliding door in the leisure room, the solana offers a protected outdoor living space for cooking, dining and great conversations by the fire.

This riverfront manor captures the essence of refined living with its majestic façade, rich in Mediterranean details, and stunning interior features that speak of exceptional living in each and every room. Designed to celebrate one-of-a-kind architecture and embrace the outdoors, *Pontedera* is a home that indulges, inspires and nurtures.

A curved wall of sectioned glass and a striking, two-story fireplace create a spectacular setting in the formal living room.

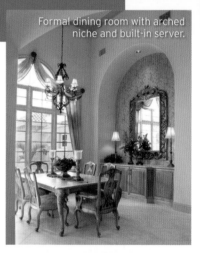

Formal dining room with arched niche and built-in server.

Polished stone columns are the only boundary separating the spacious gourmet kitchen from the view-oriented nook and leisure room.

Granite countered outdoor kitchen with solana and its fireplace beyond.

REAR ELEVATION

FIRST FLOOR

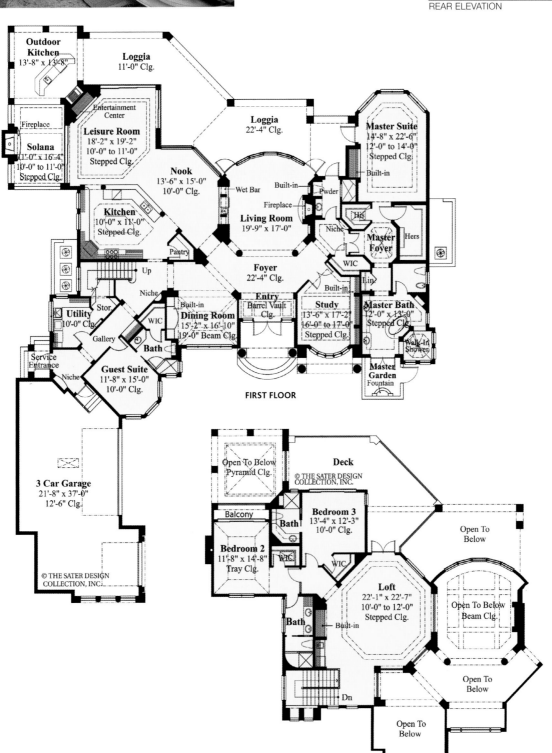

Outdoor Kitchen 13'-8" x 13'-8"

Loggia 11'-0" Clg.

Fireplace

Solana 11'-0" x 16'-4" 10'-0" to 11'-0" Stepped Clg.

Entertainment Center

Leisure Room 18'-2" x 19'-2" 10'-0" to 11'-0" Stepped Clg.

Loggia 22'-4" Clg.

Master Suite 14'-8" x 22'-6" 12'-0" to 14'-0" Stepped Clg

Built-in

Nook 13'-6" x 15'-0" 10'-0" Clg.

Wet Bar

Built-in

Powder

Fireplace

Kitchen 10'-0" x 11'-0" Stepped Clg.

Living Room 19'-9" x 17'-0"

His

Niche

Master Foyer

Hers

Pantry

Up

WIC

Lin

Niche

Foyer 22'-4" Clg.

Built-in

Utility 10'-0" Clg.

Stor.

Niche

Built-in

Dining Room 15'-2" x 16'-10" 19'-0" Beam Clg.

Entry

Barrel Vault Clg.

Study 13'-6" x 17'-2" 16'-0" to 17'-0" Stepped Clg.

Master Bath 12'-0" x 13'-0" Stepped Clg.

Gallery

WIC

Bath

Walk-In Shower

Service Entrance

Niche

Guest Suite 11'-8" x 15'-0" 10'-0" Clg.

Master Garden Fountain

3 Car Garage 21'-8" x 37'-0" 12'-6" Clg.

© THE SATER DESIGN COLLECTION, INC.

SECOND FLOOR

Open To Below Pyramid Clg.

Deck

© THE SATER DESIGN COLLECTION, INC.

Balcony

Bath

Bedroom 3 13'-4" x 12'-3" 10'-0" Clg.

Open To Below

Bedroom 2 11'-8" x 14'-8" Tray Clg.

WIC

WIC

Open To Below

Open To Below Beam Clg.

Bath

Built-in

Loft 22'-1" x 22'-7" 10'-0" to 12'-0" Stepped Clg.

Dn

Open To Below

© Sater Design Collection, Inc.

SPECIFICATIONS:

Bedrooms: **4**

Baths: **4½**

Width: **93' 9"**

Depth: **119' 10"**

1st Floor: **3873** *sf*

2nd Floor: **1289** *sf*

Total Living: **5162** *sf*

Foundation: **Slab**

Exterior Wall: **8" Block**

PLAN PRICING:

Vellum & PDF - **$4130**

CAD - **$7743**

PLAN NUMBER:

6943

PLAN NAME:

Pontedera

Huntington Lakes

Barrel dormers and cupola add architectural interest to this home, which offers Southern contemporary inspirations through the use of columns, arches, stone ornamentation and porte-cochere. Double doors open onto a bowed foyer, which introduces guests to the living room immediately ahead. The living room's two-sided fireplace is shared by the adjoining study, and sliding glass doors pocket into the wall, opening up the room to a generously sized covered lanai. The lanai embraces the rear of the home, wrapping around to the leisure room, where zero-corner sliding glass doors open up two corners-an effect that pushes the room outside.

Interesting ceilings throughout the home add elegance, visual interest and excitement. Stepped ceilings punctuate the living room, master bedroom, and dining room. Dramatic pyramid vaulted ceilings are used in the leisure room and repeated in the outdoor kitchen area of the lanai.

To the right of the plan, a gallery leads to the private master suite, which enjoys a fireplace and picturesque views of the lanai and in the front of the home, a private garden, seen from the master bath.

A great, carved-stone fireplace with tapered chimney warms this spacious living room.

The formal dining room, with its octagonal step ceiling, boasts an adjacent wet bar and a trio of front-facing bay windows.

Don't let the casual comfort of this kitchen fool you. It offers the serious chef every state-of-the-art food preparation amenity under the sun and boasts fabulous details like the stone backsplash and hood.

This cozy fireplace sitting area and impeccable outdoor kitchen are conveniently located just outside the guest suite.

REAR ELEVATION

SPECIFICATIONS:

Bedrooms: **3**

Baths: **4**

Width: **140' 7"**

Depth: **118' 3"**

1st Floor: **5170** *sf*

2nd Floor: **1600** *sf*

Total Living: **6770** *sf*

Foundation: **Slab**

Exterior Wall: **8" Block**

PLAN PRICING:

Vellum & PDF - **$6770**

PLAN NUMBER:

6900

PLAN NAME:

Huntington Lakes

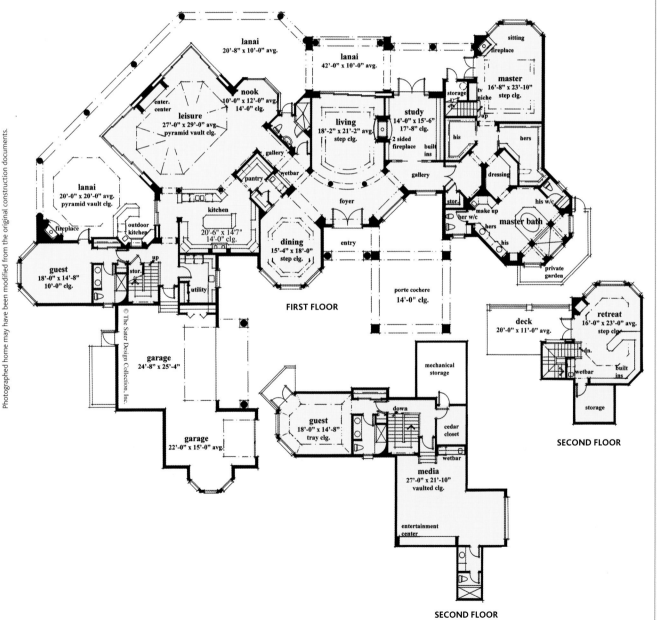

FIRST FLOOR

SECOND FLOOR

SECOND FLOOR

Windsor Court

The Windsor Court home plan is a classical modern masterpiece. It's towering entry with standing seam metal roof leads into a surprising courtyard that feels more like a tropical resort. On either side of the entry, overlooking the courtyard are two detached guest suites. Each suite is completely self contained with morning kitchen and dining alcove. The baths are like master baths with his/hers vanities and whirlpool tub with separate shower.

Upon entering one is greeted by a Koi pond that is separated by a bridge leading to a free formed pool. The covered veranda embraces the courtyard and incorporates an outdoor kitchen. Through the veranda is the entrance to the main house. Overlooking the veranda and courtyard are the dining room and study with floor to ceiling mitered glass, and gathering room with its corner-less pocketing sliding glass doors. At the end of the courtyard are two cabanas and a rock waterfall cascading into a semi-circular spa.

The main house is divided into three distinct zones. Upon entering the foyer, one is ushered into the family living zone with open leisure room, kitchen and nook. The formal dining room is adjacent, accessed via a broad gallery that leads to the utility room and garage. The central gathering room is the entertainment zone. This large diamond shaped room contains a sunken wet bar and is center stage to views of rear as well as enjoying the pool and courtyard.

Gathering room with cove lit pyramid vaulted ceiling is perfect for entertaining with sunken bar overlooking views beyond.

Dining room with floor to ceiling window walls look to home's courtyard.

Contemporary European styled dual island kitchen is ideally suited for cooking and guests simultaneously.

COURTYARD

The breakfast nook's floor-to-ceiling wall of curved glass provides panoramic, "big-screen" views – views that seem to extend for miles and miles – with the morning's first cup of coffee.

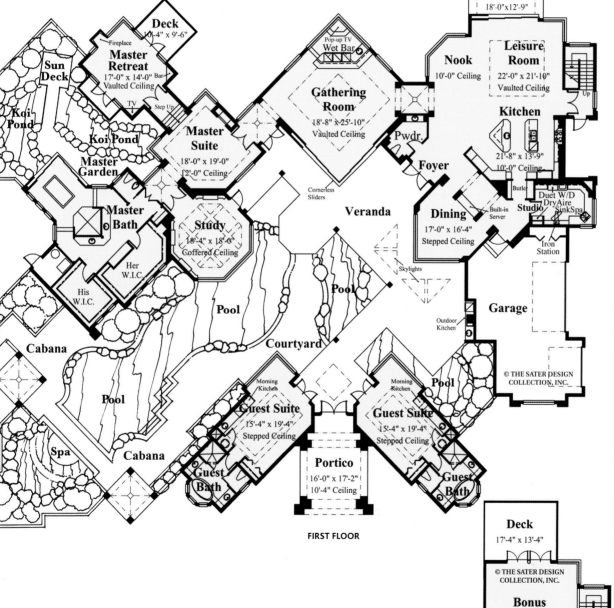

FIRST FLOOR

Deck
10'-4" x 9'-6"

Master Retreat
17'-0" x 14'-0"
Vaulted Ceiling

Sun Deck

Koi Pond

Koi Pond

Master Garden

Master Bath

Master Suite
18'-0" x 19'-0"
12'-0" Ceiling

Study
18'-4" x 18'-0"
Coffered Ceiling

Her W.I.C.

His W.I.C.

Cabana

Pool

Spa

Cabana

Pop-up TV
Wet Bar

Gathering Room
18'-8" x 25'-10"
Vaulted Ceiling

Cornerless Sliders

Veranda

Pool

Pool

Courtyard

Skylights

Lanai
18'-0"x12'-9"

Leisure Room
22'-0" x 21'-10"
Vaulted Ceiling

Nook
10'-0" Ceiling

Kitchen
21'-8" x 13'-9"
10'-0" Ceiling

Pwdr.

Foyer

Dining
17'-0" x 16'-4"
Stepped Ceiling

Built-in Server

Butler

Studio

Duet W/D
DryAire
Sink Spa

Iron Station

Garage

Outdoor Kitchen

© THE SATER DESIGN COLLECTION, INC.

Morning Kitchen

Guest Suite
15'-4" x 19'-4"
Stepped Ceiling

Guest Bath

Portico
16'-0" x 17'-2"
10'-4" Ceiling

Morning Kitchen

Guest Suite
15'-4" x 19'-4"
Stepped Ceiling

Pool

Guest Bath

SECOND FLOOR

Deck
17'-4" x 13'-4"

© THE SATER DESIGN COLLECTION, INC.

Bonus Room
22'-1" x 21'-9"

Down

Mechanical Room

SPECIFICATIONS:

Bedrooms: **3**

Baths: **3½**

Width: **137' 4"**

Depth: **103' 0"**

1st Floor: **5887** *sf*

2nd Floor: **570** *sf*

Total Living: **6457** *sf*

Foundation: **Slab**

Exterior Wall: **8" Block**

PLAN PRICING:

Vellum & PDF - **$5166**

CAD - **$9686**

PLAN NUMBER:

6751

PLAN NAME:

Windsor Court

Exquisite crown moulding gives an aura of sophistication to an otherwise very relaxed living area, while retreating sliding glass doors provide a sweeping view of the patio and landscape beyond.

St. Regis Grand

Rambling lanais and a spacious courtyard extend the living spaces, creating an environment that is relaxed and inviting. A bold turret shelters glass-paneled entry doors, which yield to a foyer defined by sculpted arches and massive decorative columns. Colonnades provide a sense of separation in the public realm without interrupting interior vistas that extend to the outdoors.

Retreating glass walls at the heart of the home permit a natural flow between the living room and lanai. Nearby a server includes a wet bar, storage and access to a cabana-style powder bath that allows sunbathers and swimmers an easy transition into the home from the pool area.

The gourmet kitchen includes a centered food-preparation island with a sink and a snack counter that overlooks the leisure room. A vaulted ceiling highlights the casual living space, which provides built-in cabinetry and wide-open links to the lanai.

Bay windows harbor an oversized shower in the private bath and a sitting area in the bedroom. An outdoor kitchen handles crowd-sized gatherings or more intimate meals by the fireplace.

The master suit offers a secluded retreat for the homeowners, with plenty of natural light. A bow window brightens the sitting area of the owners' bedroom, and separate baths provide luxe amenities, including a garden tub.

The large gourmet kitchen easily accommodates many chefs. Featuring a large walk-in pantry, double ovens and center island with vegetable sink and food-prep area. The "pièce de résistance" of this generous layout is the single paned window with hood moulding that offers a view of the outdoor fireplace just beyond the covered lanai.

REAR ELEVATION

As if dueling his-and-hers baths weren't enough, this semi-circular sitting room off the master suite, with its floor-to-ceiling radius glass, is the perfect place for relaxing – and stargazing.

SPECIFICATIONS:

Bedrooms: **4**

Baths: **6½**

Width: **106' 6"**

Depth: **106' 0"**

1st Floor: **4784** *sf*

2nd Floor: **481** *sf*

Total Living: **5265** *sf*

Foundation: **Slab**

Exterior Wall: **8" Block**

PLAN PRICING:

Vellum & PDF - **$4212**

PLAN NUMBER:

6916

PLAN NAME:

St. Regis Grand

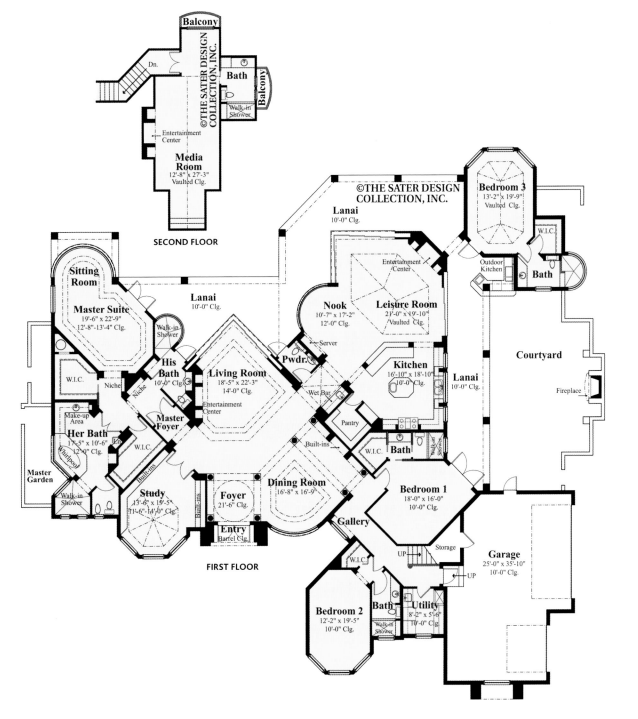

SECOND FLOOR

FIRST FLOOR

©THE SATER DESIGN COLLECTION, INC.

©THE SATER DESIGN COLLECTION, INC.

The leisure room features zero-corner pocketed glass doors. The walls disappears, highlighting the freestanding entertainment center.

A carved coffer provides a niche for a server, while the arched ceiling serves as a complement to the arch-top window in this formal dining area.

Molina

The Molina home plan has a contemporary Mediterranean flavor with arched entry, tiled roofs and towering accents. This home flows seamlessly from indoors to outside with five sets of pocketing corner-less sliding glass doors and wrap around verandas. This home is perfect for entertaining as well as relaxation.

One is greeted by the living room with pocketing corner-less sliding doors. Adjacent is the formal dining room with domed ceiling. Bridging the formal and informal areas is a centrally located wet bar. The spacious leisure room is wrapped in glass and is enjoined by the kitchen and nook. Beyond is an outdoor living space with fireplace and outdoor kitchen.

The master suite features a foyer that overlooks a private courtyard with fountain. The master bath has distinct his and hers areas with a walk-in shower and whirlpool tub that looks onto master garden.

There are two bedrooms on first floor with a bonus room above with a wet bar and expansive covered veranda. The Molina home plan has 6340 square feet of living area.

Contemporary conveniences - expansive counter space, food-prep center island and double sinks, to name just a few - abound in this casual, yet state-of-the-art kitchen.

REAR ELEVATION

Zero-corner glass doors and expansive windows in the master suite allow this space to stretch outward, encompassing both the wrap-around veranda on one side and the master garden on the other.

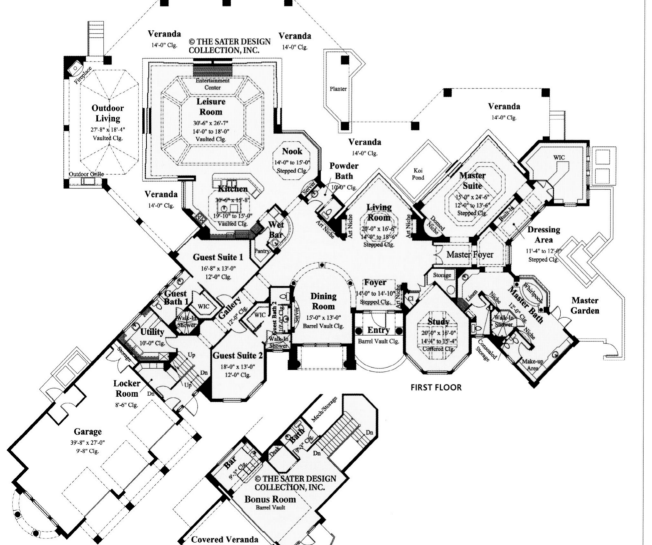

FIRST FLOOR

SECOND FLOOR

SPECIFICATIONS:

Bedrooms: **3**

Full Baths: **3**

Half Baths: **2**

Width: **146' 0"**

Depth: **132' 5"**

1st Floor: **5696** *sf*

2nd Floor: **644** *sf*

Total Living: **6340** *sf*

Foundation: **Slab**

Exterior Wall: **8" Block**

PLAN PRICING:

Vellum & PDF - **$5072**

CAD - **$9510**

PLAN NUMBER:

6931

PLAN NAME:

Molina

A curving wall of three soaring, pointed-arch windows opens the living room to the patio beyond.

An exposed-beam ceiling in the solana give the space a rustic feel. On cool evenings, the tiled, outdoor hearth makes for a perfect gathering spot.

Marrakesh

This grand villa displays an affinity for the native terrain, with natural materials and large expanses of glass that permit earthen-hued walls to absorb the scenery. Rough-hewn timbers contradict a highly refined palette of textures in the living room, and a two-sided fireplace links this formal space with a private study. Sculpted forms and elaborate arches articulate the ornate vocabulary of the revival style, offset by naïve elements, such as rugged trusses and masonry walls.

An open arrangement of the formal living and dining rooms creates an entertainment area that is completed by a wine cellar. Paneled cabinetry enhances the wet bar and pantry positioned between the dining room and kitchen to facilitate planned events. Retreating glass walls permit a fluid boundary between the casual living zone and the outdoor spaces, which include an alfresco kitchen and a rambling terrace with a pool and spa. Two über-luxe guest suites frame a spacious solana with a beamed ceiling and a massive fireplace. On the opposite side of the plan, the master wing features a secluded sitting bay and a compartmented bath with a bumped-out bay that harbors an oversized walk-in shower.

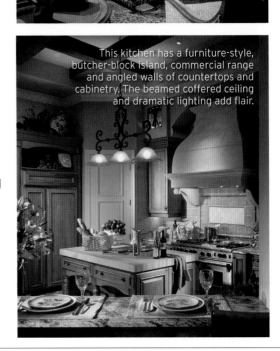

This kitchen has a furniture-style, butcher-block island, commercial range and angled walls of countertops and cabinetry. The beamed coffered ceiling and dramatic lighting add flair.

Aged wood doors open into wine cellar. Entry doors are seen in distance.

A series of pillared arches nobly lead to the master bath. An oval tub is dramatically centered under a coffered ceiling and faces a private garden through bay windows.

Lanai profiles mimic and draw attention to the pointed-arch living room window, while a secluded nook created by angled walls of glass offers an ideal spot for morning lattes.

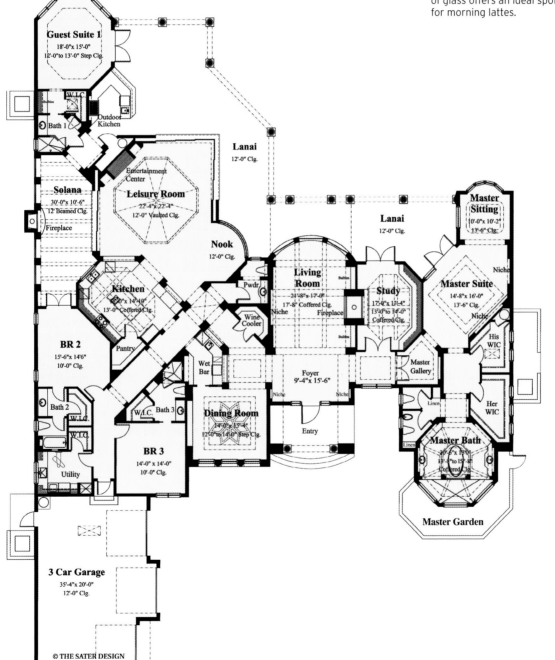

SPECIFICATIONS:

Bedrooms: **4**

Baths: **4½**

Width: **100' 0"**

Depth: **138' 10"**

1st Floor: **4705** sf

Guest Suite: **404** sf

Total Living: **5109** sf

Foundation: **Slab**

Exterior Wall: **8" Block**

PLAN PRICING:

Vellum & PDF - **$4087**

CAD - **$7664**

PLAN NUMBER:
6942

PLAN NAME:

Marrakesh

Dauphino

Virtually every room in this home opens onto or overlooks the veranda. Interesting outdoor spaces are created by the movement of the house – an effect achieved by abandoning conventionally shaped square or rectangular rooms. Architectural elements used outside – colonnades, arches, corbels and columns – are repeated inside.

Large fixed windows and moveable walls of glass welcome in natural light and offer expansive views of the home's place in the world. The leisure room seems to float into the veranda. Bayed windows in other rooms also have double French doors with direct access to these special outdoor spaces. And mitered windows used in the breakfast nook, the master suite sitting area and a sitting area in the second-floor guest room offer maximum views.

Architectural ceilings – featuring steps, a coffer in the study and a wood-clad pyramid in the leisure room – add dramatic interest. Columns lend a degree of formality and subtle definition between the grand foyer, living room and dining room. A two-sided fireplace is shared by the living room and study.

Extraordinary attention to detail is seen throughout this home.

The leisure room practically floats into the veranda with three walls of sliding glass doors that fuse the space with nature.

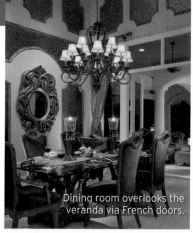

Dining room overlooks the veranda via French doors.

Granite countertops and inlaid stone floors add refined elegance to the kitchen, while commercial-grade appliances and a menu-planning desk offer state-of-the-art amenities for the serious chef. Faux and tile walls add ambient warmth.

REAR ELEVATION

Outdoor kitchen with raised serving bar.

Outdoor Kitchen 12'-0" Clg.

Veranda 12'-0" Clg.

Leisure Room 28'-2" x 26'-3" Pyramid Clg.

Nook 12'-0" Clg.

Veranda 12'-0" Clg.

Powder Bath 10'-0" Clg.

Veranda 20'-4" Clg.

Veranda 12'-0" Clg.

Sitting 10'-8" 5'-2" 12'-0" Clg.

Master Suite 21'-8" x 14'-0" 12'-0" to 14'-0" Stepped Clg.

Kitchen 24'-0" x 17'-1" 11'-0" to 12'-0" Stepped Clg.

Dining Room 13'-10" x 15'-3" 16'-0" to 18'-0" Stepped Clg.

Living Room 22'-3" x 16'-8" 20'-4" to 22'-8" Stepped Clg.

Study 18'-4" x 18'-4" 16'-0" to 17'-0" Coffered Clg.

Linen

Art Niche

WIC

Guest Suite 2 23'-6" x 13'-0" 10'-0" Clg.

Butler Pantry

Foyer 18'-0" to 18'-8" Stepped Clg.

Make-up Area

WIC

Master Bath

Guest Bath 2

Storage

Gallery 10'-0" Clg.

Up

WIC

Art Niche

Art Niche

WIC

Walk-In Shower

Guest Bath 1 10'-0" Clg.

Entry 20'-4" Clg.

Walk-In Shower

Walk-In Shower

12'-0" Clg.

Guest Suite 1 15'-5" x 14'-0" 14'-0" Clg.

Utility 10'-0" Clg.

Master Garden

Whirlpool

FIRST FLOOR

Garage 12'-0" Clg.

Balcony

Guest Suite 26'-7" x 15'-1" 10'-8" Clg.

Guest Bath 10'-0" Clg.

WIC

Art Niche

Storage

Walk-In Shower

Dn

Art Niche

SECOND FLOOR

Arch-top transom windows and doors reveal the veranda beyond. A stately fireplace radiates as a warm focal point.

SPECIFICATIONS:

Bedrooms: **4**

Baths: **4½**

Width: **132' 8"**

Depth: **117' 3"**

1st Floor: **5307** *sf*

2nd Floor: **497** *sf*

Total Living: **5804** *sf*

Foundation: **Slab**

Exterior Wall: **8" Block**

PLAN PRICING:

Vellum & PDF - **$4643**

CAD - **$8706**

PLAN NUMBER:

6933

PLAN NAME:

Dauphino

Andros Island

From hues and architectural lines that mimic the natural landscape, to disappearing walls and a spectacular courtyard that has an indoor feel, the intent of this home is to embrace the outdoors. The dining room, guest suite and study at the front of the home accomplish this with floor-to-ceiling bay windows. In the living room, retreating glass walls create flawless indoor-outdoor transitions. The kitchen flows into a leisure room that also has disappearing sliders to the lanai and courtyard.

Custom details, including a corner entertainment unit in the leisure room and sunburst-laden transoms above the kitchen bar, infuse the home with individuality. The master suite reveals elegant respite starting with the entry foyer and continuing into a walk-in shower that merges with a private outdoor garden. The second-level bonus room offers a substantial flexible space that includes a full bathroom and balcony.

Leisure room with pyramid vaulted wood ceiling and built-in entertainment center.

The richly appointed kitchen with butcher block capped island is perfect for preparing gourmet meals or serving parties.

The possibilities for entertaining are endless in this captivating courtyard adjacent to the lanai. Columns, tray ceilings and tile floors exude an indoor feel, while the island-inspired fireplace, fully appointed kitchen and hearty furniture embrace any climactic changes.

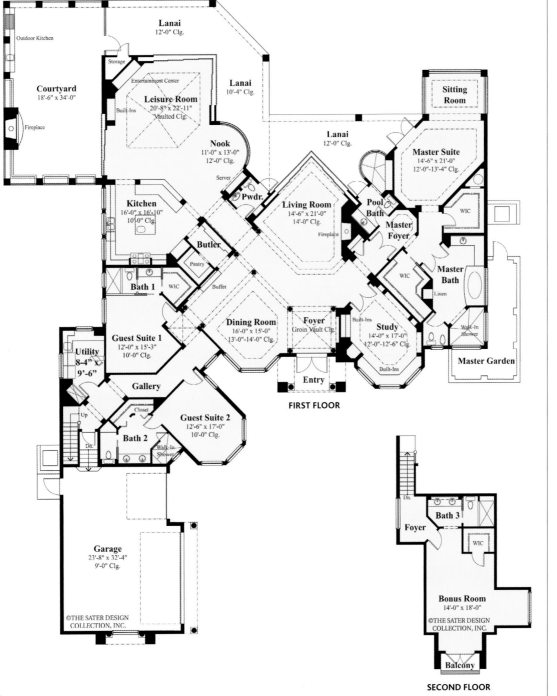

FIRST FLOOR

©THE SATER DESIGN COLLECTION, INC.

SECOND FLOOR

©THE SATER DESIGN COLLECTION, INC.

© Sater Design Collection, Inc.

Photographed home may have been modified from the original construction documents.

SPECIFICATIONS:

Bedrooms: **3**

Baths: **4½**

Width: **98' 5"**

Depth: **125' 11"**

1st Floor: **4630** *sf*

2nd Floor: **590** *sf*

Total Living: **5220** *sf*

Foundation: **Slab**

Exterior Wall: **8" Block**

PLAN PRICING:

Vellum & PDF - **$4176**

CAD - **$7830**

PLAN NUMBER:

6927

PLAN NAME:

Andros Island

The grand hall transitions seamlessly to the formal salon nestled beneath a second-story balcony. Meanwhile, an elegant radiuses staircase curves its way to the guest suites above and a sitting loft with balcony.

A 180-degree, floor-to-ceiling bay window in the dining room gives dinner guests a real taste of the great outdoors with a bigger-than-life panoramic view across the veranda.

Prestonwood

An award-winning design, this stately villa draws inspiration from classical Old-World architecture. The wide front steps lead past a barrel-vault entry into the circular-shaped grand hall, sitting under a soaring 36-foot domed ceiling. This unique space is the center focus for living spaces that stretch beyond, with columns used to provide definition and separation. Extensive use of beamed ceilings, art niches, hand-finished cabinetry and outdoor living spaces reveal a unique character of dignified livability throughout the house.

The angled layout of the main part of the home provides for a triangle-shaped veranda flanked by the private master suite on one side and family living and dining areas on the other. The intimate leisure room features built-in cabinetry and an outdoor kitchen beyond retreating glass walls. The adjacent kitchen seamlessly blends functional and decorative uses, and the formal dining room fuses with the outdoors through a wall of glass.

After dinner, guests will enjoy retreating to their rooms via the regal staircase with wrought-iron railing in the grand hall that curves elegantly to a second floor loft. The suites each feature a full bath, walk-in closet and share a deck overlooking the pool.

A massive sheet of glass draws the lush outdoors into a kitchen that glows with furniture-like cabinetry, glassy granite countertops, and a unique and seamless mix of art pieces and useful kitchen accessories.

REAR ELEVATION

Arched niches accented with custom metalwork provide a one-of-a-kind framework for the king-sized bed. An octagonal-shaped sitting room featuring a vaulted ceiling and morning kitchen complete the suite for gracious day-to-night pleasures.

SPECIFICATIONS:

Bedrooms: **3**

Baths: **3½**

Width: **117' 2"**

Depth: **131' 7"**

1st Floor: **4715** *sf*

2nd Floor: **1209** *sf*

Total Living: **5924** *sf*

Foundation: **Slab**

Exterior Wall: **8" Block**

PLAN PRICING:

Vellum & PDF - **$4739**

PLAN NUMBER:

6922

PLAN NAME:

Prestonwood

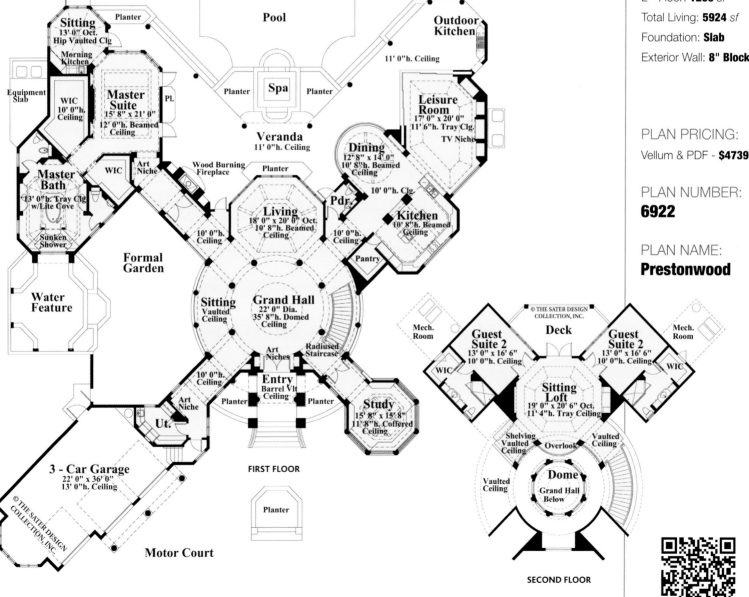

Photographed home may have been modified from the original construction documents.

FIRST FLOOR

SECOND FLOOR

Saraceno

Arches and simple lines dominate the classic architecture of this home with corbels, banding, and hipped roofs providing visual excitement. Designed to celebrate outdoor living and the views from inside, the rear elevation of this home is punctuated heavily by windows and sliding glass doors. These large openings provide wide open views of the home's surroundings and serving to bring the outside in. Designed for entertaining, an open floor plan between living and leisure room allows a wet bar to serve as the staging area for refreshments and hors d'oeuvres. Boundaries between these spaces are subtly defined by columns and changing ceilings. Natural light streams into the leisure room through zero-corner sliding glass doors and a second story band of vertical windows, opening up this room to the outdoors. This drama is heightened by a 22-foot coffered ceiling. A second floor loft overlooks the leisure room, and provides a private retreat for the fourth bedroom. Ceilings are elevated to an art form with dramatic treatments like trays and coffers taking on geometric shapes-a circle in the breakfast nook, an octagon in the master sitting area, and crisp coffers formed by diagonal beams in the leisure room. Cove and recessed lighting enhance the effect.

Arched foyer doorway opens onto living room. The formal dining and stairway to second floor is seen in the distance.

Island kitchen with walk-in pantry and serving bar overlooks leisure room.

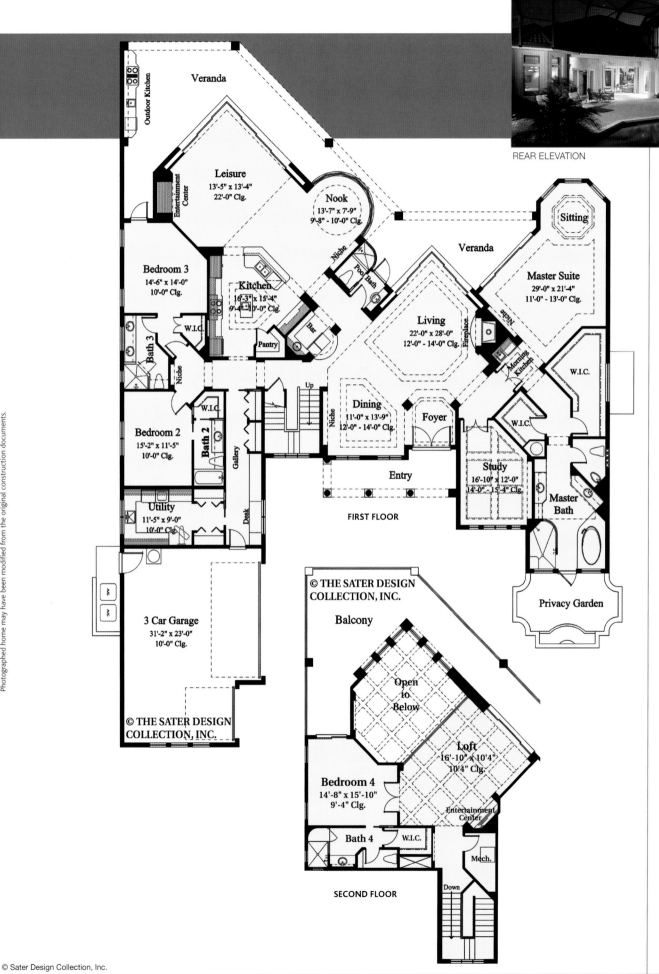

REAR ELEVATION

FIRST FLOOR

Veranda

Outdoor Kitchen

Leisure
13'-5" x 13'-4"
22'-0" Clg.

Nook
13'-7" x 7'-9"
9'-8" - 10'-0" Clg.

Sitting

Veranda

Master Suite
29'-0" x 21'-4"
11'-0" - 13'-0" Clg.

Entertainment Center

Bedroom 3
14'-6" x 14'-0"
10'-0" Clg.

Kitchen
16'-3" x 15'-4"
9'-4" - 10'-0" Clg.

Bath 3

W.I.C.

Niche

Pool Bath

Bar

Pantry

Living
22'-0" x 28'-0"
12'-0" - 14'-0" Clg.

Fireplace

Niche

Morning Kitchen

W.I.C.

W.I.C.

Bedroom 2
15'-2" x 11'-5"
10'-0" Clg.

W.I.C.

Bath 2

Gallery

Up

Dining
11'-0" x 13'-9"
12'-0" - 14'-0" Clg.

Niche

Foyer

Study
16'-10" x 12'-0"
14'-0" - 15'-4" Clg.

Entry

Utility
11'-5" x 9'-0"
10'-0" Clg.

Desk

Master Bath

3 Car Garage
31'-2" x 23'-0"
10'-0" Clg.

Privacy Garden

© THE SATER DESIGN COLLECTION, INC.

SECOND FLOOR

Balcony

© THE SATER DESIGN COLLECTION, INC.

Open to Below

Loft
16'-10" x 10'4"
10'4" Clg.

Bedroom 4
14'-8" x 15'-10"
9'-4" Clg.

Entertainment Center

Bath 4

W.I.C.

Mech.

Down

SPECIFICATIONS:

Bedrooms: **4**

Baths: **5**

Width: **81' 10"**

Depth: **113' 0"**

1st Floor: **4137** sf

2nd Floor: **876** sf

Total Living: **5013** sf

Foundation: **Slab**

Exterior Wall: **8" Block**

PLAN PRICING:

Vellum & PDF - **$4010**

CAD - **$7520**

PLAN NUMBER:

6929

PLAN NAME:

Saraceno

REAR ELEVATION

Domenico

© Sater Design Collection, Inc.

SPECIFICATIONS:

Bedrooms: **4**

Full Baths: **4**

Half Baths: **2**

Width: **92' 0"**

Depth: **157' 3"**

1st Floor: **4309** *sf*

Cabana: **400** *sf*

2nd Floor: **1417** *sf*

Total Living: **6126** *sf*

Foundation: **Slab**

PLAN PRICING:

Vellum & PDF - **$4901**

PLAN NUMBER:

8069

Past the magnificent portico entry, columns and arches define the formal spaces designed for greeting and entertaining guests, with a wet bar providing refreshments. To the rear of the plan, the leisure room flows onto the solana and loggia, with a nearby cabana offering a perfect retreat for guests. On the opposite wing, the master suite opens to a private pavilion. Upstairs, friends and family will enjoy the clubroom, wet bar and state-of-the-art theater room.

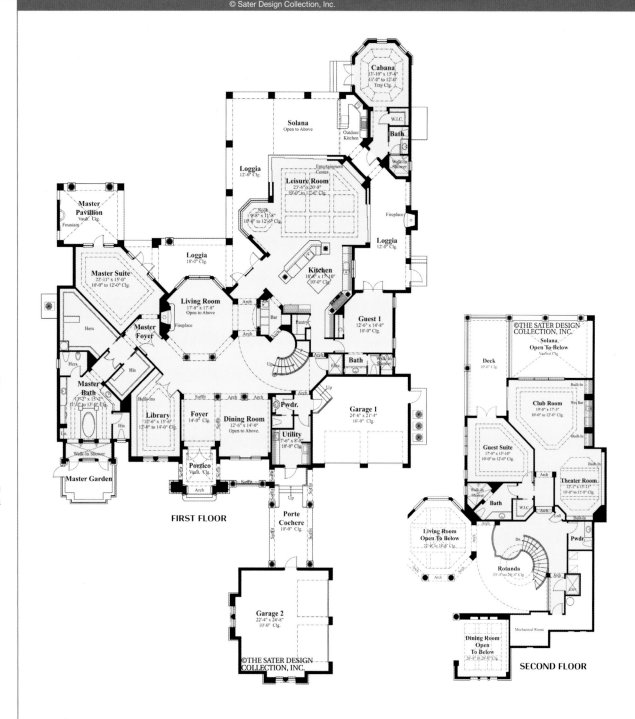

FIRST FLOOR

SECOND FLOOR

Port Royal Way

© Sater Design Collection, Inc.

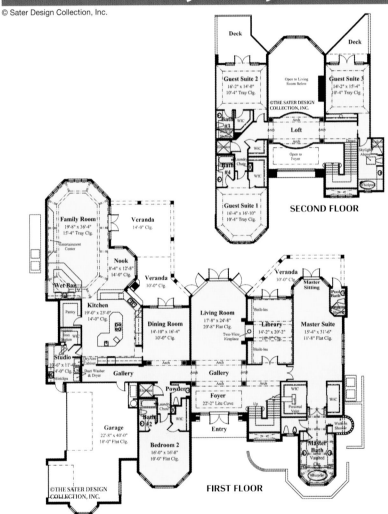

SECOND FLOOR

FIRST FLOOR

Napier

© Sater Design Collection, Inc.

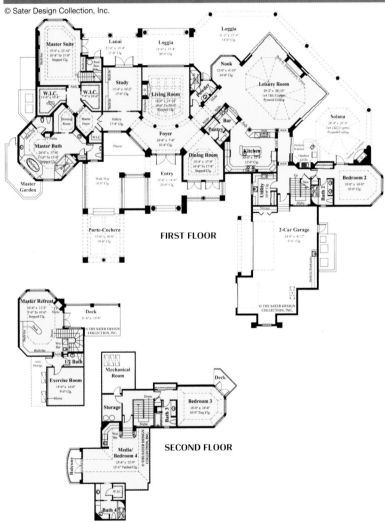

FIRST FLOOR

SECOND FLOOR

SPECIFICATIONS:

Bedrooms: **5**

Baths: **6½**

Width: **98' 0"**

Depth: **103' 8"**

1st Floor: **4879** sf

2nd Floor: **1625** sf

Total Living: **6504** sf

Foundation: **Slab**

PLAN PRICING:

Vellum & PDF - **$5203**

CAD - **$9756**

PLAN NUMBER:
6635

SPECIFICATIONS:

Bedrooms: **4**

Baths: **5½**

Width: **140' 7"**

Depth: **116' 10"**

1st Floor: **5155** sf

2nd Floor: **1937** sf

Total Living: **7092** sf

Foundation: **Slab**

PLAN PRICING:

Vellum & PDF - **$7092**

CAD - **$12056**

PLAN NUMBER:
6926

Estate Home Collection

*These homes plans range in size from **3500** square feet to **4999** square feet of living area.*

Brindisi

Our "Estate Home Collection" home plans are easily at home in a gated community as they are on acreage. These homes all contain the same expected Sater Design amenities found in all our designs. Rich and intricate exteriors, well laid out floor plans and warm detailed interiors are all an essential part of each and every house plan.

We hope you will find your new home from amongst this collection of beautiful luxury homes.

Brindisi

REAR ELEVATION

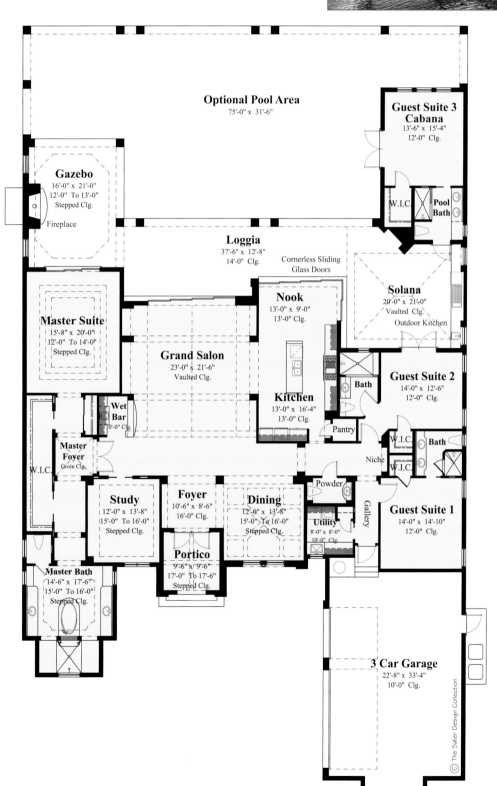

Optional Pool Area
75'-0" x 31'-6"

Gazebo
16'-0" x 21'-0"
12'-0" To 13'-0"
Stepped Clg.
Fireplace

Guest Suite 3 Cabana
13'-6" x 15'-4"
12'-0" Clg.

W.I.C. Pool Bath

Loggia
37'-6" x 12'-8"
14'-0" Clg.

Cornerless Sliding Glass Doors

Nook
13'-0" x 9'-0"
13'-0" Clg.

Solana
20'-0" x 21'-0"
Vaulted Clg.
Outdoor Kitchen

Master Suite
15'-8" x 20'-0"
12'-0" To 14'-0"
Stepped Clg.

Grand Salon
23'-0" x 21'-6"
Vaulted Clg.

Kitchen
13'-0" x 16'-4"
13'-0" Clg.

Guest Suite 2
14'-0" x 12'-6"
12'-0" Clg.

Bath

Pantry

W.I.C. Bath

Wet Bar
10'-0" Clg.

Master Foyer
Groin Clg.

W.I.C.

Study
12'-0" x 13'-8"
15'-0" To 16'-0"
Stepped Clg.

Foyer
10'-6" x 8'-6"
16'-0" Clg.

Dining
12'-0" x 13'-8"
15'-0" To 16'-0"
Stepped Clg.

Powder

Niche

Guest Suite 1
14'-0" x 14'-10"
12'-0" Clg.

Gallery

Utility
8'-0" x 8'-0"
10'-0" Clg.

Portico
9'-6" x 9'-6"
17'-0" To 17'-6"
Stepped Clg.

Master Bath
14'-6" x 17'-6"
15'-0" To 16'-0"
Stepped Clg.

3 Car Garage
22'-8" x 33'-4"
10'-0" Clg.

© The Sater Design Collection

SPECIFICATIONS:

Bedrooms: **4**

Baths: **4½**

Width: **75' 0"**

Depth: **125' 1"**

1st Floor: **3458** *sf*

Cabana: **373** *sf*

Total Living: **3831** *sf*

Foundation: **Slab**

PLAN PRICING:

Vellum & PDF - **$2490**

CAD - **$4406**

PLAN NUMBER:

6963

A blended influence of Mediterranean and Contemporary architectural styles defines Brindisi. This functional plan boasts a multitude of practical amenities throughout the casually elegant living spaces. The result is a plan that lives larger than its square footage. Perfect for hosting friends and family, this home offers three guest suites with private baths.

Not available for construction in Lee or Collier Counties, Florida.

Moderno

Aurora Award Winner!

Builders Choice & Custom Home Award Winner!

The *Moderno* home plan is a blend of clean contemporary styling and elegant casual living. It's presence gives a sense of space way beyond its 3507 square feet of living area.

Incorporating stuccoed walls with stacked stone accents give a modern yet warm appearance. The home is crowned with a standing seam metal hipped roof. Cabled railing and bronze framed windows complete the ensemble.

The great room opens to the rear via a pocketing wall of glass sliding doors. It is accented by built-ins for TV and display. The kitchen incorporates a center island for prep and serving. The adjacent dining area features a mitered glass bay window and built-in bench for seating.

The highlight of the home is it's sumptuous master retreat. The master foyer yields to another dressing vestibule that gives glances of the view beyond thru it's decorative divider, allowing an abundance of natural light. The master bath with his and hers vanities and glass enclosed shower and separate water closet gives a very Asian resort feel to the bath. The climax is the freestanding soaking tub with French door to private garden beyond.

Outdoor living is celebrated with outdoor kitchen in the background.

Great room built-ins with entry door and stairway in background.

The great room with adjacent kitchen and dining area, showcases the homes open, casual lifestyle as well as its view oriented floor plan.

The spacious master bathroom features his and her vanities, a freestanding tub and access to a private garden.

The master suite faces the verandah, making it the perfect location for waking up to beautiful water views.

The outdoor cabana is located right off of the master suite.

The master suite faces the verandah, making it the perfect location for waking up to beautiful water views.

*~ Any plan can be customized to meet your needs, find out how by calling **800-718-7526**. ~*

Study with views of the front yard and master garden.

First floor full bath with access to the verandah in the distance.

Outdoor kitchen and eating area just outside of the great room.

Second floor guest bedroom with sliders that open out to the balcony and sun deck.

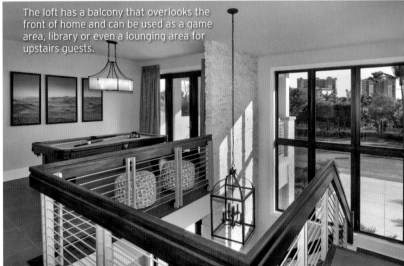

The loft has a balcony that overlooks the front of home and can be used as a game area, library or even a lounging area for upstairs guests.

Second floor guest room's bathroom with granite countertops and glass enclosed walk-in shower.

Foyer and staircase with beautiful metal railing with wood handrail gives contrast to a two story stone wall.

A beautiful view from the solana through to the great room and beyond to the front door showcases the homes open, casual lifestyle.

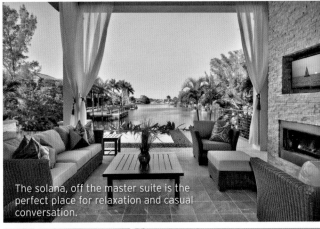

The solana, off the master suite is the perfect place for relaxation and casual conversation.

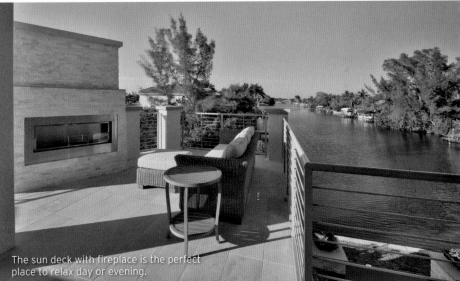

The sun deck with fireplace is the perfect place to relax day or evening.

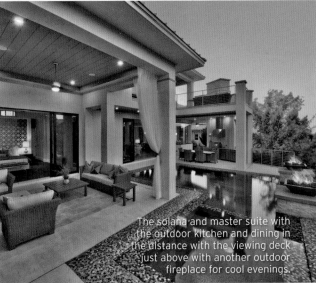

The solana and master suite with the outdoor kitchen and dining in the distance with the viewing deck just above with another outdoor fireplace for cool evenings.

Moderno's outdoor solana, off the master suite with TV and fireplace is counter balanced by its outdoor kitchen and dining area. The infinity edge pool with dual pillared fire pots set the stage.

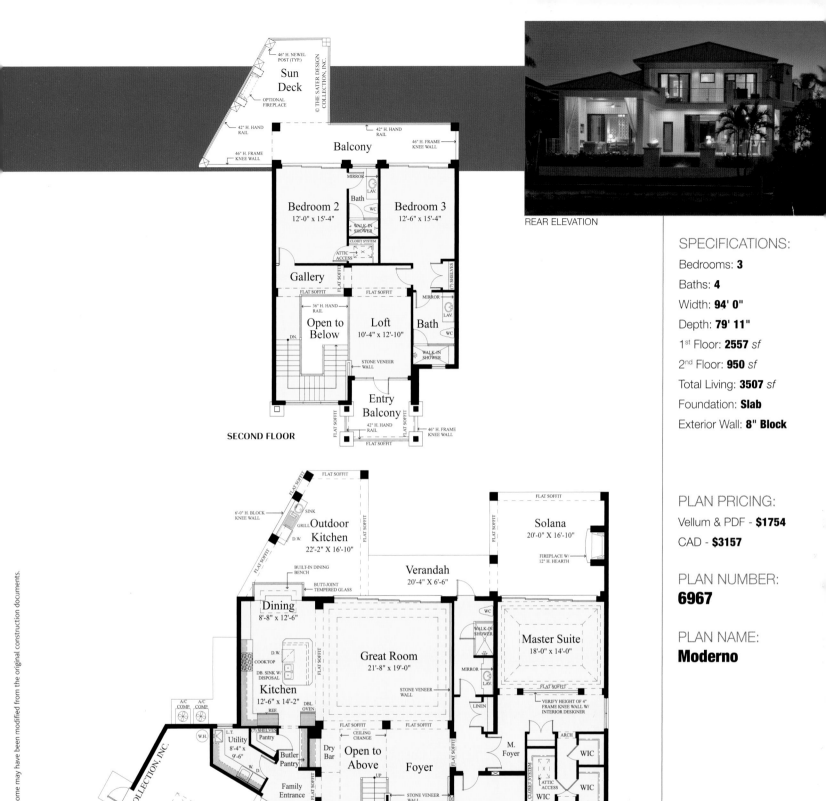

Sun Deck

46" H. NEWEL POST (TYP.)

OPTIONAL FIREPLACE

42" H. HAND RAIL

46" H. FRAME KNEE WALL

Balcony

42" H. HAND RAIL

46" H. FRAME KNEE WALL

MIRROR

Bath

LAV.

WC

Bedroom 2
12'-0" x 15'-4"

Bedroom 3
12'-6" x 15'-4"

WALK-IN SHOWER

CLOSET SYSTEM

ATTIC ACCESS

Gallery

FLAT SOFFIT

(7) SHELVES

MIRROR

36" H. HAND RAIL

Open to Below

DN.

Loft
10'-4" x 12'-10"

Bath

LAV.

WC

WALK-IN SHOWER

STONE VENEER WALL

Entry Balcony

42" H. HAND RAIL

46" H. FRAME KNEE WALL

FLAT SOFFIT

SECOND FLOOR

REAR ELEVATION

FLAT SOFFIT

6'-0" H. BLOCK KNEE WALL

SINK

GRILL

D.W.

Outdoor Kitchen
22'-2" X 16'-10"

BUILT-IN DINING BENCH

BUTT-JOINT TEMPERED GLASS

Dining
8'-8" x 12'-6"

D.W.

COOKTOP

DB. SINK W/ DISPOSAL

Kitchen
12'-6" x 14'-2"

REF.

DBL. OVEN

Verandah
20'-4" X 6'-6"

Great Room
21'-8" x 19'-0"

STONE VENEER WALL

FLAT SOFFIT

Solana
20'-0" X 16'-10"

FIREPLACE W/ 12" H. HEARTH

WC

WALK-IN SHOWER

WIC

MIRROR

LAV.

Master Suite
18'-0" x 14'-0"

FLAT SOFFIT

VERIFY HEIGHT OF 4" FRAME KNEE WALL W/ INTERIOR DESIGNER

A/C COMP.

A/C COMP.

W.H.

L.T.

Utility
8'-4" x 9'-6"

(7) SHELVES

Pantry

Butler Pantry

W. D.

Dry Bar

Open to Above

Family Entrance

FLAT SOFFIT

UP

Foyer

CEILING CHANGE

FLAT SOFFIT

STONE VENEER WALL

LINEN

M. Foyer

ATTIC ACCESS

WIC

CLOSET SYSTEM

ARCH

WIC

WIC

M. Bath

LAV.

LAV.

MIRROR

MIRROR

Study
12'-0" x 12'-8"

Master Bath

3 Car Garage
21'-0" x 26'-8"

ATTIC ACCESS

Portico

CONC. STEPS

STONE VENEER

FLAT SOFFIT

STONE VENEER WALL

STONE VENEER

Seat

WALK-IN SHOWER

TUB

WC

FIRST FLOOR

Master Garden

6'-4" H. BLOCK KNEE WALL

STONE VENEER

SPECIFICATIONS:

Bedrooms: **3**

Baths: **4**

Width: **94' 0"**

Depth: **79' 11"**

1st Floor: **2557** *sf*

2nd Floor: **950** *sf*

Total Living: **3507** *sf*

Foundation: **Slab**

Exterior Wall: **8" Block**

PLAN PRICING:

Vellum & PDF - **$1754**

CAD - **$3157**

PLAN NUMBER:

6967

PLAN NAME:

Moderno

Not available for construction in Lee or Collier Counties, Florida.

Casoria

With its terra-cotta-hued barrel roof tiles, limestone sheathed walls, stone accents and golden-hued stucco façade, this is a quintessential Tuscan-inspired home. Entering the courtyard through a pair of wrought iron gates, a loggia of stone-covered pillars and arched openings travels the length of the home. Myriad windows and glass doors grace the interior walls resulting in an instant and irrevocable synergy that connects the interior and exterior spaces.

To the left of the foyer, the master suite faces the pool and seemingly draws the outdoors inward. The library is located near the foyer and adjacent to the airy kitchen, dining and great room, which naturally transition outward onto the covered loggia and ensuing pool area. Facing the enclosed courtyard, two second-story guest suites share a common loft that opens up onto a covered balcony and pergola-shaded deck. Anchored on one side by a private guesthouse, a privacy wall encloses the courtyard, enhancing the home's oasis-like ambiance. The courtyard area is highlighted by an outdoor solana featuring a fireplace and outdoor kitchen adjacent to the cabana.

Casoria's imposing entry with balcony overlook.

Home's casita in distance as viewed from main loggia.

View from dining and kitchen with great room and stairway to second floor beyond

ABOVE: Master bath with garden tub and walk-in shower.

BELOW: An expansive wall of glass-fronted doors connects the master suite, with its softly hued walls and elegantly tiered ceiling, to the stunningly designed pool and spa area.

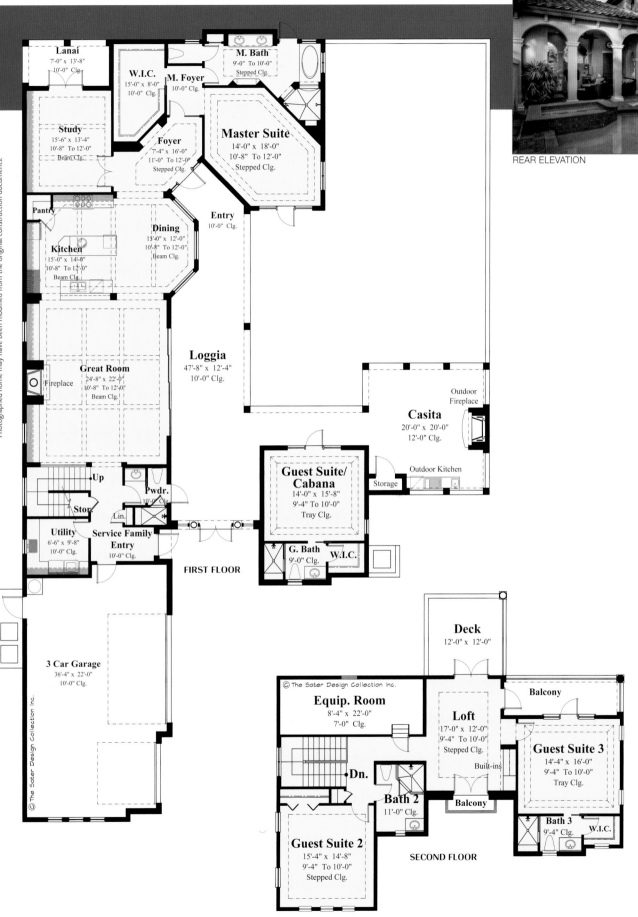

Lanai
7'-0" x 13'-8"
10'-0" Clg.

W.I.C.
15'-0" x 8'-0"
10'-0" Clg.

M. Foyer
10'-0" Clg.

M. Bath
9'-0" To 10'-0"
Stepped Clg.

Study
15'-6" x 13'-4"
10'-8" To 12'-0"
Beam Clg.

Foyer
7'-4" x 16'-0"
11'-0" To 12'-0"
Stepped Clg.

Master Suite
14'-0" x 18'-0"
10'-8" To 12'-0"
Stepped Clg.

Pantry

Dining
15'-0" x 12'-0"
10'-8" To 12'-0"
Beam Clg.

Entry
10'-0" Clg.

Kitchen
15'-0" x 14'-0"
10'-8" To 12'-0"
Beam Clg.

Great Room
24'-8" x 22'-0"
10'-8" To 12'-0"
Beam Clg.

Fireplace

Loggia
47'-8" x 12'-4"
10'-0" Clg.

Outdoor Fireplace

Casita
20'-0" x 20'-0"
12'-0" Clg.

Up

Pwdr.
10'-0"

Stor.

Guest Suite/ Cabana
14'-0" x 15'-8"
9'-4" To 10'-0"
Tray Clg.

Storage

Outdoor Kitchen

Utility
6'-6" x 9'-8"
10'-0" Clg.

Service Family Entry
10'-0" Clg.

Lin.

G. Bath
9'-0" Clg.

W.I.C.

FIRST FLOOR

3 Car Garage
36'-4" x 22'-0"
10'-0" Clg.

© The Sater Design Collection Inc.

REAR ELEVATION

SPECIFICATIONS:

Bedrooms: **4**

Baths: **5**

Width: **73' 2"**

Depth: **118' 8"**

1st Floor: **2392** *sf*

Cabana: **351** *sf*

2nd Floor: **1034** *sf*

Total Living: **3777** *sf*

Foundation: **Slab**

Exterior Wall: **8" Block**

PLAN PRICING:

Vellum & PDF - **$2455**

CAD - **$4344**

PLAN NUMBER:

6797

PLAN NAME:

Casoria

© The Sater Design Collection Inc.

Deck
12'-0" x 12'-0"

Balcony

Equip. Room
8'-4" x 22'-0"
7'-0" Clg.

Loft
17'-0" x 12'-0"
9'-4" To 10'-0"
Stepped Clg.

Built-ins

Guest Suite 3
14'-4" x 16'-0"
9'-4" To 10'-0"
Tray Clg.

Dn.

Bath 2
11'-0" Clg.

Balcony

Bath 3
9'-4" Clg.

W.I.C.

Guest Suite 2
15'-4" x 14'-8"
9'-4" To 10'-0"
Stepped Clg.

SECOND FLOOR

Barletta

This Andalusian flavored home's exterior features a barrel tile roof, warmly colored stucco walls, stone corbels and an arched entry tower. Entering the home one is greeted by a pocketing wall of glass sliding doors. The home's open layout is immediately apparent.

Casual elegant living with view oriented living spaces and open layout is thoughtfully accomplished without sacrificing each spaces richly detailed character. Myriad windows and glass doors grace the interior walls resulting in an instant synergy that connects the interior and exterior spaces.

This homes highlight is the luxurious master suite with private foyer, view oriented bedroom, oversized his/her walk-in closets and beautiful bath with island tub and walk-in shower.

The home also features two nicely sized guest suites with walk-in closets and private access baths. The study is conveniently located off public areas yet feels secluded and has open views to the veranda. It's direct access to guest suite 2's bath makes for easily doubling as an overflow guest suite.

The kitchen features an island layout with walk-in pantry and has commanding views of home's interior and exterior. The home's elegant powder bath and large utility room with view to motor court round out this winning home plan's features.

Home's nook with cornerless pocketing sliding glass doors.

The Barletta's open island kitchen with dramatic arched soffits is the central hub in this open floor plan.

RIGHT: Great room with coffered ceiling is open to kitchen.

ABOVE: Dining room is spacious and open to the great room.

BELOW: The great room with kitchen, dining, and foyer in the distance.

Master bath with his and hers vanities and island tub with the walk-in shower beyond.

This intimate master suite is highlighted with a stepped tray ceiling and arched bed niche.

The study with its arched niches and built-in desk overlooks the expansive veranda by the outdoor kitchen.

The arched doorways form an elegant passage from the master suite to the master bath with the island tub framed in the center by the arches to the walk-in shower beyond.

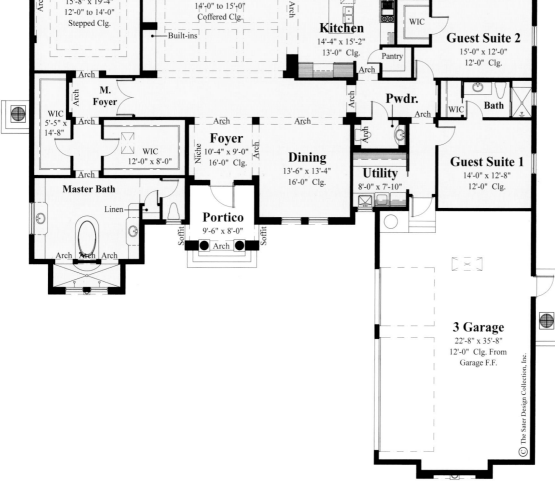

Veranda
36'-6" x 18'-0" Avg.
12'-0" Clg.

Outdoor Kitchen

Study
20'-5" x 15'-0"
12'-0" to 13'-0"
Stepped Clg.

Veranda
37'-10" x 11'-4"
12'-0" Clg.

Nook
14'-4" x 12'-2"
13'-0" Clg.

Bath

Closet

WIC

Master Retreat
15'-8" x 19'-4"
12'-0" to 14'-0"
Stepped Clg.

Grand Salon
19'-0" x 17'-10"
14'-0" to 15'-0"
Coffered Clg.

Built-ins

Kitchen
14'-4" x 15'-2"
13'-0" Clg.

Pantry

Guest Suite 2
15'-0" x 12'-0"
12'-0" Clg.

M. Foyer

WIC
5'-5" x
14'-8"

WIC
12'-0" x 8'-0"

Pwdr.

WIC

Bath

Master Bath

Linen

Foyer
10'-4" x 9'-0"
16'-0" Clg.

Niche

Dining
13'-6" x 13'-4"
16'-0" Clg.

Guest Suite 1
14'-0" x 12'-8"
12'-0" Clg.

Utility
8'-0" x 7'-10"

Portico
9'-6" x 8'-0"

3 Garage
22'-8" x 35'-8"
12'-0" Clg. From
Garage F.F.

Arch

SPECIFICATIONS:

Bedrooms: **3**

Baths: **3½**

Width: **75' 0"**

Depth: **105' 9"**

1st Floor: **3543** *sf*

Total Living: **3543** *sf*

Foundation: **Slab**

Exterior Wall: **8" Block**

PLAN PRICING:

Vellum & PDF - **$1772**

CAD - **$3189**

PLAN NUMBER:

6964

PLAN NAME:

Barletta

Not available for construction in Lee or Collier Counties, Florida.

Leighton

Quiet elegance is found throughout Leighton, a stunning British Colonial home that boasts multiple outdoor living spaces, specialty ceiling treatments and state-of-the-art amenities. Details both romantic and practical are found around every corner, like the living room's striking bow windows.

A soaring portico and stately turret create an unforgettable façade. Inside, the foyer opens to views of a grand staircase, formal dining room and a wide-open living room that is as impressive for its soaring two-story ceiling as it is for the gorgeously detailed, two-sided fireplace that it shared with the study.

But Leighton's treasures don't end there. The master suite encompasses one whole side of the plan and delights with an art niche foyer, private lanai access, dual walk-in closets and dual vanities in a luxurious bath overlooking a private master garden.

A casual living zone is on the opposite side of the first floor arranged in an open layout. The gourmet kitchen is open to a dining nook and leisure room with built-ins

Through French doors on the far side of the leisure room, a lanai with a full outdoor kitchen and fireplace beckons.

The second story echoes the classic elegance of the first floor with tray and vaulted ceilings in the bedrooms, walk-in closets and overlooks to both the living and leisure rooms.

Just inside the foyer, stately columns and a tray ceiling define the intimate dining room. This creates an open, but warm, gathering place conveniently located near the wet bar and kitchen.

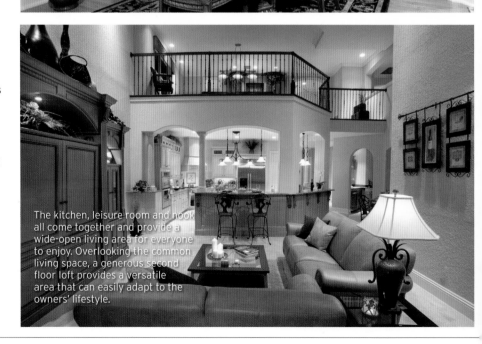

The kitchen, leisure room and nook all come together and provide a wide-open living area for everyone to enjoy. Overlooking the common living space, a generous second floor loft provides a versatile area that can easily adapt to the owners' lifestyle.

The formal living room, with its dramatic two-story, coffered ceiling, is filled with light and views thanks to the wall of bow windows that display the home's outdoor living areas. The striking fireplace, crafted in handsome detail, provides a grand and comfortable centerpiece.

The master suite combines exquisite elegance with quiet solitude, creating a welcome retreat. Resplendent in its details, the suite features a step-up tray ceiling and arched entryways with stately columns to access the lanai. *(Photo reflects customer modified sitting room.)*

To create a romantic ambiance, the luxurious master bath is flooded with views from wide, beautiful windows with arched transoms over the whirlpool tub.

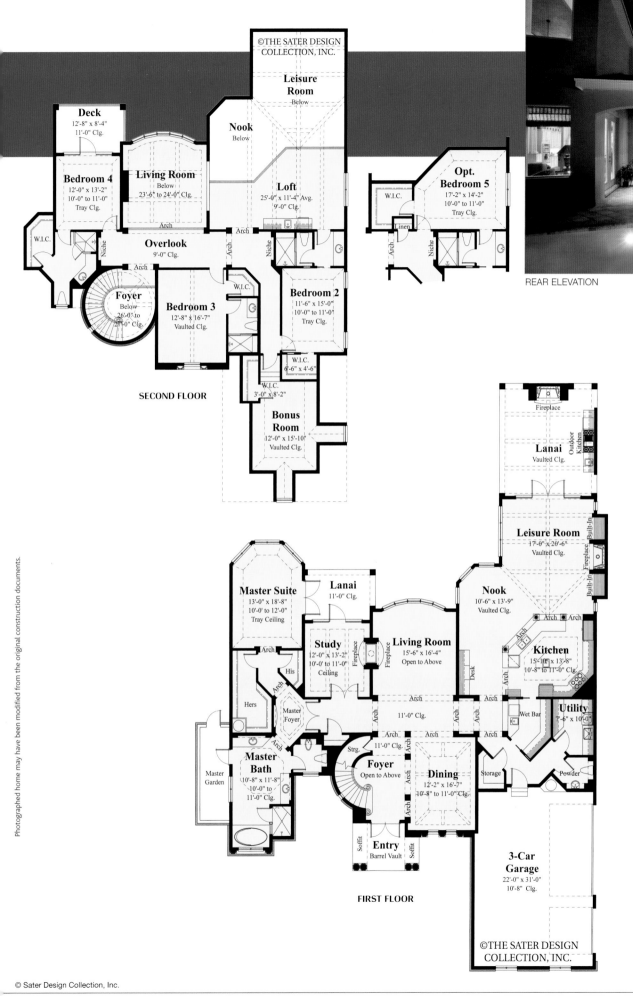

©THE SATER DESIGN COLLECTION, INC.

Deck
12'-8" x 8'-4"
11'-0" Clg.

Bedroom 4
12'-0" x 13'-2"
10'-0" to 11'-0"
Tray Clg.

W.I.C.

Living Room
Below
23'-6" to 24'-0" Clg.
Arch

Leisure Room
Below

Nook
Below

Loft
25'-0" x 11'-4" Avg.
9'-0" Clg.

Overlook
9'-0" Clg.
Arch

Foyer
Below
26'-0" to 27'-0" Clg.

Bedroom 3
12'-8" x 16'-7"
Vaulted Clg.

W.I.C.

Bedroom 2
11'-6" x 15'-0"
10'-0" to 11'-0"
Tray Clg.

W.I.C.
6'-6" x 4'-6"

W.I.C.
3'-0" x 8'-2"

Bonus Room
12'-0" x 15'-10"
Vaulted Clg.

SECOND FLOOR

Opt. Bedroom 5
17'-2" x 14'-2"
10'-0" to 11'-0"
Tray Clg.

W.I.C.

Linen

Master Suite
13'-0" x 18'-8"
10'-0" to 12'-0"
Tray Ceiling

Lanai
11'-0" Clg.

Study
12'-0" x 13'-2"
10'-0" to 11'-0"
Ceiling

His

Hers

Master Foyer

Master Bath
10'-8" x 11'-8"
10'-0" to 11'-0" Clg.

Master Garden

Living Room
15'-6" x 16'-4"
Open to Above

Lanai
Vaulted Clg.

Outdoor Kitchen

Fireplace

Leisure Room
17'-0" x 20'-6"
Vaulted Clg.

Built-In
Fireplace
Built-In

Built-In

Nook
10'-6" x 13'-9"
Vaulted Clg.

Kitchen
15'-4" x 13'-8"
10'-8" to 11'-0" Clg.

Desk

Wet Bar

Utility
7'-6" x 10'-0"

Foyer
Open to Above

Strg.

Dining
12'-2" x 16'-7"
10'-8" to 11'-0" Clg.

Storage

Powder

Entry
Barrel Vault

Soffit

3-Car Garage
22'-0" x 31'-0"
10'-8" Clg.

FIRST FLOOR

©THE SATER DESIGN COLLECTION, INC.

REAR ELEVATION

SPECIFICATIONS:

Bedrooms: **4**

Baths: **4½**

Width: **70' 0"**

Depth: **104' 0"**

1st Floor: **3054** *sf*

2nd Floor: **1904** *sf*

Total Living: **4958** *sf*

Foundation: **Slab**

Exterior Wall: **2x6 Wood**

PLAN PRICING:

Vellum & PDF - **$3966**

CAD - **$7437**

PLAN NUMBER:
8070

PLAN NAME:
Leighton

Martinique

Clearly Mediterranean-inspired, with a barrel-tile roof in terra-cotta hues, lancet arches and Tuscan columns, the sun-drenched façade of this home extends a formal welcome. Crisp, white trim speaks of Spanish influence, and iron detailing adds a hint of sun–drenched Tuscan charm.

Past the foyer, an open floor plan emphasizes outdoor living with a seamless transition of indoor and outdoor spaces. Columns, built-ins and ceiling treatments define rooms, while a flowing floor plan creates natural movement.

The formal living room is punctuated by natural light welcomed in by floor-to-ceiling windows. The openness of the leisure room, nook and kitchen create casual gathering areas extended by ample outdoor spaces.

Spacious guest accommodations on both floors assure that visitors stay in comfort. Guests enjoy private or semi-private full baths and private spaces – a garden on the first floor and a loft upstairs.

Well-appointed and well-planned, this kitchen boasts ample storage for tools of the trade and two large islands that add lots of workspace.

~ Any plan can be customized to meet your needs, find out how by calling **800-718-7526.** *~*

ABOVE: Elegant arches and stunning wood columns define the dining space while giving it a unique connection to the diamond-shaped living room. More wood adds drama to a stepped ceiling, and three dramatic windows provide natural light and an effortless connection to the veranda.

RIGHT: Draped floor to ceiling bay picture windows immerse the living room with natural light and open it upon the views beyond. The beamed ceiling gives a rich canopy to this beautiful room.

A stepped ceiling with molding details and elegant lighting crowns a generous master suite. An art niche separates two walk-in closets and provides a visually appealing entry to a fully appointed master bedroom.

A whirlpool tub in the master bath is anything but ordinary, nestled between dark wood columns and overlooking a private garden.

The veranda features twelve-foot ceilings and wraps along the entire back of the house and around the pool for first-class outdoor living and entertaining.

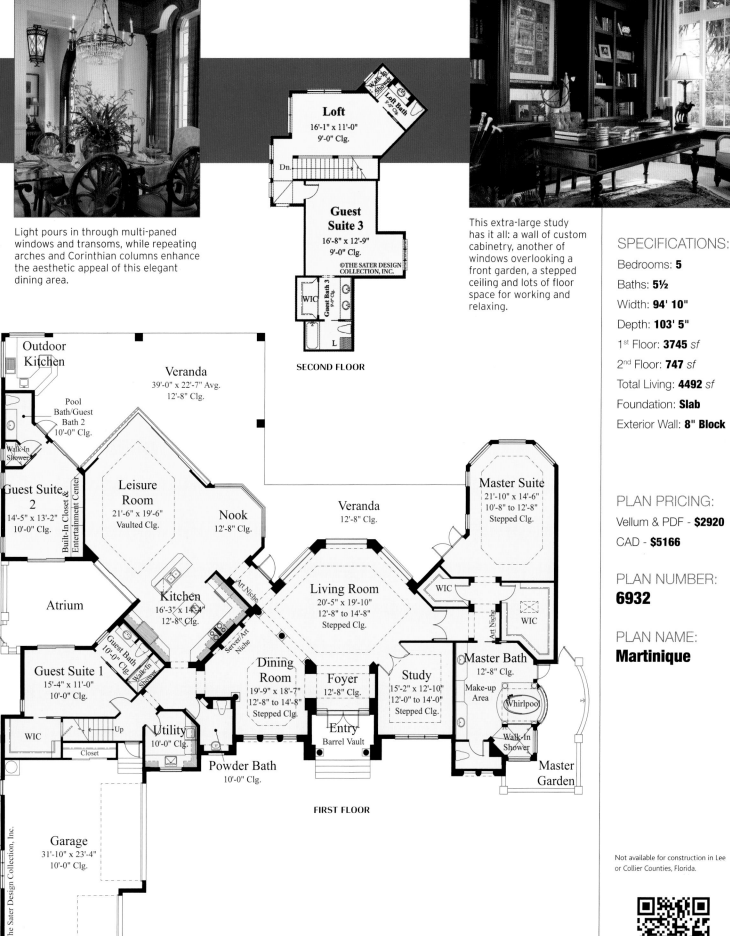

Light pours in through multi-paned windows and transoms, while repeating arches and Corinthian columns enhance the aesthetic appeal of this elegant dining area.

This extra-large study has it all: a wall of custom cabinetry, another of windows overlooking a front garden, a stepped ceiling and lots of floor space for working and relaxing.

SECOND FLOOR

Second Floor

- **Loft** 16'-1" x 11'-0" 9'-0" Clg.
- Walk-In Shower
- Loft Bath 9'-0" Clg.
- Dn.
- **Guest Suite 3** 16'-8" x 12'-9" 9'-0" Clg.
- ©THE SATER DESIGN COLLECTION, INC.
- WIC
- Guest Bath 3 9'-0" Clg.
- L

First Floor

FIRST FLOOR

- Outdoor Kitchen
- Pool Bath/Guest Bath 2 10'-0" Clg.
- Walk-In Shower
- **Guest Suite 2** 14'-5" x 13'-2" 10'-0" Clg.
- Built-In Closet & Entertainment Center
- Atrium
- **Veranda** 39'-0" x 22'-7" Avg. 12'-8" Clg.
- **Leisure Room** 21'-6" x 19'-6" Vaulted Clg.
- **Nook** 12'-8" Clg.
- **Veranda** 12'-8" Clg.
- **Master Suite** 21'-10" x 14'-6" 10'-8" to 12'-8" Stepped Clg.
- WIC
- **Kitchen** 16'-3" x 14'-4" 12'-8" Clg.
- Art Niche
- **Living Room** 20'-5" x 19'-10" 12'-8" to 14'-8" Stepped Clg.
- WIC
- Art Niche
- Guest Bath 10'-0" Clg.
- Walk-In Shower
- **Guest Suite 1** 15'-4" x 11'-0" 10'-0" Clg.
- Server/Art Niche
- **Dining Room** 19'-9" x 18'-7" 12'-8" to 14'-8" Stepped Clg.
- **Foyer** 12'-8" Clg.
- **Study** 15'-2" x 12'-10" 12'-0" to 14'-0" Stepped Clg.
- **Master Bath** 12'-8" Clg.
- Make-up Area
- Whirlpool
- WIC
- **Utility** 10'-0" Clg.
- Closet
- Up
- **Entry** Barrel Vault
- Walk-In Shower
- **Powder Bath** 10'-0" Clg.
- **Master Garden**
- **Garage** 31'-10" x 23'-4" 10'-0" Clg.

SPECIFICATIONS:

Bedrooms: **5**

Baths: **5½**

Width: **94' 10"**

Depth: **103' 5"**

1st Floor: **3745** sf

2nd Floor: **747** sf

Total Living: **4492** sf

Foundation: **Slab**

Exterior Wall: **8" Block**

PLAN PRICING:

Vellum & PDF - **$2920**

CAD - **$5166**

PLAN NUMBER:

6932

PLAN NAME:

Martinique

Not available for construction in Lee or Collier Counties, Florida.

Porto Velho

From private guest suites to a wide-open floor plan that melds with a wrapping verandah, the Porto Velho offers infinite charm and function without sacrificing the ultimate in luxury living appointments. The façade invites, with a dramatic, recessed and turreted entry enhanced by multiple arched windows framed with balusters. Inside, the foyer opens to a vaulted great room with views stretching well beyond the retreating glass wall. The master suite is allotted an entire wing and a forward dining room and study, both with octagonal stepped ceilings, provide first-class environments for entertaining and private studies.

A spacious, centralized great room anchors the 4,500 square foot plan. A wall of built-ins is perfect for media components, books and treasures. Another wall is lined with pocketing glass doors, throwing the room open to the verandah and pool area. The gourmet kitchen is accessed through three archways that mimic the Mediterranean windows gracing the front of the home. A breakfast nook, walk-in pantry and powder bath complete the core of the home.

Even the home's small spaces are intimately planned, such as the entry foyer to the master suite. The full-length niche is art in itself, with its elegant wall treatment, soft lighting and tasteful accessories.

Tall Tuscan columns and a wooden pergola frame a stunning courtyard. Located near the outdoor kitchen, this plein air living room is idyllic for a lazy Sunday brunch.

Dining room with its elegantly detailed beamed ceiling and arched windows overlooks the patio.

An elaborately carved center island, hand-rubbed cabinetry and a stunning carved-stone hood add drama to this has-it-all gourmet kitchen. There's even a desk nook through the arched doorway.

ABOVE: The great room's built-ins with its stone trimmed arch make a impacting focal point of the space.

RIGHT: Rustic beams lend texture to the vaulted ceiling of the wide open great room, where glass doors pocket into the walls to extend the room outdoors and elegant arches grant access to the kitchen and its gracious serving counter.

LEFT: The molded, stepped ceiling is a dramatic canopy to this regal master bedroom, where floor-to-ceiling windows frame a cozy sitting nook and glass doors disappear to access a private corner of the verandah. Two walk-in closets and a sumptuous bath complete the suite.

BELOW: A center spa tub rests inside gleaming wood and granite, offering an opulent focal point for the master bath. A window-framed, walk-in shower is tucked beneath the curved and wrought iron-adorned wall behind the tub. Her vanity is ultra-pampering, with two sinks, a restful bench and elegant lighting. On the other side of the tub is a vanity just for him.

The study, located near the gallery leading to the master bedroom, glows with recessed custom cabinetry, a stepped ceiling, and tall windows embracing a forward view.

REAR ELEVATION

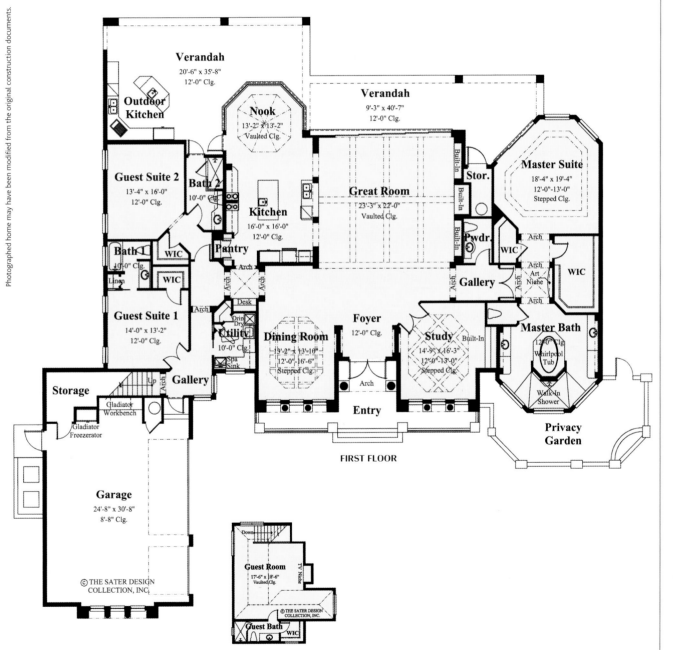

Verandah
20'-6" x 35'-8"
12'-0" Clg.

Outdoor Kitchen

Nook
13'-2" x 13'-2"
Vaulted Clg.

Verandah
9'-3" x 40'-7"
12'-0" Clg.

Guest Suite 2
13'-4" x 16'-0"
12'-0" Clg.

Bath 2
10'-0" Clg.

Great Room
23'-3" x 22'-0"
Vaulted Clg.

Stor.

Master Suite
18'-4" x 19'-4"
12'-0"-13'-0"
Stepped Clg.

Kitchen
16'-0" x 16'-0"
12'-0" Clg.

Built-In

Built-In

Bath 1
10'-0" Clg.

WIC

Pantry

WIC

Pwdr.

Art Niche

WIC

Arch

Arch

Arch

WIC

Gallery

Guest Suite 1
14'-0" x 13'-2"
12'-0" Clg.

Arch

Desk

Foyer
12'-0" Clg.

Study
14'-9" x 16'-3"
12'-0"-13'-0"
Stepped Clg.

Built-In

Master Bath
12'-0" Clg.

Whirlpool Tub

Utility
10'-0" Clg.

Drip Dry

Spa Sink

Dining Room
13'-2" x 13'-10"
12'-0"-16'-6"
Stepped Clg.

Arch

Entry

Arch

Walk-In Shower

Storage

Gladiator Workbench

Up

Gallery

Privacy Garden

Gladiator Freezerator

Garage
24'-8" x 30'-8"
8'-8" Clg.

FIRST FLOOR

© THE SATER DESIGN COLLECTION, INC.

Down

Guest Room
17'-6" x 18'-6"
Vaulted Clg.

TV Niche

© THE SATER DESIGN COLLECTION, INC.

Guest Bath

WIC

SECOND FLOOR

SPECIFICATIONS:

Bedrooms: **4**

Baths: **4½**

Width: **105' 9"**

Depth: **100' 9"**

1st Floor: **3947** *sf*

2nd Floor: **545** *sf*

Total Living: **4492** *sf*

Foundation: **Slab**

Exterior Wall: **8" Block**

PLAN PRICING:

Vellum & PDF - **$2920**

CAD - **$5166**

PLAN NUMBER:

6950

PLAN NAME:

Porto Velho

Not available for construction in Lee or Collier Counties, Florida.

La Reina

Derived from a blend of cultural influences including Moorish and Renaissance, this clearly Mediterranean elevation creates an impressive, yet not imposing, street presence. Trios of windows bring light to interior spaces, and accentuate rows of decorative tile vents that line the façade. Carved balusters enhance a side balcony that's spacious enough to serve as an outdoor room. The paneled portal opens to a portico and courtyard, which creates a procession to the formal entry of the home. To the front of the courtyard, a casita, or guesthouse, offers space that easily converts to a workshop or home office. The foyer opens directly to the grand room and through an arched opening, to the formal dining room. Glass bayed walls in the central living area and in the study help meld inside and outside spaces, and the dining room leads to a loggia—for open-air meals.

Centrally located between the formal and informal rooms, the gourmet-caliber kitchen serves both realms with ease. A wraparound eating bar offers "patrons" a place to sit, while the center island with prep sink provides ample counter space for the family "chef".

Soaring two-story ceilings allow for voluminous views and light to stream in through numerous windows that encircle the room. A grand fireplace provides a central gathering area, and a flowing design offers an open avenue to the dining room nearby.

LEFT: Designed for privacy and appointed in elegance, the master suite features a high stepped ceiling and generous views through the suite's multi-paned windows and transoms. French doors provide access to the loggia.

BELOW: This master bath opens to the impressive courtyard area and features a whirlpool tub soaked in light from the outdoors, a beautifully stepped ceiling and arches setting off the suite's vanities.

Balcony
10'-12" x 9'-4"

Grand Room
Beamed Clg.

Bedroom 2
10'-11" x 13'-4"
10'-0" Clg.

Open to Below

©THE SATER DESIGN COLLECTION, INC.

WIC

Open to Below

Bath 2
10'-0" Clg.

Dn.   Linen

Balcony
10'-7" x 14'-4"

Bath 3
10'-0" Clg.
Walk-In Shower

Bedroom 3
15'-0" x 11'-6"
10'-0" Clg.

WIC   WIC

SECOND FLOOR

WIC

Bedroom 4
11'-6" x 16'-8"
10'-0" Clg.

COURTYARD AND PORTICO

Loggia
26'-10" x 11'-8"
Open to Above

Loggia
15'-6" x 10'-0"
10'-0" Clg.

Master Suite
14'-8" x 22'-4"
12'-0" to 14'-0"
Stepped Clg.

Grand Room
19'-0" x 19'-5"
21'-0" to 22'-4"
Open to Above

Dining Room
10'-6" x 13'-4"
10'-0" Clg.

Built-In

WIC

Whirlpool

M. Bath
12'-0" to 14'-0"
Stepped Clg.

Pwdr.
9'-4" Clg.

Foyer

Up

Built-in Server

Utility
6'-8" x 9'-
10'-0" Clg.

WIC

Linen

Desk

Balcony

Walk-In Shower

Study
14'-4" x 15'-0"
12'-0" to 13'-0"
Stepped Clg.

Loggia
10'-0" Clg.

Nook
10'-0" Clg.

Kitchen
13'-8" x 15'-4"
10'-0" Clg.

Pantry

Fountain

Spa

Optional Pool

Courtyard

Loggia
16'-8" Clg.

Leisure Room
18'-6" x 17'-10"
10'-0" to 14'-6"
Stepped Clg.

Garage
11'-6" x 16'-10"
10'-0" Clg.

Fireplace

Built-In Entertainment

Loggia
10'-0" Clg.

Outdoor Kitchen

WIC

Guest Suite
14'-4" x 13'-5"
10'-0" Clg.

Pool Bath

Portico
14'-8" X 14'-4"
Groin Vault

©THE SATER DESIGN COLLECTION, INC.

Garage
22'-4" x 25'-6"
10'-0" Clg.

FIRST FLOOR

SPECIFICATIONS:

Bedrooms: **5**

Baths: **4½**

Width: **80' 0"**

Depth: **96' 0"**

1st Floor: **2852** *sf*

Cabana: **330** *sf*

2nd Floor: **969** *sf*

Total Living: **4151** *sf*

Foundation: **Slab**

Exterior Wall: **2x6 Wood**

PLAN PRICING:

Vellum & PDF - **$2698**

CAD - **$4774**

PLAN NUMBER:

8046

PLAN NAME:

La Reina

Grimaldi Court

ARDA Award Winner!

A striking mix of arches, columns, carved balusters and arch-top windows foretell of the beauty waiting within this Mediterranean home. A view-oriented design, guests are immediately greeted with stunning vistas past the wall of curved glass to the wraparound verandah. A two-sided fireplace warms the formal areas comprised of the living and dining rooms, its boundary with the foyer defined by a line of decorative columns.

Arched entry ways lead to the generous common living area. A beautiful and functional gourmet kitchen boasts a center prep island, walk-in pantry and a wraparound eating bar to the leisure room. The kitchen's open connection with the nook and leisure room creates a family-friendly environment that's perfect for large family get-togethers as well as intimate movie nights for two. Retreating glass walls further expand the area to the wraparound verandah. The outdoor kitchen is located just outside the leisure room, making indoor/outdoor entertaining a breeze.

Nearby, three guest suites offer friends and family a quiet place to relax at the end of the day. On the opposite side of the home, the master suite is a four-star retreat designed to pamper the homeowners after a busy day.

Earth tones—as well as a two-sided fireplace—warm the living and dining area. A line of columns creates a boundary between the foyer and living areas.

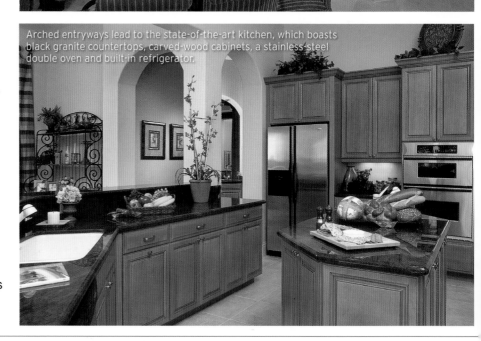

Arched entryways lead to the state-of-the-art kitchen, which boasts black granite countertops, carved-wood cabinets, a stainless-steel double oven and built-in refrigerator.

ABOVE: The leisure room is enveloped in glass with pocketing sliding glass doors and TV niche.

RIGHT: The early morning sun shines through the bay window of the breakfast nook, giving it a golden glow and making it one of the most warm and welcoming spaces in the home.

With its scenic view of the master garden, the master bath becomes a private oasis.

The study has bay with views and access to the veranda through the French doors.

Arch-top windows and retreating glass doors invite the exterior landscape into the master bedroom, transforming the outdoors into an ever-changing work of art for this elegant retreat

~ Any plan can be customized to meet your needs, find out how by calling 800-718-7526. ~

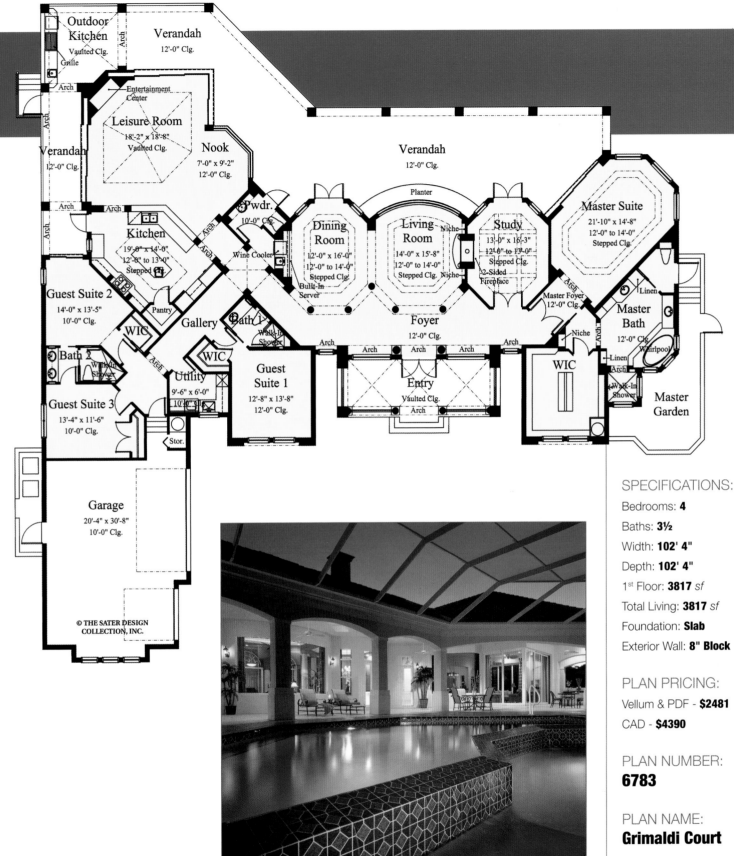

Outdoor Kitchen
Vaulted Clg.
Grille

Verandah
12'-0" Clg.

Leisure Room
18'-2" x 18'-8"
Vaulted Clg.

Entertainment Center

Nook
7'-0" x 9'-2"
12'-0" Clg.

Verandah
12'-0" Clg.

Verandah
12'-0" Clg.

Master Suite
21'-10" x 14'-8"
12'-0" to 14'-0"
Stepped Clg.

Planter

Pwdr.
10'-0" Clg.

Kitchen
19'-0" x 14'-0"
12'-0" to 13'-0"
Stepped Clg.

Dining Room
12'-0" x 16'-0"
12'-0" to 14'-0"
Stepped Clg.

Living Room
14'-0" x 15'-8"
12'-0" to 14'-0"
Stepped Clg.

Study
13'-0" x 16'-3"
12'-0" to 13'-0"
Stepped Clg.
2-Sided Fireplace

Niche

Niche

Wine Cooler

Guest Suite 2
14'-0" x 13'-5"
10'-0" Clg.

Pantry

WIC

Gallery

Bath 1
Walk-In Shower

Built-In Server

Foyer
12'-0" Clg.

Master Foyer
12'-0" Clg.

Niche

Master Bath
12'-0" Clg.
Whirlpool

Linen

Linen

Bath 2
Walk-In Shower

WIC

Utility
9'-6" x 6'-0"
10'-0" Clg.

Guest Suite 1
12'-8" x 13'-8"
12'-0" Clg.

Entry
Vaulted Clg.

WIC

Walk-In Shower

Master Garden

Guest Suite 3
13'-4" x 11'-6"
10'-0" Clg.

Stor.

Garage
20'-4" x 30'-8"
10'-0" Clg.

© THE SATER DESIGN COLLECTION, INC.

Arch (multiple)

Photographed home may have been modified from the original construction documents.

Accessible from almost every room to the rear of the home, the wraparound verandah offers endless entertaining opportunities.

SPECIFICATIONS:

Bedrooms: **4**

Baths: **3½**

Width: **102' 4"**

Depth: **102' 4"**

1st Floor: **3817** *sf*

Total Living: **3817** *sf*

Foundation: **Slab**

Exterior Wall: **8" Block**

PLAN PRICING:

Vellum & PDF - **$2481**

CAD - **$4390**

PLAN NUMBER:

6783

PLAN NAME:

Grimaldi Court

La Serena

ARDA Award Winner!

Hipped rooflines, carved eave brackets and varied gables evoke a sense of the past in this Italianate-style design. Inside, an engaging blend of old and new prevails where beamed and coffered ceilings play counterpoint to modern amenities— cutting-edge appliances in the kitchen, a state-of-the-art utility room and retreating glass walls in the leisure room.

Past the dramatic entryway, columns line the formal rooms and foyer. The hand-carved fireplace is nestled between built-in cabinetry and lies underneath the cove-lit coffered-ceiling. Nearby, the leisure room is an open and comfortable retreat for family and guests. Centrally located between the main living areas, snacks are just a few feet away in the kitchen, retreating glass walls open up to the lanai—making indoor/outdoor entertaining a breeze and a fun-filled game room lays just beyond the art-niche foyer.

A split-bedroom floor plan ensures privacy to the master wing of the home. A generous walk-in closet provides ample storage while the master bath features luxe amenities. On the opposite wing, three guest bedrooms offer plenty of space for overnight guests.

Light streams in to the foyer through the sleek curved sidelights surrounding the elegant paneled door. Hand-carved Crema Maya stone columns and arches define the space.

Powder bath accessed from the expansive veranda.

The "heart of the home"—the kitchen features a step-up tray ceiling, spacious pantry, state-of-the-art appliances, a convenient island workstation and an open counter connecting to the leisure room.

Hand-carved Crema Maya stone columns, weighing over one-ton apiece, line the formal living room and foyer. A stunning focal point, the hand-carved fireplace surround is nestled between built-in cabinetry and lies underneath the cove-lit coffered-ceiling.

A split-bedroom floor plan provides privacy to the master wing of the home. Muted lighting creates a relaxing environment while the sitting nook provides a quiet spot for reading. A step-tray ceiling adds an elegant touch to the spacious room.

This elegant dining room is adorned with a built-in niche and stepped ceiling. Moonlight pours in through the sunburst-arch transom, creating a romantic and intimate ambiance.

To create a warm and organic feel, earth-toned slate tiles flow throughout the entire master bath. A cove-lit tray ceiling, his-and-hers vanities, spa-style tub and walk-in shower complete the luxurious retreat.

With an octagonal coffered ceiling, centrally located between the main living areas and just a few feet away from the kitchen the leisure room is a relaxing retreat.

REAR ELEVATION

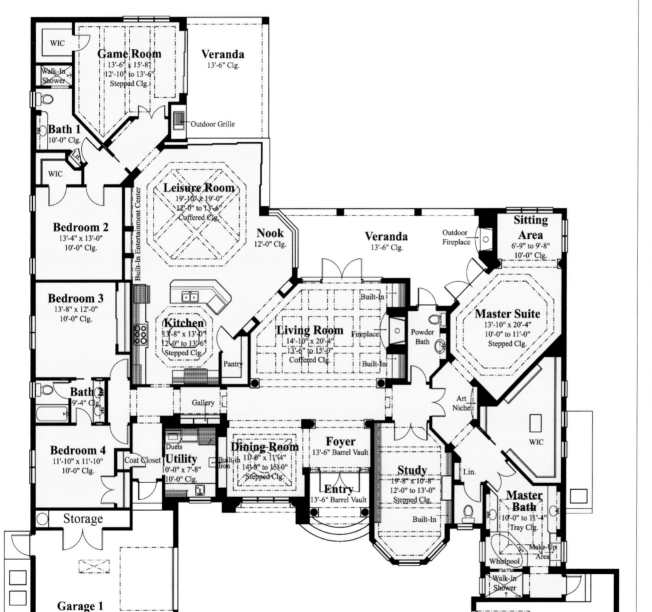

Photographed home may have been modified from the original construction documents.

WIC

Game Room
13'-6" x 15'-8"
12'-10" to 13'-6"
Stepped Clg.

Veranda
13'-6" Clg.

Walk-In Shower

Bath 1
10'-0" Clg.

WIC

Outdoor Grille

Bedroom 2
13'-4" x 13'-0"
10'-0" Clg.

Leisure Room
19'-10" x 19'-0"
12'-0" to 13'-6"
Coffered Clg.

Nook
12'-0" Clg.

Veranda
13'-6" Clg.

Outdoor Fireplace

Sitting Area
6'-9" to 9'-8"
10'-0" Clg.

Built-In

Bedroom 3
13'-8" x 12'-0"
10'-0" Clg.

Built-In Entertainment Center

Kitchen
13'-8" x 13'-0"
12'-0" to 13'-6"
Stepped Clg.

Living Room
14'-10" x 20'-4"
13'-6" to 15'-0"
Coffered Clg.

Fireplace

Powder Bath

Master Suite
13'-10" x 20'-4"
10'-0" to 11'-0"
Stepped Clg.

Built-In

Pantry

Bath 2
9'-4" Clg.

Gallery

Art Niche

WIC

Bedroom 4
11'-10" x 11'-10"
10'-0" Clg.

Coat Closet

Ducts

Utility
10'-0" x 7'-8"
10'-0" Clg.

Built-in Iron

Dining Room
11'-6" x 11'-4"
14'-0" to 15'-0"
Stepped Clg.

Foyer
13'-6" Barrel Vault

Study
19'-8" x 10'-8"
12'-0" to 13'-0"
Stepped Clg.

Lin.

Built-In

Master Bath
10'-0" to 11'-4"
Tray Clg.

Storage

Entry
13'-6" Barrel Vault

Make-Up Area

Whirlpool

Walk-In Shower

Garage 1
26'-0" x 20'-8"
10'-0" Clg. A.F.F.

Garage 2
11'-8" x 20'-8"
10'-0" Clg. A.F.F.

©THE SATER DESIGN COLLECTION, INC.

SPECIFICATIONS:

Bedrooms: **4**

Baths: **3½**

Width: **88' 0"**

Depth: **98' 8"**

1st Floor: **4049** *sf*

Total Living: **4049** *sf*

Foundation: **Slab**

Exterior Wall: **8" Block**

PLAN PRICING:

Vellum & PDF - **$2632**

CAD - **$4656**

PLAN NUMBER:
8076

PLAN NAME:
La Serena

Valdivia

ARDA Award Winner!

This elegantly detailed façade features a pergola, tiled roof, wrought-iron accents, arch-top windows and a majestic entry turret. A blended influence of Andalusian and Spanish Colonial architectural styles creates a stately ambiance.

Inside, this functional plan boasts a multitude of practicable amenities throughout the casually elegant living spaces. The result is a plan that lives larger than its square footage.

Most suitable for temperate climates, Valdivia offers a host of outdoor living space accessible from many public and private places throughout the home. Two outdoor fireplaces and an outdoor kitchen create natural gathering areas under a beautifully crafted wooden ceiling that provides an organic-feeling atmosphere.

The central grand salon has a wet bar and is open to the kitchen, where a spacious eating bar invites casual entertaining, though a formal dining space is dedicated to fine meals in style. Perfect for hosting friends and family, the home offers three complete guest suites with private baths and walk-in closets, including one secluded suite fully detached from the main home, but connected by the outdoor living room.

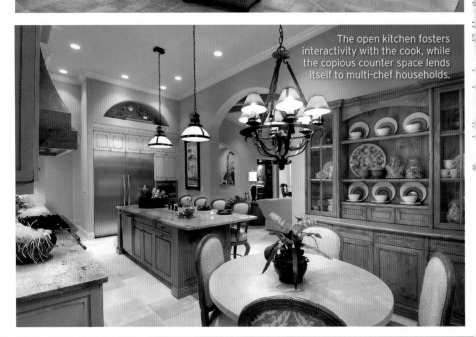

Guest suite has French doors that open out to the loggia next to the outdoor fireplace and solana.

The open kitchen fosters interactivity with the cook, while the copious counter space lends itself to multi-chef households.

ABOVE: The great room offers a centralized social area with refreshments available from the wet bar with brick-look tiling, and rear views of the pool through a wall of retreating glass.

RIGHT: One of the two outdoor fireplaces warms an outdoor dining area adjacent to an outdoor kitchen and the entry of the secluded guest cabana.

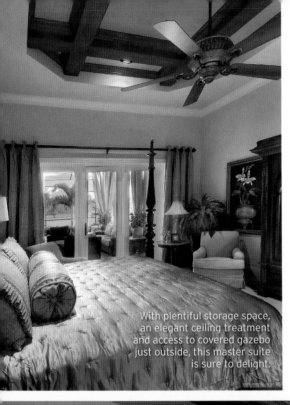

With plentiful storage space, an elegant ceiling treatment and access to covered gazebo just outside, this master suite is sure to delight.

An amenity-rich master bath hosts his-and-hers matching vanities, which frame the walls of the spacious bath. A center tub and shower with multiple luxury showerheads reside beneath an intricate stepped ceiling.

A mosaic tile surround frames the outdoor fireplace outside the master retreat.

REAR ELEVATION

The home's entry is open to both the formal dining and great rooms with space delineated by elongated arches, supportive columns and unique ceiling treatments.

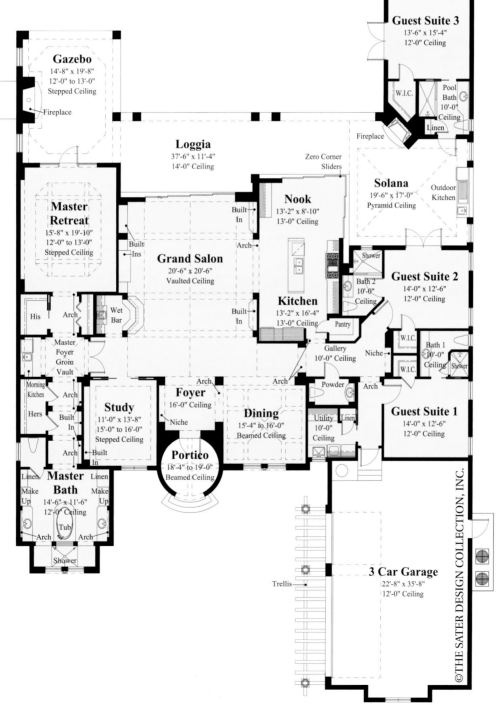

Gazebo
14'-8" x 19'-8"
12'-0" to 13'-0"
Stepped Ceiling

Fireplace

Guest Suite 3
13'-6" x 15'-4"
12'-0" Ceiling

W.I.C.

Pool Bath
10'-0" Ceiling

Linen

Loggia
37'-6" x 11'-4"
14'-0" Ceiling

Zero Corner Sliders

Fireplace

Master Retreat
15'-8" x 19'-10"
12'-0" to 13'-0"
Stepped Ceiling

Built Ins

Built In

Nook
13'-2" x 8'-10"
13'-0" Ceiling

Solana
19'-6" x 17'-0"
Pyramid Ceiling

Outdoor Kitchen

Grand Salon
20'-6" x 20'-6"
Vaulted Ceiling

Arch

Shower

Guest Suite 2
14'-0" x 12'-6"
12'-0" Ceiling

His

Arch

Wet Bar

Built In

Kitchen
13'-2" x 16'-4"
13'-0" Ceiling

Bath 2
10'-0" Ceiling

Master Foyer Groin Vault

Morning Kitchen

Arch

Hers

Built In

Pantry

Gallery
10'-0" Ceiling

Niche

W.I.C.

Bath 1
10'-0" Ceiling

Shower

W.I.C.

Arch

Arch

Powder

Arch

Study
11'-0" x 13'-8"
15'-0" to 16'-0"
Stepped Ceiling

Foyer
16'-0" Ceiling

Niche

Dining
15'-4" to 16'-0"
Beamed Ceiling

Utility
10'-0" Ceiling

Linen

Guest Suite 1
14'-0" x 12'-6"
12'-0" Ceiling

Built In

Arch

Arch

Portico
18'-4" to 19'-0"
Beamed Ceiling

Linen

Master Bath
14'-6" x 11'-6"
12'-0" Ceiling

Make Up

Linen

Make Up

Tub

Arch

Arch

Shower

Trellis

3 Car Garage
22'-8" x 35'-8"
12'-0" Ceiling

©THE SATER DESIGN COLLECTION, INC.

Photographed home may have been modified from the original construction documents.

© Sater Design Collection, Inc.

SPECIFICATIONS:

Bedrooms: **4**

Baths: **4½**

Width: **75' 0"**

Depth: **115' 0"**

1st Floor: **3790** *sf*

Total Living: **3790** *sf*

Foundation: **Slab**

Exterior Wall: **8" Block**

PLAN PRICING:

Vellum & PDF - **$2464**

CAD - **$4359**

PLAN NUMBER:

6959

PLAN NAME:

Valdivia

Not available for construction in Lee or Collier Counties, Florida.

Dimora

Corbeled cornices, decorative quoin elements and keystone enhanced arches, coupled with a capriciously gabled roofline reinforce the home's Italian inspired design. The true essence of the home is the amalgamation of interior and exterior spaces, thus maximizing the spatiality and functionality of the home. While myriad windows and glass doors strengthen the constant connection between the inside and outdoors, the study, dining and living rooms transition freely into one another.

To the left of the foyer, the wet bar differentiates the informal and formal venues. In the kitchen and family room, retreating glass walls open onto the covered lanai and pool deck, creating a "room without walls." To the right of the foyer, the master suite, with its large sitting alcove, oversized walk-in closet and luxuriously appointed bath and private courtyard, is a serene milieu that is unsurpassed.

The detailed, triple-tiered ceiling envelops the magnificent dining room with glass-fronted French doors which open out to the verandah.

The wet bar serves as an anchor, joining the casual family room and kitchen to the formal living and dining areas.

The kitchen, with its octagonal-shaped, beamed coffered ceiling and center prep island, opens up into the family room and nook.

The tile surround and deck of the oval-shaped tub incorporates the same intricate detailing as in the stunning walk-in shower in the master bath.

REAR ELEVATION

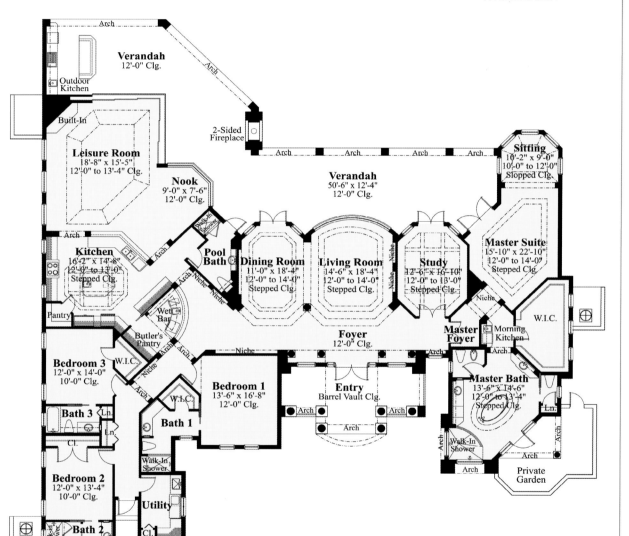

Verandah 12'-0" Clg.

Outdoor Kitchen

Built-In

Leisure Room 18'-8" x 15'-5" 12'-0" to 13'-4" Clg.

Nook 9'-0" x 7'-6" 12'-0" Clg.

2-Sided Fireplace

Verandah 50'-6" x 12'-4" 12'-0" Clg.

Sitting 10'-2" x 9'-0" 10'-0" to 12'-0" Slopped Clg.

Arch Arch Arch Arch

Kitchen 16'-2" x 14'-8" 12'-0" to 13'-0" Stepped Clg.

Pool Bath

Dining Room 11'-0" x 18'-4" 12'-0" to 14'-0" Stepped Clg.

Living Room 14'-6" x 18'-4" 12'-0" to 14'-0" Stepped Clg.

Study 12'-6" x 16'-10" 12'-0" Stepped Clg.

Master Suite 15'-10" x 22'-10" 12'-0" to 14'-0" Stepped Clg.

Pantry

Wet Bar

Butler's Pantry

W.I.C.

Foyer 12'-0" Clg.

Master Foyer

Morning Kitchen

W.I.C.

Bedroom 3 12'-0" x 14'-0" 10'-0" Clg.

W.I.C.

Niche

Bedroom 1 13'-6" x 16'-8" 12'-0" Clg.

Entry Barrel Vault Clg.

Master Bath 13'-6" x 14'-6" 12'-0" to 13'-4" Stepped Clg.

Bath 3

Bath 1

Walk-In Shower

Bedroom 2 12'-0" x 13'-4" 10'-0" Clg.

Walk-In Shower

Utility

Walk-In Shower

Private Garden

Bath 2

3-Car Garage 22'-4" x 32'-0" 10'-0" Clg.

©THE SATER DESIGN COLLECTION, INC.

Photographed home may have been modified from the original construction documents.

Retreating glass walls pull the outdoors inside toward the leisure room, kitchen and nook, creating a large, wide-open living space. Enhanced by custom millwork elements, the leisure room's exaggerated sloped tray ceiling creates a cozy ambiance.

SPECIFICATIONS:

Bedrooms: **4**

Baths: **5**

Width: **94' 2"**

Depth: **131' 6"**

1st Floor: **4664** *sf*

Total Living: **4664** *sf*

Foundation: **Slab**

Exterior Wall: **8" Block**

PLAN PRICING:

Vellum & PDF - **$3032**

CAD - **$5364**

PLAN NUMBER:

6954

PLAN NAME:

Dimora

San Filippo

ARDA Award Winner!

Spacious, light-filled rooms allow unencumbered views throughout the interior. The pure geometry of the plan plays raw nature against historic details and 21st century accoutrements. A massive hearth in the living room reinforces the ancient charm of tapered columns along the gallery, while French doors bring in scenery and light. Angled lines melt into the outdoors with walls of retreating glass in the morning nook and kitchen. A family valet, conveniently located, provides the perfect place to drop your keys and packages.

From the old-country styling of the central turret to the high ceilings and gracefully arched doorways and windows, San Filippo melds award-winning design with comfortable living. Experience breathtaking vistas immediately upon entering the foyer, where an open floor plan allows views directly into the formal dining and living rooms and out through multiple French doors to the veranda.

The open kitchen also affords unobstructed views of the nook and leisure room. Retreating glass doors expand the common living space to the outdoor living areas. Upstairs, French doors open two of the four guest bedrooms to a private deck overlooking the veranda.

The two-story barrel-vault ceiling and transom-topped glass doors leading to the veranda is sure to impress.

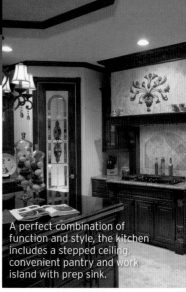

A perfect combination of function and style, the kitchen includes a stepped ceiling, convenient pantry and work island with prep sink.

Designed to be an indulgent retreat, the master bath offers repose with a whirlpool tub and a generous walk-thru shower framed by a triple set of circular windows and repeating arches.

~ *Any plan can be customized to meet your needs, find out how by calling* **800-718-7526**. ~

Veranda
29'-9" x 24'-4" Avg.
10'-0" Clg.

Pool Bath

Outdoor Grille

Leisure Room
20'-4" x 17'-4"
9'-4" to 10'-0"
Stepped Clg.

Built-In Entertainment

Nook
9'-4" Clg.

Kitchen
13'-8" x 14'-8"
9'-4" to 10'-0"
Stepped Clg.

Courtyard

Pantry

Veranda
18'-2" x 8'-8"
14'-2" Clg.

Master Suite
15'-0" x 21'-6"
12'-0" to 13'-0"
Stepped Clg.

Dining Room
10'-0" x 14'-2"
9'-0" to 10'-0"
Stepped Clg.

Living Room
18'-2" x 14'-2"
Open to Above

Fireplace

WIC

WIC

Study/ Bedroom 5
12'-2" x 13'-8"
10'-0" Clg.

Bath 1
10'-0" Clg.

Laundry Chute

Foyer
16'-0" Clg.

Art Niche

Opt. Closet

Storage

Walk-In Shower

Family Valet

Wine Cellar

Coat Closet

Up

Portico
18'-8" x 7'-4"
13'-4" Clg.

FIRST FLOOR

Whirlpool

M. Bath
12'-0" to 12'-8"
Stepped Clg.

Walk-In Shower

Utility
8'-2" x 6'-0"
10'-0" Clg.

Garage
23'-0" x 31'-2"
10'-0" Clg.

©THE SATER DESIGN COLLECTION, INC.

Photographed home may have been modified from the original construction documents.

REAR ELEVATION

©THE SATER DESIGN COLLECTION, INC.

Deck
35'-1" x 8'-0"

Walk-In Shower

Bedroom 2
14'-0" x 13'-0"
9'-4" Clg.

Bath 2
9'-4" Clg.

Bedroom 1
13'-5" x 13'-10"
9'-4" Clg.

WIC

WIC

Bedroom 3
16'-2" x 12'-0"
9'-4" Clg.

Loft
10'-10" x 13'-8"
9'-4" Clg.

Open to Below
18'-4" to 19'-4"
Vaulted Clg.

Bath 3
9'-4" Clg.

WIC

Bedroom 4
12'-4" x 14'-0"
9'-4" Clg.

WIC

Laundry Chute

Storage Room

Dn.

Open to Below

SECOND FLOOR

© Sater Design Collection, Inc.

SPECIFICATIONS:

Bedrooms: **6**

Baths: **4½**

Width: **69' 4"**

Depth: **95' 4"**

1st Floor: **2913** *sf*

2nd Floor: **1471** *sf*

Total Living: **4384** *sf*

Foundation: **Slab**

Exterior Wall: **2x6 Wood**

PLAN PRICING:

Vellum & PDF - **$2850**

CAD - **$5042**

PLAN NUMBER:
8055

PLAN NAME:
San Filippo

Vittoria

The Vittoria home plan blends Old World Andalusian architecture with modern styling. This three bedroom, three and a half bath plan features a game room and bar than can be converted into a fourth bedroom and full bath. Outdoor living is front and center in this plan's layout with a connecting series of lanais. A large lanai off of the leisure room includes an expansive island, outdoor kitchen and fire-pit.

Once in the home guests are drawn into the coffer ceilinged living room and the views beyond. Through an arch, the home's casual area features the nook, island kitchen and leisure room. The leisure room is wrapped in glass with its cornerless disappearing sliding glass doors.

The sumptuous master suite features an elegant foyer entry, morning kitchen, his/hers closets, and a resort-like master bath with island tub and walk-in shower.

The Vittoria showcases an optional wine cellar with fixed glass window in the dining room where it becomes a focal point of dinner conversations with guests.

The home's powder bath is ideally located for privacy and doubles as a pool bath. It is not hard to see the attraction of the Vittoria home plan.

Beautiful arched wrought iron entry doors and arches grace the foyer and dining beyond.

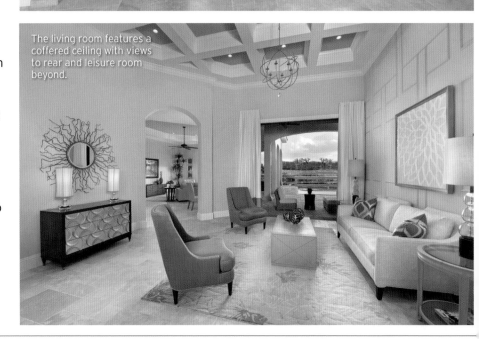

The living room features a coffered ceiling with views to rear and leisure room beyond.

~ *Any plan can be customized to meet your needs, find out how by calling 800-718-7526.* ~

REAR ELEVATION

Outdoor living is the focus of this home's lanai with outdoor kitchen and seating spaces.

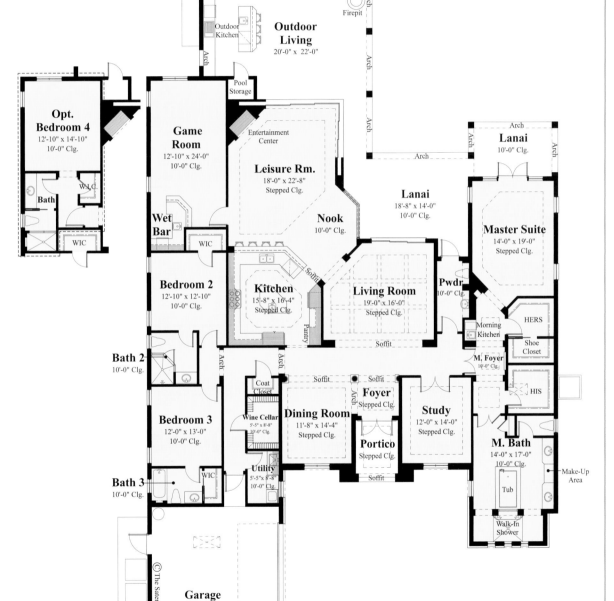

© Sater Design Collection, Inc.

© The Sater Design Collection, Inc.

SPECIFICATIONS:

Bedrooms: **3**

Baths: **3½**

Width: **70' 0"**

Depth: **123' 4"**

1st Floor: **3877** *sf*

Total Living: **3877** *sf*

Foundation: **Slab**

Exterior Wall: **8" Block**

PLAN PRICING:

Vellum & PDF - **$2520**

CAD - **$4460**

PLAN NUMBER:

6966

PLAN NAME:

Vittoria

Not available for construction in Lee or Collier Counties, Florida.

The formal living room greets guests and offers a wall of windows to enjoy views of the pool area. A two-sided fireplace is shared with the study.

Palazzo Ripoli

ARDA Award Winner!

The elegant European façade will provide an Old-World flair to any street-scape. Arches line the cloister flowing from the detached guest suite to the barrel-vault entry of this innovative design. Inside, the grand salon welcomes with commanding views past the loggia and a two-sided fireplace shared with the study. A walk-in wet bar adjoins the kitchen and provides a servery to the formal areas. Retreating glass walls open the leisure room to the outside amenities. Multiple connections to the outdoors are present throughout the plan courtesy of French doors, walls of windows, and retreating walls of glass. To the left of the plan the master wing is an indulgent retreat for the owners, particularly with its luxurious his-and-hers amenities located throughout the spacious retreat. Two additional guest suites have en suite baths and are located on the opposite side of the plan, enhancing privacy for all.

Two kitchen islands, one with an eating bar, dual sinks, and plentiful cabinetry come together to make this spacious kitchen spectacular.

REAR ELEVATION

Solana
20'-0" x 11'-0"
12'-0" Clg.

Arch   Arch   Arch

Outdoor Grill
10'-0" Clg.

Pool Bath

Leisure Room
18'-0" x 23'-2"
10'-0" to 11'-4" Clg.

Built-Ins
Built-Ins
Built-Ins
Built-In

Sitting
10'-0" to 10'-8" Clg.

Arch

Arch

Arch

Arch   Arch

Master Suite
14'-0" x 18'-0"
10'-0" to 11'-4" Clg.

Loggia
12'-0" Clg.

Nook
12'-0" x 15'-0"
10'-0" to 10'-8" Clg.

Kitchen
17'-0" x 15'-6"
10'-0" to 10'-8" Clg.

Hers
10'-0" Clg.

Arch

Arch

Study
12'-2" x 16'-4"
10'-0" to 10'-8" Clg.

Grand Salon
19'-4" x 20'-4"
12'-0" to 12'-8" Clg.

Built-In

Bar

Arch

Arch

Arch

His
10'-0" Clg.

Arch

Master Foyer
10'-0" Clg.

Guest 2
15'-0" x 12'-10"
10'-0" to 10'-8" Clg.

Soffit

Soffit

Arch

Arch

Arch

Arch

Arch

Niche

Soffit

Dining Room
10'-10" x 17'-9"
11'-0" to 11'-8" Clg.

Bath2
10'-0" Clg.

Bath3
10'-0" Clg.

Master Bath
14'-6" x 11'-4"
Barrel Vault Clg.

Powder

Foyer
Barrel Vault Clg.

Gallery

Cloisters
10'-0" Clg.

Portico
Barrel Vault Clg.

Linen

Guest 3
15'-0" x 12'-10"
10'-0" to 10'-8" Clg.

Arch

Arch

Master Garden
10'-0" Clg.

Arch

Utility
8'-0" x 8'-6"
10'-0" Clg.

Arch

Arch

Motor Court

Arch

3-Car Garage
23'-8" x 32'-4"
10'-0" Clg.

Arch

Guest Studio
14'-6" x 15'-4"
10'-0" to 10'-8" Clg.

SPECIFICATIONS:

Bedrooms: **4**

Full Baths: **4**

Half Baths: **2**

Width: **69' 10"**

Depth: **120' 0"**

1st Floor: **4266** sf

Total Living: **4266** sf

Foundation: **Slab**

Exterior Wall: **8" Block**

PLAN PRICING:

Vellum & PDF - **$2773**

CAD - **$4906**

PLAN NUMBER:
8074

PLAN NAME:
Palazzo Ripoli

Sunningdale Cove

Sunningdale Cove is a unique home that successfully brings the outdoors inside for all to enjoy. What appears to be a traditional entry is, in fact, a portico that grants access to a spacious courtyard. The courtyard provides a serene outdoor retreat no matter the configuration, but is well matched with a pool and spa. This floor plan is a perennial favorite and remains a best-seller year after year.

The main house, with its generous master suite, dramatic grand salon and well-crafted family living spaces, flanks the courtyard on two sides, while an extended garage and full guest suite border the third. A pool and spa, built-in planters and a fireplace take the courtyard to a level of sublime luxury.

Past the foyer, a sculpted arch delineates the dining room from the grand room, where oversized windows, arch-top transoms and a box-beamed ceiling create an airy warmth that spreads throughout the house.

Nearby, the kitchen features a center island, an angled serving bar and a niche for a desk, while the adjacent family room boasts a built-in media wall.

Upstairs, the partial second story completes the home with two guest bedrooms, a full bath and two observation decks that overlook the courtyard and rear loggia.

With a soaring seventeen-foot ceiling, two-story bay windows facing the lanai, carved coffers and decorative columns, this grand room truly lives up to its name in every respect.

In keeping with a theme of casual comfort, the common area shared by the kitchen, breakfast nook and leisure room feels festive and informal, making it the ideal place for casual, impromptu entertaining.

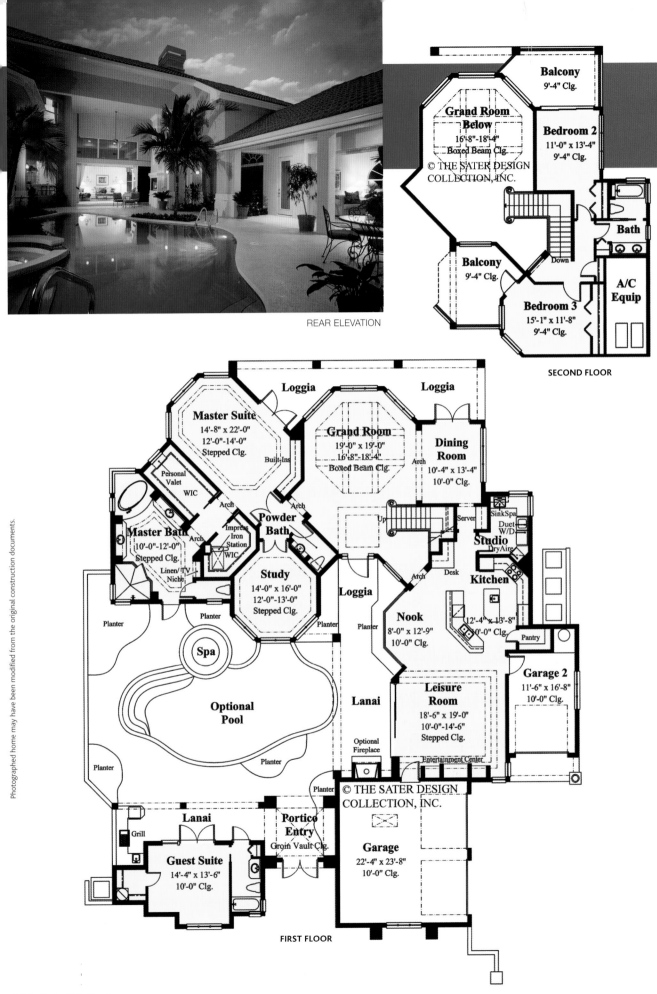

REAR ELEVATION

Balcony
9'-4" Clg.

Grand Room Below
16'-8"-18'-4"
Boxed Beam Clg.

© THE SATER DESIGN COLLECTION, INC.

Bedroom 2
11'-0" x 13'-4"
9'-4" Clg.

Bath

Down

A/C Equip

Balcony
9'-4" Clg.

Bedroom 3
15'-1" x 11'-8"
9'-4" Clg.

SECOND FLOOR

Loggia

Loggia

Master Suite
14'-8" x 22'-0"
12'-0"-14'-0"
Stepped Clg.

Built-Ins

Grand Room
19'-0" x 19'-0"
16'-8"-18'-4"
Boxed Beam Clg.

Dining Room
10'-4" x 13'-4"
10'-0" Clg.

Arch

Personal Valet
WIC

Arch

Powder Bath

Arch

Master Bath
10'-0"-12'-0"
Stepped Clg.

Impress Iron Station
WIC

Linen/TV Niche

Study
14'-0" x 16'-0"
12'-0"-13'-0"
Stepped Clg.

Up

Server

Sink Spa

Duet W/D

Studio
DryAire

Desk

Kitchen
12'-4" x 13'-8"
10'-0" Clg.

Arch

Loggia

Planter

Planter

Planter

Planter

Planter

Nook
8'-0" x 12'-9"
10'-0" Clg.

Pantry

Spa

Optional Pool

Planter

Lanai

Optional Fireplace

Leisure Room
18'-6" x 19'-0"
10'-0"-14'-6"
Stepped Clg.

Garage 2
11'-6" x 16'-8"
10'-0" Clg.

Entertainment Center

Planter

© THE SATER DESIGN COLLECTION, INC.

Planter

Lanai

Grill

Portico Entry
Groin Vault Clg.

Guest Suite
14'-4" x 13'-6"
10'-0" Clg.

Garage
22'-4" x 23'-8"
10'-0" Clg.

FIRST FLOOR

Photographed home may have been modified from the original construction documents.

© Sater Design Collection, Inc.

SPECIFICATIONS:

Bedrooms: **4**

Baths: **3½**

Width: **80' 0"**

Depth: **96' 0"**

1st Floor: **3165** *sf*

2nd Floor: **627** *sf*

Total Living: **3792** *sf*

Foundation: **Slab**

Exterior Wall: **2x6 Wood**

PLAN PRICING:

Vellum & PDF - **$2465**

CAD - **$4361**

PLAN NUMBER:

6660

PLAN NAME:

Sunningdale Cove

Carved entry doors and an ornate barrel-vault ceiling are hallmarks of this stately, Moorish-influenced foyer.

Monticello

Sunlight and moonlight filter into the foyer through glass walls that frame the entry doors and showcase the lush landscaping surrounding the entry. Straight ahead of the foyer, the corner of the living room is mere steps from the pool - a boundary that is erased with the opening of zero-corner sliding glass doors. An elegant stepped ceiling, accented by moldings, lends a finishing touch to the living room. Columns offer decorative support to an archway that defines the space between the formal living room and dining room. The open arrangement of the kitchen, leisure room and nook provides a continuum of space that is roomy, yet comfortable. The leisure room boasts an appealing corner fireplace, built-in entertainment center, pyramid ceiling and zero-corner doors, which open onto a special place off the lanai-an outdoor kitchen with bar seating. The master suite encompasses a sitting area with bay window, two walk-in closets and a large bathroom with garden tub overlooking a private garden spot-a soulful sojourn for lucky homeowners. A butler's pantry is cleverly accessible to both dining room and kitchen, as is a grotto wet bar with wine cellar. A groin-vaulted ceiling and wrought-iron gates create a quaint setting for storing favorite vintages.

Nook, leisure room and kitchen converge to create a spacious - and gracious - living area. Courtesy of retreating glass walls, spectacular exterior vistas become part of the equally spectacular interior landscape.

Island kitchen with arched niche over gas cook-top and stone backdrop.

~ Any plan can be customized to meet your needs, find out how by calling 800-718-7526. ~

Elegant-yet-sturdy ten-foot columns support soft slump arches, loosely defining the living room and generous dining room beyond.

REAR ELEVATION

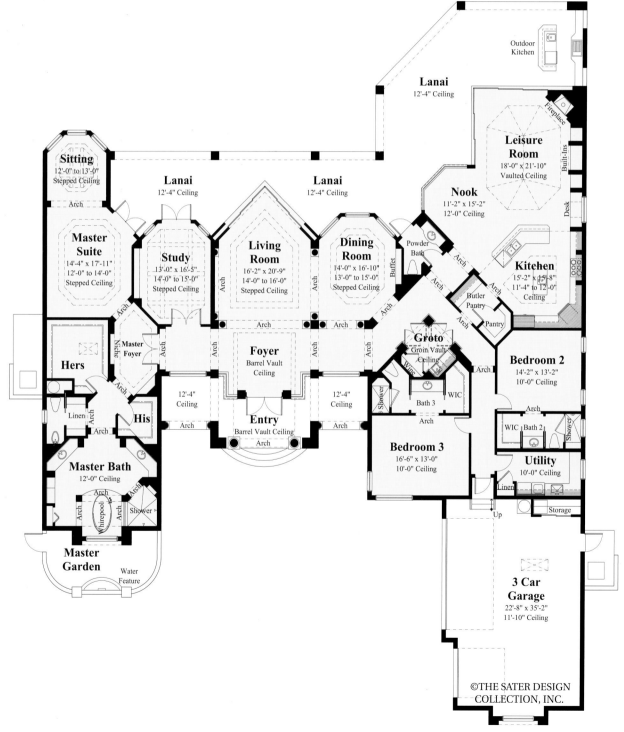

Outdoor Kitchen

Lanai 12'-4" Ceiling

Leisure Room 18'-0" x 21'-10" Vaulted Ceiling

Lanai 12'-4" Ceiling

Lanai 12'-4" Ceiling

Nook 11'-2" x 15'-2" 12'-0" Ceiling

Sitting 12'-0" to 13'-0" Stepped Ceiling

Master Suite 14'-4" x 17'-11" 12'-0" to 14'-0" Stepped Ceiling

Study 13'-0" x 16'-5" 14'-0" to 15'-0" Stepped Ceiling

Living Room 16'-2" x 20'-9" 14'-0" to 16'-0" Stepped Ceiling

Dining Room 14'-0" x 16'-0" 13'-0" to 15'-0" Stepped Ceiling

Powder Bath

Kitchen 15'-2" x 15'-8" 11'-4" to 12'-0" Ceiling

Buffet

Butler Pantry

Pantry

Hers

Master Foyer

Niche

Foyer Barrel Vault Ceiling

Groto Groin Vault Ceiling

Wine

Bedroom 2 14'-2" x 13'-2" 10'-0" Ceiling

Shower

Bath 3

WIC

12'-4" Ceiling

12'-4" Ceiling

His

Linen

Entry Barrel Vault Ceiling

WIC

Bath 2

Shower

Master Bath 12'-0" Ceiling

Whirlpool

Shower

Bedroom 3 16'-6" x 13'-0" 10'-0" Ceiling

Utility 10'-0" Ceiling

Linen

Up

Storage

Master Garden

Water Feature

3 Car Garage 22'-8" x 35'-2" 11'-10" Ceiling

©THE SATER DESIGN COLLECTION, INC.

Photographed home may have been modified from the original construction documents.

SPECIFICATIONS:

Bedrooms: **3**

Baths: **3½**

Width: **91' 6"**

Depth: **117' 0"**

1st Floor: **4255** *sf*

Total Living: **4255** *sf*

Foundation: **Slab**

Exterior Wall: **8" Block**

PLAN PRICING:

Vellum & PDF - **$2766**

CAD - **$4893**

PLAN NUMBER:
6907

PLAN NAME:
Monticello

Cantadora

A stately entry distinguishes this Mediterranean estate from the rest. Varied roof lines and wrought-iron accents provide visual interest in the façade. Guests are welcomed into the formal living room, where a soaring ceiling and walls of glass are sure to make a lasting impression.

The kitchen is open to a casual dining nook and leisure room, an open arrangement that provides a family-friendly atmosphere. From the leisure room, stairs lead to the roomy upstairs loft with wet bar.

The master retreat offers a host of features in a rambling arrangement that encompasses one entire side of the home.

Three self-contained guest suites are not only secluded from the master, they're also secluded from each other, offering the ultimate in privacy for overnight guests.

Outdoor living is at its finest in Cantadora, with retreating glass walls eliminating boundaries between inside and out, as well as walls of windows highlighting the beautiful outdoors. Amenities include an outdoor kitchen under the veranda and an outdoor fireplace in the courtyard.

A regal master bath features an elevated marble garden tub and elegant walk-in shower framed by handsome columns.

The leisure room has custom built-ins for media equipment.

Casual and comfortable, yet equipped to meet any culinary challenge, the kitchen flows into both the leisure room and the breakfast nook.

REAR ELEVATION

SECOND FLOOR

Guest Suite 3
13'-2" x 15'-6"
9'-4" Clg.

Balcony
19'-6" x 16'-1"

© THE SATER DESIGN
COLLECTION, INC.

Bath 3
9'-4" Clg.

Loft
27'-0" x 26'-1"
9'-4" Clg.

Down

Wet Bar

FIRST FLOOR

Guest Suite 2
13'-6" x 15'-4"
12'-0" Clg.

Outdoor Kitchen

Veranda
12'-0" Clg.

Bath 2
10'-0" Clg.

Storage

Leisure Room
21'-3" x 29'-0"
11'-3"–12'-0"
Stepped Clg.

Built-Ins

Veranda
Sloped Clg.

Up

Nook
8'-7" x 10'-0"
12'-0" Clg.

Veranda
12'-0" Clg.

Master Suite
19'-11" x 20'-1"
12'-0"-14'-0"
Stepped Clg.

Courtyard

Fireplace

Kitchen
11'-10" x 15'-2"
12'-0"-13'-0"
Stepped Clg.

Living Room
26'-3" x 18'-11"
15'-0"-16'-0"
Stepped Clg.

Pwdr.

WIC

Bath
10'-0" Clg.

Dining Room
13'-0" x 11'-2"
14'-0"-15'-0"
Stepped Clg.

Foyer
15'-0" Clg.

Study
13'-0" x 13'-0"
14'-0"-15'-0"
Stepped Clg.

Built-Ins

WIC

Master Bath
10'-0" Clg.

Guest Suite 1
16'-4" x 14'-10"
10'-0" Clg.

Utility
10'-0" Clg.

Entry
Barrel Vault Clg.

Walk-In Shower

Storage

WIC

Arch

4-Car Garage
23'-4" x 44'-4"
10'-0" Clg.

© THE SATER DESIGN
COLLECTION, INC.

Arch

SPECIFICATIONS:

Bedrooms: **4**

Baths: **4½**

Width: **91' 6"**

Depth: **122' 3"**

1st Floor: **3641** *sf*

2nd Floor: **894** *sf*

Total Living: **4535** *sf*

Foundation: **Slab**

Exterior Wall: **8" Block**

PLAN PRICING:

Vellum & PDF - **$2948**

CAD - **$5215**

PLAN NUMBER:

6949

PLAN NAME:

Cantadora

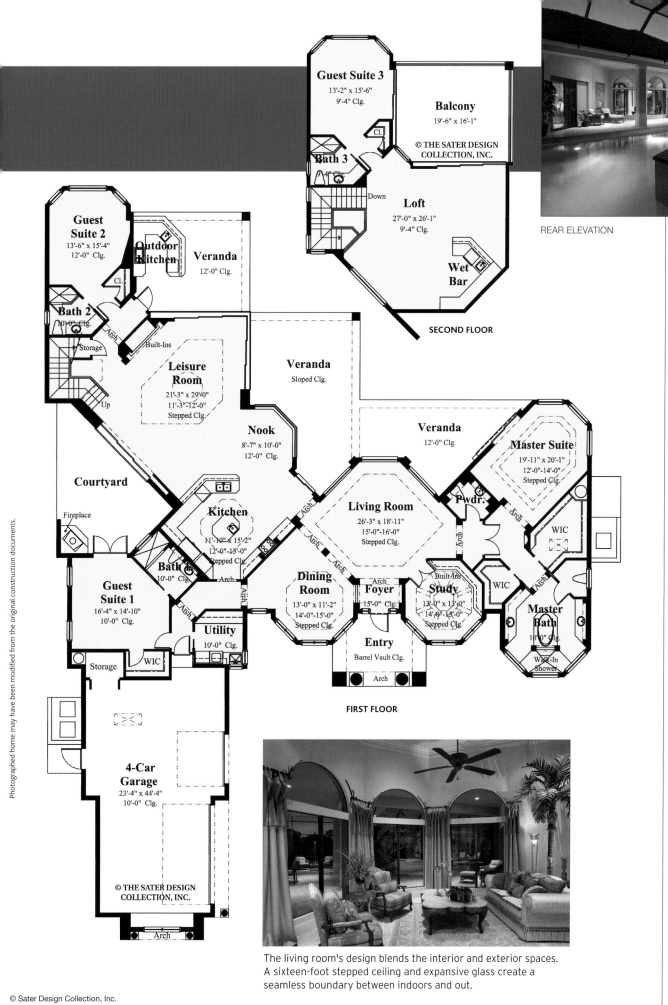

The living room's design blends the interior and exterior spaces. A sixteen-foot stepped ceiling and expansive glass create a seamless boundary between indoors and out.

Vasari

A stunning window-lined turret, classic columns and repeating arches create a striking façade. An uninhibited spirit prevails within, where a gallery foyer and loft deepen the central living/dining room, allowing a stepped ceiling to soar above open vistas defined only by decorative columns. A two-sided fireplace warms the central area as well as a study that boasts a private porch. A view-oriented leisure room enjoys multiple connections with the outdoors. The openness of the kitchen/nook/leisure room creates a flexible, informal area that is perfect for spending time with friends and family. Above the entry, a sun porch with French doors permits sunlight to invigorate the loft. An inviting space that connects the family's sleeping quarters with a private guest suite. The main level brags a cabana-style guest suite, with access to a compartmented bath and shower from the veranda.

Decorative wrought-iron railing flows up the stairs in the glass-encased turret to the lot overlooking the well-appointed formal rooms.

Overlooking the stairway and landing embraced with an arched bay of windows.

Home's open island kitchen (modified with a single island by designer)

FIRST FLOOR

Porch
10'-0" Clg.

Leisure Room
17'-8" x 19'-11"
9'-4" to 10'-0"
Stepped Clg.

Entertainment Center

Nook
9'-0" x 9'-8"
9'-4" Clg.

Kitchen
17'-4" x 13'-8"
9'-4" to 10'-0"
Stepped Clg.

Cabana/Guest Suite
13'-0" x 13'-4"
10'-0" Clg.

WIC

Veranda
26'-6" x 10'-2"
Open to Above

Outdoor Grille

Guest Bath

Walk-In Shower

Living/Dining Room
21'-11" x 11'-9"
Open to Above

Two Sided Fireplace

Built-Ins

Library / Study
12'-3" x 15'-0"
9'-4" to 10'-0"
Stepped Clg.

Foyer
10'-0" Clg.

Pantry

Pwdr.

Stor.

Elev.

Up

Stor.

Porch
10'-0" Clg.

Entry
10'-0" Clg.

Garage
29'-0" x 23'-8"
10'-0" Clg.

©THE SATER DESIGN COLLECTION, INC.

SECOND FLOOR

©THE SATER DESIGN COLLECTION, INC.

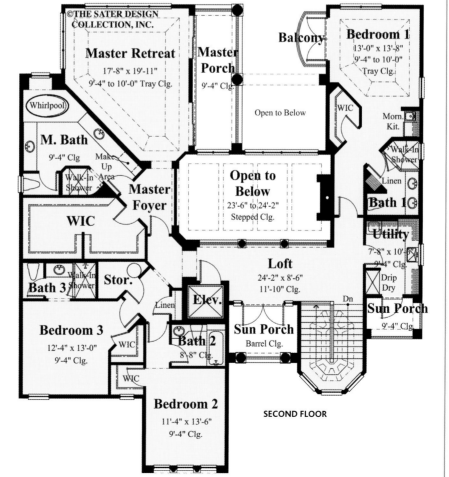

Master Retreat
17'-8" x 19'-11"
9'-4" to 10'-0" Tray Clg.

Master Porch
9'-4" Clg.

Balcony

Bedroom 1
13'-0" x 13'-8"
9'-4" to 10'-0" Tray Clg.

Whirlpool

M. Bath
9'-4" Clg.

Make Up Area

WIC

Morn. Kit.

Walk-In Shower

Open to Below
23'-6" to 24'-2"
Stepped Clg.

Master Foyer

Open to Below

Bath 1

Walk-In Shower

Linen

WIC

Bath 3

Walk-In Shower

Stor.

Elev.

Linen

Utility
7'-8" x 10'-
9'-4" Clg.

Drip Dry

Loft
24'-2" x 8'-6"
11'-10" Clg.

Bedroom 3
12'-4" x 13'-0"
9'-4" Clg.

WIC

Bath 2
8'-8" Clg.

WIC

Sun Porch
Barrel Clg.

Dn

Sun Porch
9'-4" Clg.

Bedroom 2
11'-4" x 13'-6"
9'-4" Clg.

REAR ELEVATION

SPECIFICATIONS:

Bedrooms: **5**

Baths: **5½**

Width: **58' 0"**

Depth: **65' 0"**

1st Floor: **1995** *sf*

2nd Floor: **2165** *sf*

Total Living: **4160** *sf*

Foundation: **Slab**

Exterior Wall: **2x6 Wood**

PLAN PRICING:

Vellum & PDF - **$2704**

CAD - **$4784**

PLAN NUMBER:

8025

PLAN NAME:

Vasari

Autumn Woods

A bold entry turret shelters glass-paneled doors recessed behind a sculpted, Palladio-influenced arch. Fractured symmetry heightens the street presentation and creates a progression of spaces within. A gallery hall links an open arrangement of the formal rooms, with decorative columns providing subtle separation and definition. Retreating doors open the central living area to the outdoors, where a wrapping lanai leads to an alfresco kitchen. A cabana bath permits sunbathers and swimmers a transition area before re-entering the home.

The formal dining room provides a bay window and splendid views of the front property. Linked to the gourmet kitchen via a butler's pantry, the dining room easily facilitates planned events.

The kitchen's food preparation counter, which provides a vegetable sink, serves easy meals and overlooks the casual living zone. An entertainment center anchors the spacious leisure room, enriched by panoramas of scenery through retreating glass doors. The opposing wall also features retractable doors leading out to a spacious side courtyard, which offers an outdoor fireplace.

The formal dining room opens from the foyer through graceful sculpted archways.

Panoramic floor-to-ceiling windows in the breakfast nook bring magnificent view.

In the Old World tradition, the kitchen is both friendly and intimate, making it as much a place for casual conversation as for cooking.

The diamond-shaped leisure room is conveniently located adjacent to the kitchen. The paneled, vaulted ceiling casts a warm glow over this comfortable and relaxing space.

REAR ELEVATION

Floor Plan

Lanai
10'-0" Clg.

Outdoor Kitchen

Storage

Entertainment Center

Leisure Room
17'-0" x 20'-10"
Vaulted Clg.

Fireplace

Master Sitting

Lanai
12'-0" Clg.

Nook
11'-8" x 11'-1"
12'-0" Clg.

Walk-In Shower

Master Suite
24'-0" x 17'-11"
13'-4" Clg.

Kitchen
16'-9" x 18'-8"
10'-0" Clg.

W.I.C.

Personal Valet

His Bath
10'-0" Clg.

Living Room
22'-9" x 17'-8"
14'-0" Clg.

Powder
10'-0" Clg.

Art Niche

Fireplace

Butler's Pantry

Pantry

Her Bath
12'-0" Clg.

W.I.C.

W.I.C.

Whirlpool

Bath #1
10'-0" Clg.

Linen

Study
16'-11" x 20'-0"
Tongue & Groove Clg.

Foyer
Groin Vault Clg.

Dining Room
17'-6" x 18'-5"
14'-0" Clg.

Art Niche

Guest Suite #1
14'-1" x 15'-4"
10'-0" Clg.

Studio

Walk-In Shower

Master Garden

SinkSpa Iron Station

Duet W/D DryAire

Entry

Gallery

Guest Suite #2
12'-6" x 17'-2"
10'-0" Clg.

Bath #2
10'-0" Clg.

Built In

Walk-In Shower

Casual and cozy, this living room offers visitors a warm welcome, courtesy of its beautifully crafted tile fireplace and angled view.

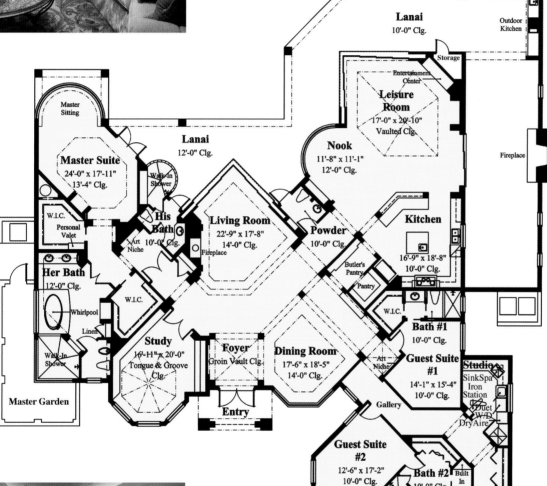

Garage
23'-8" x 36'-1"
11'-0" Clg.

© THE SATER DESIGN COLLECTION, INC.

SPECIFICATIONS:

Bedrooms: **3**

Baths: **4½**

Width: **87' 2"**

Depth: **127' 11"**

1st Floor: **4534** *sf*

Total Living: **4534** *sf*

Foundation: **Slab**

Exterior Wall: **8" Block**

PLAN PRICING:

Vellum & PDF - **$2947**

CAD - **$5214**

PLAN NUMBER:

6753

PLAN NAME:

Autumn Woods

Starwood

The entry's dramatic barrel-vaulted ceiling begins a welcoming introduction; the foyer with its sweeping views of the scenery beyond the living room windows gives a warming embrace.

The casual areas of this home are to the left of the plan, including the leisure room, guest wing, and kitchen with its large island and pantry. An elegant gallery leads to two guest rooms, each with private full bathrooms and spacious walk-in closets.

The arches and columns from the facade add a flourish to interior spaces, defining boundaries between the open living room and dining room, creating a dramatic entry or a finishing touch to a niche. A covered veranda rambles freely along the rear of this home, providing secluded areas for intimate conversation or larger gathering spots for grand soirees. A scenic backdrop for six rooms, this outdoor area is showcased through floor-to-ceiling windows, including curved walls of glass in the nook and living room, as well as French doors from the dining room and private study, and a sliding glass door from the master suite. Zero-corner sliding glass doors pocket into the walls of the leisure room, eliminating boundaries between outside and inside.

An open foyer eases the transition from the outdoors to the elegant living and dining rooms, which are suffused with natural light.

Open airy island kitchen with cook-top hood and granite countertops

Floor-to-ceiling glass permits nature to intrude, and grants spacious views of the veranda.

REAR ELEVATION

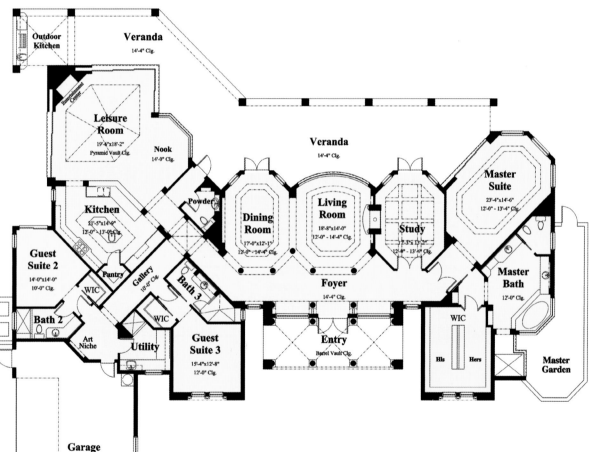

Outdoor Kitchen

Veranda
14'-4" Clg.

Leisure Room
19'-6"x18'-2"
Pyramid Vault Clg.

Nook
14'-0" Clg.

Kitchen
21'-5"x14'-0"
12'-0" - 13'-0" Clg.

Powder

Veranda
14'-4" Clg.

Dining Room
17'-0"x12'-1"
12'-0" - 14'-4" Clg.

Living Room
18'-8"x14'-0"
12'-0" - 14'-4" Clg.

Study
17'-3"x13'-2"
12'-0" - 13'-4" Clg.

Master Suite
23'-4"x14'-6"
12'-0" - 13'-4" Clg.

Guest Suite 2
14'-0"x14'-0"
10'-0" Clg.

WIC

Pantry

Gallery
10'-0" Clg.

Bath 3

Foyer
14'-4" Clg.

Master Bath
12'-0" Clg.

Bath 2

WIC

Art Niche

Utility

Guest Suite 3
15'-4"x12'-8"
12'-0" Clg.

Entry
Barrel Vault Clg.

WIC
His   Hers

Master Garden

Garage
36'-10"x22'-4"
12'-0" Clg.

© THE SATER DESIGN COLLECTION, INC.

SPECIFICATIONS:

Bedrooms: **3**

Baths: **3½**

Width: **102' 4"**

Depth: **98' 10"**

1st Floor: **3877** *sf*

Total Living: **3877** *sf*

Foundation: **Slab**

Exterior Wall: **8" Block**

PLAN PRICING:

Vellum & PDF - **$2520**

CAD - **$4459**

PLAN NUMBER:

6911

PLAN NAME:

Starwood

Sand-hued cabinets and countertops subdue a seamless bay window that permits views of a lush private garden outside the master bath.

Cadenwood

An inviting wraparound porch announces the relaxed ambience of the interior, while the symmetry of a series of classic columns and a triple-window dormer perfect the curb appeal of the façade. Built-in cabinetry, a fireplace and a series of French doors highlight the great room, which also features a wet bar.

To the left of the plan, an island kitchen establishes a link between the nook and the main living area, and easily serves the formal dining room. Bay windows bring in natural light along the rear perimeter, which connects to the outdoors via a covered porch and terrace that step down into the property.

The upper level boasts a catwalk that connects two secondary suites with a staircase that leads to a sizeable bonus room above the garage. Both of the guest bedrooms open to a rear deck, which overlooks the pool and spa area.

Deeply carved coffers serve as home to a pair of armoires that bookend the fireplace. A second floor balcony provides access to the guest suites and, at the same time, a "scenic overlook" of the great room and foyer.

Multiple workstations and state-of-the-art appliances combine with a beamed ceiling and granite countertops create an inviting and functional kitchen.

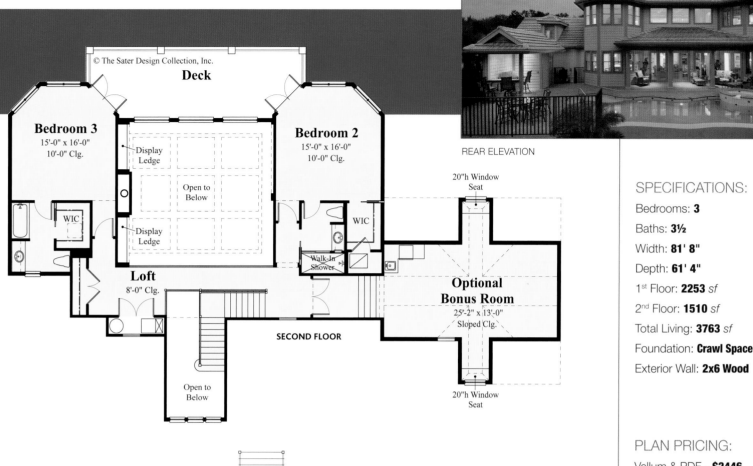

© The Sater Design Collection, Inc.

Deck

Bedroom 3
15'-0" x 16'-0"
10'-0" Clg.

Display Ledge

Open to Below

Display Ledge

WIC

Bedroom 2
15'-0" x 16'-0"
10'-0" Clg.

WIC

Walk-In Shower

Loft
8'-0" Clg.

REAR ELEVATION

20"h Window Seat

Optional Bonus Room
25'-2" x 13'-0"
Sloped Clg.

SECOND FLOOR

Open to Below

20"h Window Seat

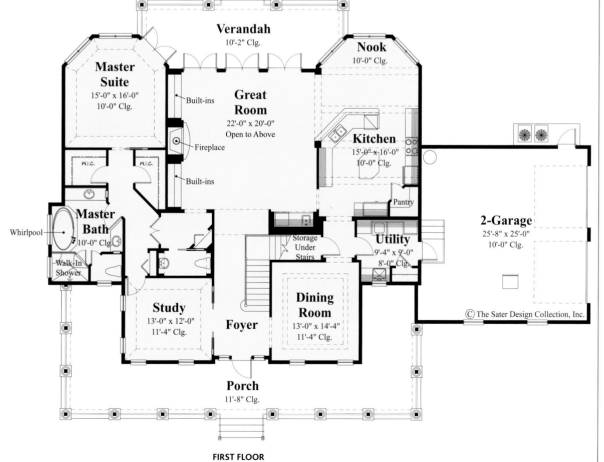

Verandah
10'-2" Clg.

Nook
10'-0" Clg.

Master Suite
15'-0" x 16'-0"
10'-0" Clg.

Built-ins

Great Room
22'-0" x 20'-0"
Open to Above

Fireplace

Built-ins

Kitchen
15'-0" x 16'-0"
10'-0" Clg.

Pantry

W.I.C.   W.I.C.

Master Bath
10'-0" Clg.

Whirlpool

Walk-In Shower

Storage Under Stairs

Utility
9'-4" x 9'-0"
8'-0" Clg.

2-Garage
25'-8" x 25'-0"
10'-0" Clg.

© The Sater Design Collection, Inc.

Study
13'-0" x 12'-0"
11'-4" Clg.

Foyer

Dining Room
13'-0" x 14'-4"
11'-4" Clg.

Porch
11'-8" Clg.

© Sater Design Collection, Inc.

FIRST FLOOR

SPECIFICATIONS:

Bedrooms: **3**

Baths: **3½**

Width: **81' 8"**

Depth: **61' 4"**

1st Floor: **2253** *sf*

2nd Floor: **1510** *sf*

Total Living: **3763** *sf*

Foundation: **Crawl Space**

Exterior Wall: **2x6 Wood**

PLAN PRICING:

Vellum & PDF - **$2446**

PLAN NUMBER:

7076

PLAN NAME:

Cadenwood

Megan's Bay

Whether it's the wide, handsome porches or the classic simplicity of the pillars, you'll feel the very definition of the word "inviting" as you approach Megan's Bay. Inside, the pleasures are even more abundant. The wide entrance hallway is a study in simplicity and elegance. High, detailed ceilings, stately pillars and a view up the stairs as well as through to the back verandah all combine to make even your visitors feel as though they've come home again.

Everyone will notice the wide, comfortable great room, opening through French doors to the veranda beyond; also, an open kitchen with a bay nook that simply begs for long weekend breakfasts complete with coffee, the newspaper and plenty of relaxation.

Speaking of relaxing—with its own small foyer, the master suite becomes a separated, private refuge designed for comfort and calm. With convenient access to the back verandah, this room is a spacious sanctuary.

And you'll find more flexibility and roomy comfort on the second level, where four extra bedrooms and two baths, a sizeable media room, and even a bonus room that can double as an apartment or artist's retreat.

The great room is a balance of classic beauty and comfortable living. Striking pillars draw the eye upward, where a beamed ceiling tops the room off in style. French doors and a convenient pass-thru to the kitchen – creates a casual and cozy living space.

With three sets of windows and a door to the verandah nearby, light will stream into the airy breakfast nook and kitchen area.

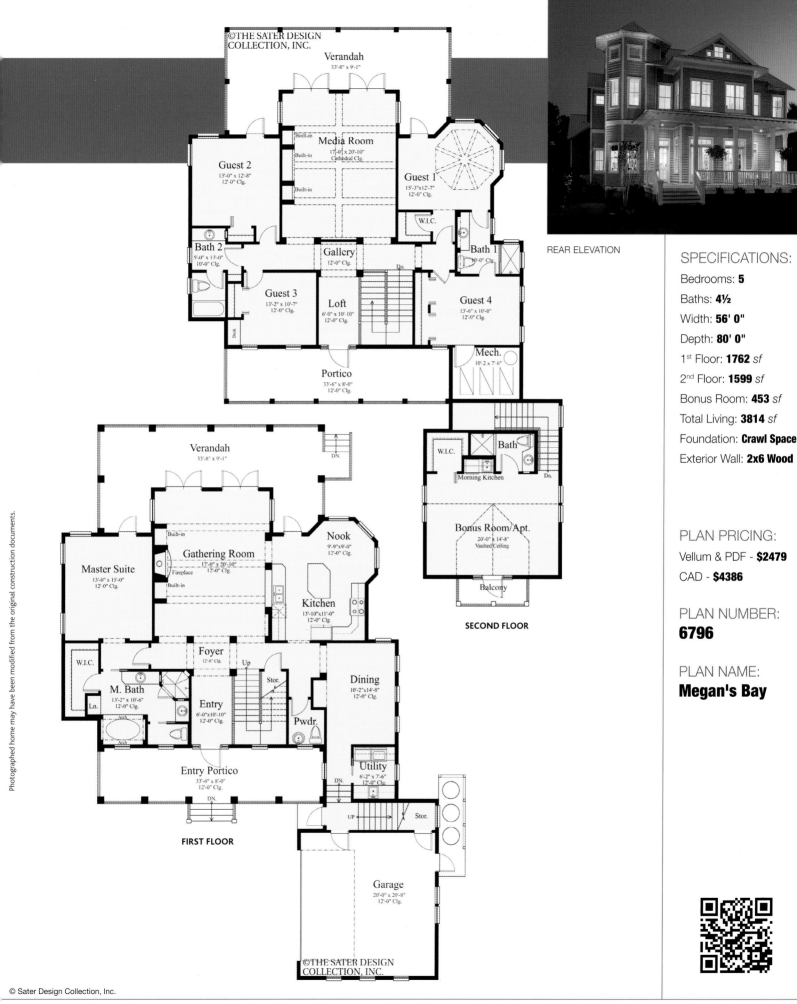

©THE SATER DESIGN
COLLECTION, INC.

Verandah
33'-8" x 9'-1"

Media Room
17'-0" x 20'-10"
Cathedral Clg.

Built-in

Built-in

Built-in

Guest 2
13'-0" x 12'-8"
12'-0" Clg.

Guest 1
15'-3"x12'-7"
12'-0" Clg.

W.I.C.

Bath 2
5'-0" x 13'-0"
10'-0" Clg.

Gallery
12'-0" Clg.

Bath 1
10'-0" Clg.

REAR ELEVATION

Dn.

Guest 3
13'-2" x 10'-7"
12'-0" Clg.

Loft
6'-0" x 10'-10"
12'-0" Clg.

Guest 4
13'-6" x 10'-0"
12'-0" Clg.

Desk

Portico
33'-6" x 8'-0"
12'-0" Clg.

Mech.
10'-2 x 7'-6"

DN.

Verandah
33'-8" x 9'-1"

W.I.C.

Bath

Master Suite
13'-0" x 15'-0"
12'-0" Clg.

Gathering Room
17'-0" x 20'-10"
12'-0" Clg.

Built-in

Fireplace

Built-in

Nook
9'-9"x9'-0"
12'-0" Clg.

Morning Kitchen

Dn.

Kitchen
13'-10"x11'-0"
12'-0" Clg.

Bonus Room/Apt.
20'-0" x 14'-8"
Vaulted Ceiling

W.I.C.

Foyer
12'-0" Clg.

Up

Stor.

Dining
10'-2"x14'-8"
12'-0" Clg.

M. Bath
13'-2" x 10'-6"
12'-0" Clg.

Ln.

Arch

Entry
6'-0"x10'-10"
12'-0" Clg.

Pwdr.

Balcony

SECOND FLOOR

Arch

Entry Portico
33'-6" x 8'-0"
12'-0" Clg.

Utility
6'-2" x 7'-6"
12'-0" Clg.

DN.

DN.

UP

Stor.

FIRST FLOOR

Garage
20'-0" x 20'-8"
12'-0" Clg.

©THE SATER DESIGN
COLLECTION, INC.

SPECIFICATIONS:

Bedrooms: **5**

Baths: **4½**

Width: **56' 0"**

Depth: **80' 0"**

1st Floor: **1762** sf

2nd Floor: **1599** sf

Bonus Room: **453** sf

Total Living: **3814** sf

Foundation: **Crawl Space**

Exterior Wall: **2x6 Wood**

PLAN PRICING:

Vellum & PDF - **$2479**

CAD - **$4386**

PLAN NUMBER:
6796

PLAN NAME:
Megan's Bay

Portofino

Our Portofino home Plan reflects the elegance of an Italian Villa with its distinct Mediterranean styling. The home's turreted entry portico with wrought iron niches and corbeled stone accents is the elevation's centerpiece. Frescoed stucco walls and barrel tiled roofs complete it's charm.

Inside the foyer one is greeted by the formal dining and living room beyond. The coffered ceiling living room opens via French doors to the veranda and view beyond. To the right is the study and master suite beyond. The master bath with walk-in shower and whirlpool tub looks onto a private walled garden. The master suite has its own sitting area for relaxation, reading a good book or just enjoying the view.

The home's casual area with leisure room, nook and kitchen enjoy panoramic views of the veranda and pool area. The leisure room's entertainment wall serves as a divider for the adjacent game room.

To the rear of the home is a bath with a special guest suite that feels secluded and enjoys views of the pool area. The home has another two guest suites with private baths and utility room enroute to the garage.

The Portofino home plan melds the best of the old and the new in this spectacular design.

Rustic tile floors and convenient built-ins create warmth and charm throughout the living room, while expansive glass doors bring the outside in.

The kitchen, nook, and leisure room join together to make this an open and welcoming home. High, coffered ceilings and a generous kitchen island make this plan ideal for entertaining.

This spacious master bath feels like a private spa. Marble tile, a freestanding tub, his and her vanities, and a walk in shower make this a perfect space to relax in.

REAR ELEVATION

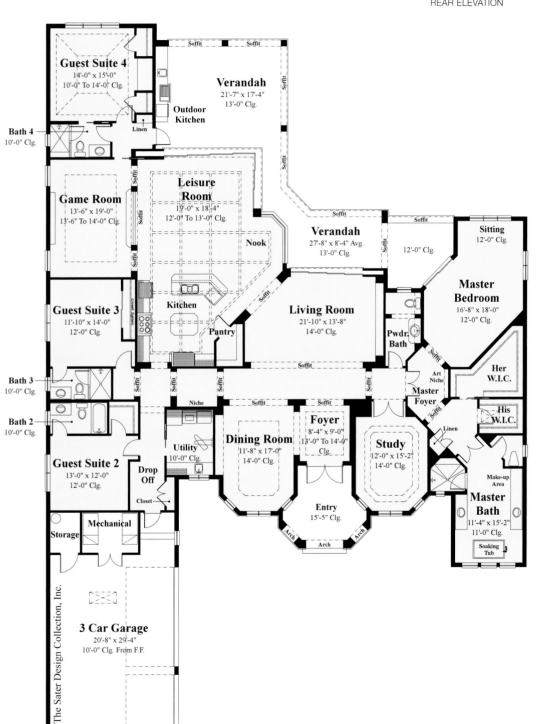

Floor plan labels:

Guest Suite 4
14'-0" x 15'-0"
10'-0" To 14'-0" Clg.

Bath 4
10'-0" Clg.

Outdoor Kitchen

Linen

Verandah
21'-7" x 17'-4"
13'-0" Clg.

Game Room
13'-6" x 19'-0"
13'-6" To 14'-0" Clg.

Leisure Room
19'-0" x 18'-4"
12'-0" To 13'-0" Clg.

Nook

Verandah
27'-8" x 8'-4" Avg.
13'-0" Clg.

Sitting
12'-0" Clg.

12'-0" Clg.

Master Bedroom
16'-8" x 18'-0"
12'-0" Clg.

Guest Suite 3
11'-10" x 14'-0"
12'-0" Clg.

Kitchen

Pantry

Living Room
21'-10" x 13'-8"
14'-0" Clg.

Pwdr. Bath

Her W.I.C.

Bath 3
10'-0" Clg.

Master Foyer

Art Niche

His W.I.C.

Bath 2
10'-0" Clg.

Niche

Soffit

Utility
10'-0" Clg.

Dining Room
11'-8" x 17'-0"
14'-0" Clg.

Foyer
8'-4" x 9'-0"
13'-0" To 14'-0" Clg.

Study
12'-0" x 15'-2"
14'-0" Clg.

Linen

Make-up Area

Guest Suite 2
13'-0" x 12'-0"
12'-0" Clg.

Drop Off

Closet

Entry
15'-5" Clg.

Arch

Master Bath
11'-4" x 15'-2"
11'-0" Clg.

Soaking Tub

Storage

Mechanical

3 Car Garage
20'-8" x 29'-4"
10'-0" Clg. From F.F.

SPECIFICATIONS:

Bedrooms: **4**
Baths: **4½**
Width: **80' 0"**
Depth: **116' 10"**
1st Floor: **4287** sf
Total Living: **4287** sf
Foundation: **Slab**
Exterior Wall: **8" Block**

PLAN PRICING:

Vellum & PDF - **$3429**
CAD - **$4930**

PLAN NUMBER:

6968

PLAN NAME:

Portofino

Not available for construction in Lee, Collier, Sarasota, and Manatee Counties, Florida.

Sherbrooke

Winner of 4 National Awards

Highly influenced by Italianate style, the layered elevation incorporates an array of details melded from renaissance themes. Pilasters line an arcade of windows that repeat the sculpted form of the entry. The open foyer grants extensive vistas through the living room, with wide outdoor panoramas that include the wrapping lanai. A graceful colonnade borders the formal dining room, which allows its own views to the front property.

Conveniently located near the dining room, state-of-the-art amenities prepare the gourmet kitchen for any occasion. The kitchen easily serves the connected breakfast nook and leisure room. Near the walk-in pantry, a window seat with storage below and views of the side courtyard through a large picture window. An angled hearth in the leisure room extends warmth and creates a comfortable atmosphere that flows all the way to the breakfast nook. A stair hall connects the casual living space with secluded guest quarters and leads to a single glass door, which provides access to an outdoor kitchen. The entire wing opens through retreating doors to the side courtyard, which includes an outdoor fireplace.

The living room has access to the lanai via two sets of French doors, is set apart from the dining and foyer area by Tuscan columns and features an octagonal ceiling with inlaid wood.

The kitchen has plenty of counter space, double ovens and a large walk-in pantry. The recessed window with window seat overlooks a courtyard. A convenient eating bar connects the kitchen to the leisure room.

Topped with decorative corbels, a stately, ornately carved partition wall separates the Roman tub from a spacious walk-in shower designed for two. Arch-top windows supply ample panoramas of the master garden.

REAR ELEVATION

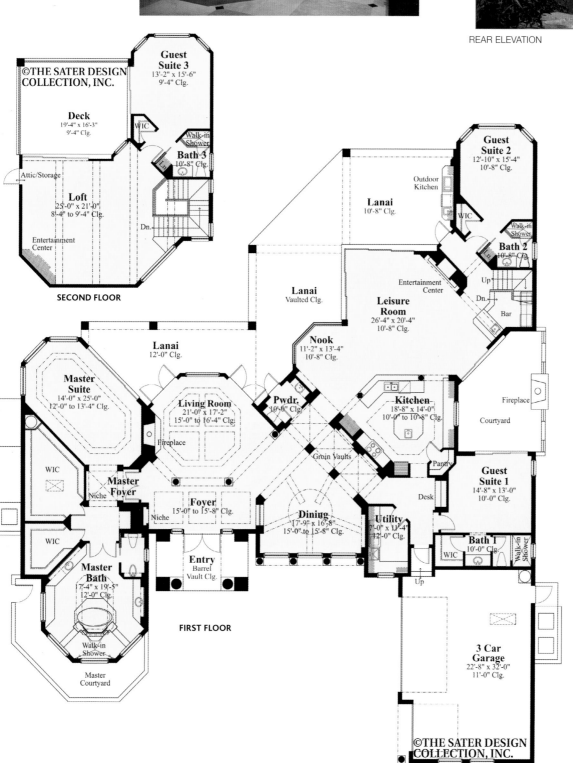

©THE SATER DESIGN COLLECTION, INC.

Guest Suite 3
13'-2" x 15'-6"
9'-4" Clg.

Deck
19'-4" x 16'-3"
9'-4" Clg.

WIC

Walk-in Shower

Bath 3
10'-8" Clg.

Attic/Storage

Loft
25'-0" x 21'-0"
8'-4" to 9'-4" Clg.

Dn.

Entertainment Center

SECOND FLOOR

Guest Suite 2
12'-10" x 15'-4"
10'-8" Clg.

Lanai
10'-8" Clg.

Outdoor Kitchen

WIC

Walk-in Shower

Bath 2
10'-8" Clg.

Up

Dn.

Bar

Lanai
Vaulted Clg.

Entertainment Center

Leisure Room
26'-4" x 20'-4"
10'-8" Clg.

Nook
11'-2" x 13'-4"
10'-8" Clg.

Lanai
12'-0" Clg.

Master Suite
14'-0" x 25'-0"
12'-0" to 13'-4" Clg.

Living Room
21'-0" x 17'-2"
15'-0" to 16'-4" Clg.

Fireplace

Pwdr.
10'-0" Clg.

Kitchen
18'-8" x 14'-0"
10'-0" to 10'-8" Clg.

Fireplace

Courtyard

WIC

WIC

Master Foyer

Niche

Foyer
15'-0" to 15'-8" Clg.

Niche

Groin Vaults

Pantry

Desk

Guest Suite 1
14'-8" x 13'-0"
10'-0" Clg.

Dining
17'-9" x 16'-8"
15'-0" to 15'-8" Clg.

Utility
7'-0" x 11'-4"
12'-0" Clg.

WIC

Bath 1
10'-0" Clg.

Walk-in Shower

Master Bath
17'-4" x 19'-5"
12'-0" Clg.

Entry
Barrel Vault Clg.

Up

Master Courtyard

Walk-in Shower

FIRST FLOOR

3 Car Garage
22'-8" x 32'-0"
11'-0" Clg.

©THE SATER DESIGN COLLECTION, INC.

SPECIFICATIONS:

Bedrooms: **4**

Baths: **4½**

Width: **91' 4"**

Depth: **109' 0"**

1st Floor: **3943** *sf*

2nd Floor: **859** *sf*

Total Living: **4802** *sf*

Foundation: **Slab**

Exterior Wall: **2x6 Wood**

PLAN PRICING:

Vellum & PDF - **$3842**

CAD - **$7203**

PLAN NUMBER:

6742

PLAN NAME:

Sherbrooke

REAR ELEVATION

© Sater Design Collection, Inc.

Rosewood Court

SPECIFICATIONS:

Bedrooms: **3**

Baths: **3½**

Width: **101' 8"**

Depth: **128' 4"**

1ˢᵗ Floor: **3891** *sf*

Total Living: **3891** *sf*

Foundation: **Slab**

PLAN PRICING:

Vellum & PDF - **$2529**

CAD - **$4475**

PLAN NUMBER:

6733

This highly livable floor plan begins with open, generously sized rooms. French doors open the formal living room to the spacious veranda. Located alongside the nook and spacious leisure room, the kitchen provides counter-style seating, ample storage space and a food-prep island. On the opposite side of the home, the master retreat features glass doors opening to the veranda and garden.

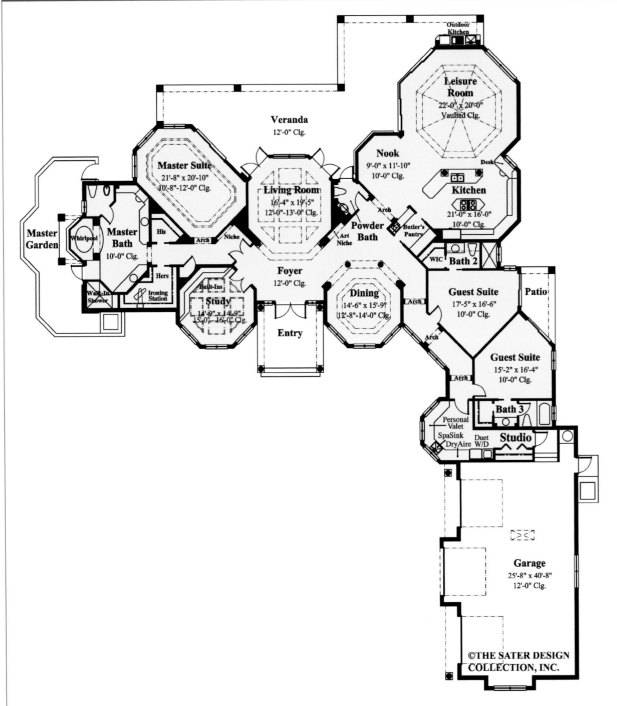

~ Any plan can be customized to meet your needs, find out how by calling 800-718-7526. ~

REAR ELEVATION

Oak Island

© Sater Design Collection, Inc.

ARDA Award Winner!

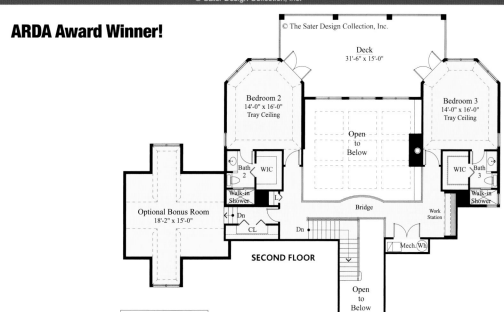

© The Sater Design Collection, Inc.

Deck
31'-6" x 15'-0"

Bedroom 2
14'-0" x 16'-0"
Tray Ceiling

Bedroom 3
14'-0" x 16'-0"
Tray Ceiling

Open to Below

Bath 2
WIC
Walk-in Shower

WIC
Bath 3
Walk-in Shower

Optional Bonus Room
18'-2" x 15'-0"

Dn
CL
Bridge
Dn
Work Station

Mech. Wh

SECOND FLOOR

Open to Below

Plant shelf

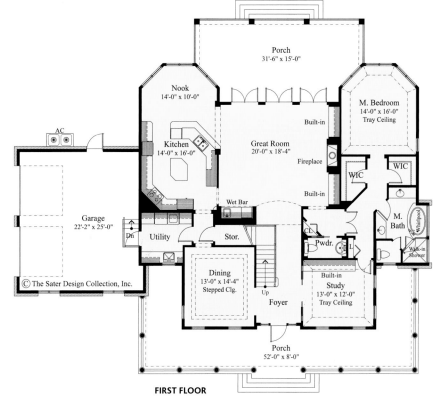

Porch
31'-6" x 15'-0"

Nook
14'-0" x 10'-0"

Kitchen
14'-0" x 16'-0"

Great Room
20'-0" x 18'-4"

Built-in

M. Bedroom
14'-0" x 16'-0"
Tray Ceiling

Fireplace

Built-in

WIC
WIC

Wet Bar

M. Bath
Whirlpool

AC

Garage
22'-2" x 25'-0"

Dn
Utility
Stor.

© The Sater Design Collection, Inc.

CL
Pwdr.
Walk-in Shower

Dining
13'-0" x 14'-4"
Stepped Clg.

Up
Foyer

Built-in
Study
13'-0" x 12'-0"
Tray Ceiling

Porch
52'-0" x 8'-0"

FIRST FLOOR

SPECIFICATIONS:

Bedrooms: **3**

Baths: **3½**

Width: **76' 8"**

Depth: **64' 0"**

1st Floor: **2138** *sf*

2nd Floor: **1371** *sf*

Total Living: **3509** *sf*

Opt. Bonus Room: **427** *sf*

Foundation: **Crawl Space**

PLAN PRICING:

Vellum & PDF - **$1755**

CAD - **$3158**

PLAN NUMBER:
7062

Style and elegance are found in Oak Island's window dormers, mirrored stone chimneys and split-shake tile roof. A big, welcoming great room with multiple sets of French doors features built-ins and open access to the kitchen and nook. Double doors access the master retreat, which also reveals private access to a large study. Upstairs, two guest bedrooms, each with large baths and walk-in closets, adjoin the bonus room.

REAR ELEVATION

© Sater Design Collection, Inc.

Rosemary Bay

SPECIFICATIONS:

Bedrooms: **3**

Baths: **3½**

Width: **75' 0"**

Depth: **111' 4"**

1st Floor: **3555** *sf*

Total Living: **3555** *sf*

Foundation: **Slab**

PLAN PRICING:

Vellum & PDF - **$1778**

CAD - **$3200**

PLAN NUMBER:

6781

The well-thought-out floor plan allots one entire side of the home to a sizeable master retreat and dedicates the other to a flexible leisure room/ kitchen/breakfast nook common area. Designed with friends and family in mind, the leisure room is a comfy gathering place. The kitchen is a gourmet chef's, busy family's, delight with its double island and abundant workplace for multiple cooks.

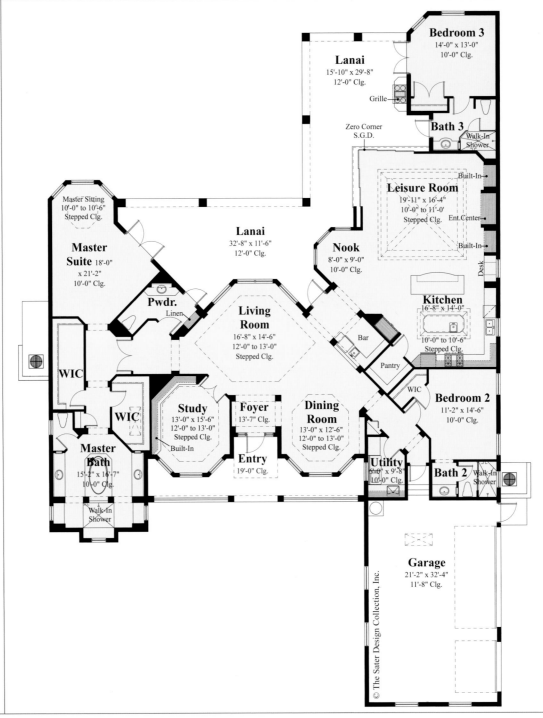

REAR ELEVATION

Monterrey Lane

© Sater Design Collection, Inc.

Golden ARDA Award Winner!

Photographed home may have been modified from the original construction documents.

Lanai
28'-4" Avg. x 10'-0"

Outdoor Kitchen

Zero Corner S.G.D.

Sitting Area

Leisure Room
21'-4" x 19'-3"
Vaulted Clg.

Entertainment Center

Built-ins

Master Suite
18'-10" x 19'-11"
11'-0" to 13'-0"
Stepped Clg.

bed art niche

Lanai

Nook
12'-0" Clg.

Zero Corner S.G.D.

Built-in

Arch

WH

Pool Room

Living Room
17'-0" x 23'-2"
12'-0" to 14'-0"
Stepped Ceiling

Fireplace

Wet Bar

Kitchen
17'-0" x 16'-3"
10' Clg.

Arch

Optional Valet
Her WIC

Niche

Arch

His WIC

Arch

Pantry

Built-ins

WIC

Bath 2

M. Bath
13'-4" x 13'-9"
12'-0" Stepped Clg.

Niche

Linen

Arch

Foyer
16'-8" Clg.

Built-in

Dining
14'-0" x 14'-6"
13'-0" to 14'-0"
Stepped Clg.

Arch

Guest Suite 2
13'-3" x 14'-6"
10'-0" Clg.

Study
14'-5" x 14'-9"
12'-0" to 14'-0"
Stepped Clg.

Niche   Niche

Gallery

Guest Suite 1
11'-8" x 15'-0"
10'-0" Clg.

WIC

Bath 1

WH

© The Sater Design Collection, Inc.

2 Car Garage
23'-0" x 26'-10"
11'-0" Clg.

AC
AC

Golf Cart

SPECIFICATIONS:

Bedrooms: **3**

Baths: **4**

Width: **79' 0"**

Depth: **117' 2"**

1ˢᵗ Floor: **4123** *sf*

Total Living: **4123** *sf*

Foundation: **Slab**

PLAN PRICING:

Vellum & PDF - **$2680**

CAD - **$4741**

PLAN NUMBER:
6672

Commanding architectural details, open living spaces and spectacular views combine to create this sophisticated, yet relaxed, home. Exciting outdoor spaces include an elevated spa and swimming pool combination, vast sitting areas and an outdoor kitchen. An island workstation and a corner oven, plus a U-shaped walk-in pantry, top the kitchen's amenities, which overlooks the massive leisure room.

REAR ELEVATION

Coach Hill

© Sater Design Collection, Inc.

SPECIFICATIONS:

Bedrooms: **4**

Baths: **4½**

Width: **70' 0"**

Depth: **100' 0"**

1st Floor: **3030** *sf*

2nd Floor: **1638** *sf*

Total Living: **4668** *sf*

Bonus Room: **290** *sf*

Foundation: **Slab**

PLAN PRICING:

Vellum & PDF - **$3034**

CAD - **$5368**

PLAN NUMBER:

8013

A striking balcony, bay turret and pediment dormers add curb appeal to this English country design. The foyer surrounds a spiral staircase, enhanced with a dome ceiling and clerestory windows. A stepped ceiling and arched columns define the forward formal room. Plenty of natural light enters the interior through the two-story bow window in the living room, which shares a two-sided fireplace with the study.

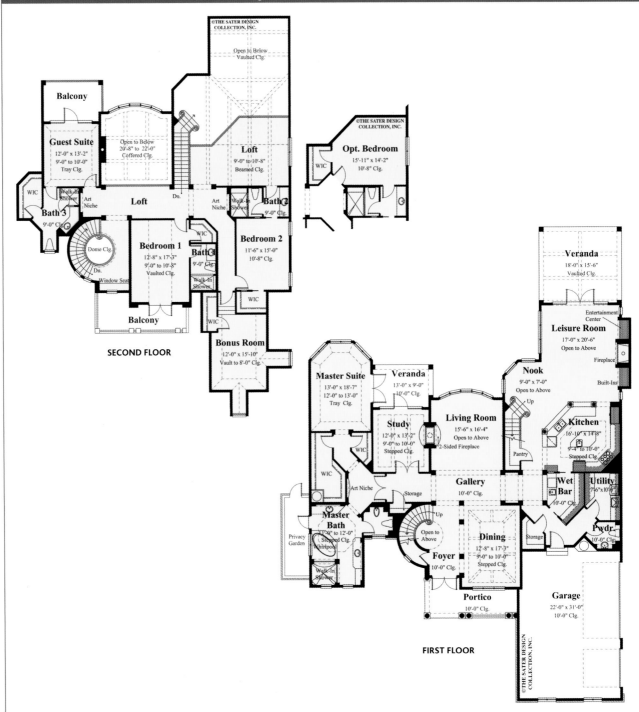

SECOND FLOOR

FIRST FLOOR

Photographed home may have been modified from the original construction documents.

REAR ELEVATION

Gambier Court

© Sater Design Collection, Inc.

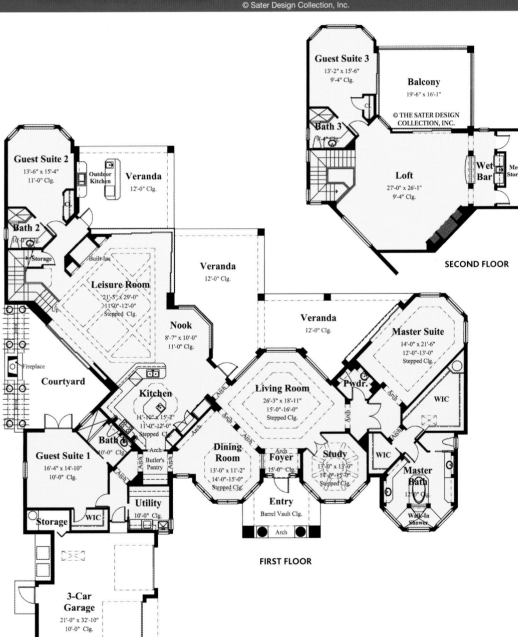

SECOND FLOOR

Guest Suite 3
13'-2" x 15'-6"
9'-4" Clg.

Balcony
19'-6" x 16'-1"

© THE SATER DESIGN COLLECTION, INC.

Bath 3

Loft
27'-0" x 26'-1"
9'-4" Clg.

Wet Bar

Mech. Storage

Guest Suite 2
13'-6" x 15'-4"
11'-0" Clg.

Outdoor Kitchen

Veranda
12'-0" Clg.

Bath 2

Storage

Built-Ins

Leisure Room
21'-3" x 29'-0"
11'0"-12'-0"
Stepped Clg.

Veranda
12'-0" Clg.

Nook
8'-7" x 10'-0"
11'-0" Clg.

Veranda
12'-0" Clg.

Master Suite
14'-0" x 21'-6"
12'-0"-13'-0"
Stepped Clg.

Fireplace

Courtyard

Kitchen
11'-0" x 15'-2"
11'-0"-12'-0"
Stepped Clg.

Living Room
26'-3" x 18'-11"
15'-0"-16'-0"
Stepped Clg.

Pwdr.

WIC

Bath

Guest Suite 1
16'-4" x 14'-10"
10'-0" Clg.

Butler's Pantry

Dining Room
13'-0" x 11'-2"
14'-0"-15'-0"
Stepped Clg.

Foyer
15'-0" Clg.

Study
13'-0" x 13'-0"
14'-0"-15'-0"
Stepped Clg.

WIC

Master Bath
12'-0" Clg.

Utility
10'-0" Clg.

Storage

WIC

Walk-In Shower

Entry
Barrel Vault Clg.

Arch

FIRST FLOOR

3-Car Garage
21'-0" x 32'-10"
10'-0" Clg.

© THE SATER DESIGN COLLECTION, INC.

SPECIFICATIONS:

Bedrooms: **4**

Baths: **4½**

Width: **93' 10"**

Depth: **113' 8"**

1st Floor: **3789** *sf*

2nd Floor: **1123** *sf*

Total Living: **4912** *sf*

Foundation: **Slab**

PLAN PRICING:

Vellum & PDF - **$3930**

CAD - **$7368**

PLAN NUMBER:
6948

The front-entry turret – with its wrought iron-filled friezes and recessed glass doors makes an impressive Mediterranean statement and imparts a warm welcome to this unique and impressive, outdoor-focused manor.

REAR ELEVATION

© Sater Design Collection, Inc.

Hillcrest Ridge

SPECIFICATIONS:

Bedrooms: **4**

Baths: **3½**

Width: **95' 4"**

Depth: **83' 0"**

1st Floor: **3546** *sf*

2nd Floor: **1213** *sf*

Total Living: **4759** *sf*

Foundation: **Basement**

PLAN PRICING:

Vellum & PDF - **$3807**

CAD - **$7139**

PLAN NUMBER:

6651

This grand traditional home offers a wonderful blend of open and formal spaces in design that feels much larger than it really is. From the street, the brick triple arched entryway warmly welcomes one into the home. Inside the grand foyer area, double arches lead past the formal living room and out to the rear yard views.

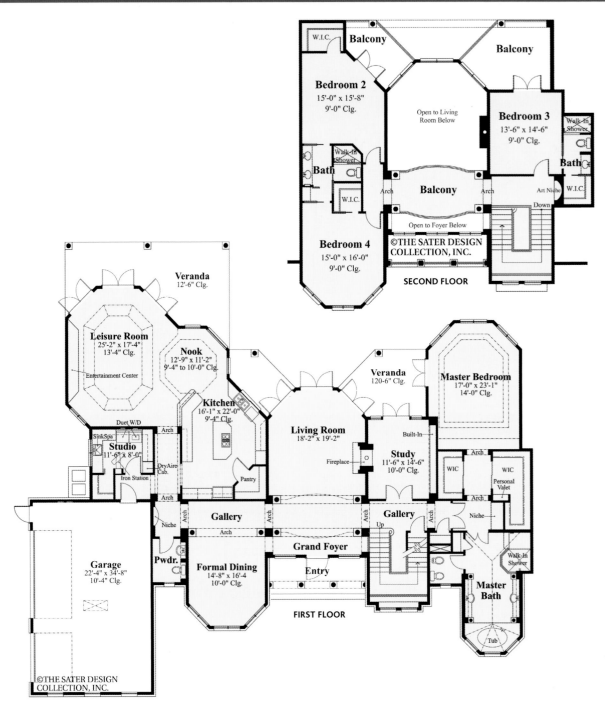

REAR ELEVATION

Castlepines Trace

© Sater Design Collection, Inc.

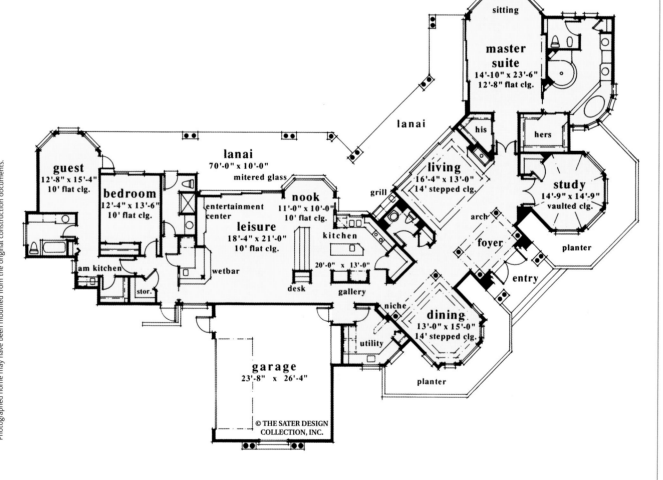

master suite
14'-10" x 23'-6"
12'-8" flat clg.

sitting

lanai

his

hers

guest
12'-8" x 15'-4"
10' flat clg.

bedroom
12'-4" x 13'-6"
10' flat clg.

lanai
70'-0" x 10'-0"
mitered glass

nook
11'-0" x 10'-0"
10' flat clg.

living
16'-4" x 13'-0"
14' stepped clg.

grill

study
14'-9" x 14'-9"
vaulted clg.

entertainment center

leisure
18'-4" x 21'-0"
10' flat clg.

am kitchen

kitchen

arch

foyer

planter

wetbar

20'-0" x 13'-0"

stor.

desk

gallery

entry

niche

dining
13'-0" x 15'-0"
14' stepped clg.

utility

garage
23'-8" x 26'-4"

planter

© THE SATER DESIGN COLLECTION, INC.

Photographed home may have been modified from the original construction documents.

SPECIFICATIONS:

Bedrooms: **3**

Baths: **3½**

Width: **120' 0"**

Depth: **89' 0"**

1st Floor: **3844** *sf*

Total Living: **3844** *sf*

Foundation: **Slab**

PLAN PRICING:

Vellum & PDF - **$2499**

CAD - **$4421**

PLAN NUMBER:
6640

A turret, varied rooflines, built-in planters, and lots of windows add elegant street appeal to this elevation. The main living areas open to the lanai and offer broad views to the rear through large expanses of retreating glass walls. The family kitchen, nook, and leisure room focus on the lanai, the built-in entertainment center and the wet bar.

REAR ELEVATION

© Sater Design Collection, Inc.

Stoney Creek Way

SPECIFICATIONS:

Bedrooms: **4**

Baths: **3½**

Width: **87' 4"**

Depth: **80' 4"**

1st Floor: **3053** *sf*

2nd Floor: **1087** *sf*

Total Living: **4140** *sf*

Foundation: **Basement**

PLAN PRICING:

Vellum & PDF - **$2691**

PLAN NUMBER:

6656

Inside the foyer, the living room features a warming fireplace, a two-story ceiling and bayed glass doors that overlook the rear yard views. A gallery hallway leads you down each wing of the home. The leisure room features a fireplace, built-in shelves and French doors. The kitchen is full of amenities like a walk-in pantry and pass-thru to veranda.

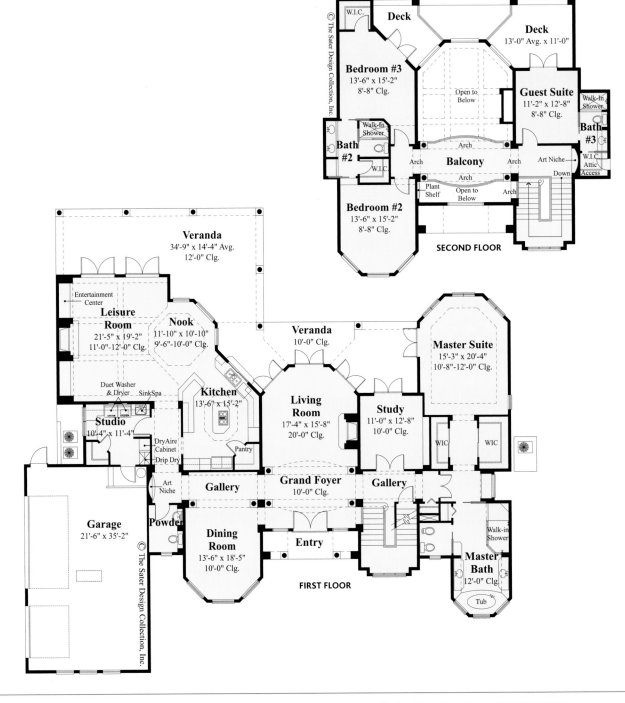

REAR ELEVATION

Griffith Parkway

© Sater Design Collection, Inc.

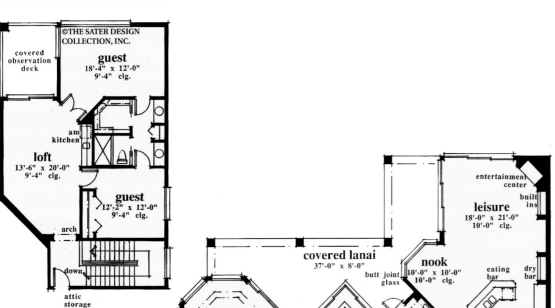

©THE SATER DESIGN COLLECTION, INC.

covered observation deck

guest
18'-4" x 12'-0"
9'-4" clg.

loft
13'-6" x 20'-0"
9'-4" clg.

mor. kitchen

guest
12'-2" x 12'-0"
9'-4" clg.

arch

down

attic storage

SECOND FLOOR

covered lanai
37'-0" x 8'-0"

butt joint glass

nook
10'-0" x 10'-0"
10'-0" clg.

eating bar

dry bar

leisure
18'-0" x 21'-0"
10'-0" clg.

entertainment center

built ins

kitchen
15' x 15'

arch

pantry

gallery

master
17'-0" x 14'-9"
step clg.

living
16'-0" x 16'-0"
step clg.

arch

arch

up

storage

arch

walk in wardrobe

dressing

mirror

arch

books

arch

dining
11'-0" x 16'-0"
step clg.

foyer

gallery

study
10'-0" x 14'-0"
step clg.

books

his

hers

guest
14'-6" x 11'-8"
10'-0" clg.

utility

workbench

covered entry

FIRST FLOOR

privacy wall

private garden

covered entry

garage
21'-0" x 26'-0"

©THE SATER DESIGN COLLECTION, INC.

SPECIFICATIONS:

Bedrooms: **4**

Baths: **3½**

Width: **65' 0"**

Depth: **91' 0"**

1st Floor: **2924** *sf*

2nd Floor: **948** *sf*

Total Living: **3872** *sf*

Foundation: **Slab**

PLAN PRICING:

Vellum & PDF - **$2517**

CAD - **$4453**

PLAN NUMBER:
6721

The formal core of the home is elegantly expressed in the stepped ceilings, while an open arrangement creates an easy flow to the spacious casual living area comprised of a dining nook, kitchen with eating bar and a leisure room with built-in entertainment center. A full guest suite on the first floor complements two more guest suites that share a loft, morning kitchen and spacious bath.

REAR ELEVATION

Grand Cypress Lane

SPECIFICATIONS:

Bedrooms: **3**

Baths: **3½**

Width: **88' 0"**

Depth: **95' 0"**

1st Floor: **4565** *sf*

Total Living: **4565** *sf*

Foundation: **Slab**

PLAN PRICING:

Vellum & PDF - **$2967**

CAD - **$5250**

PLAN NUMBER:

6636

The soaring arch design is carried through to the rear using a gable roof and a vaulted ceiling. This plan boasts a very elongated master wing, two secondary bedrooms with full baths, a deluxe fabric care center, as well as elegant ceiling treatments and arches throughout. An outdoor kitchen is built into the verandah.

Built-Ins

Bedroom 2
14'-2" x 14'-6"
Tray Clg.

Bath #2

Built-In

Fireplace

Family Room
27'-0" x 19'-6"
Stepped Clg.

Breakfast Nook
9'-6" x 10'-4"
13'-4" Clg.

Bedroom 3
12'-8" x 12'-4"
9'-4" Clg.

Bath #3

Cl

Kitchen
14'-2" x 17'-10"
13'-4" Clg.

Linen

Built-in

Personal Valet

Studio

Duet W/D   Sink   Spa

Cabinet Pantry

Dry Aire

Up

Verandah
Vaulted Clg.

Living Room
15'-3" x 23'-4"
Vaulted Clg.

Gallery

Dining Room
11'-4" x 21'-2"
Vaulted Clg.

Foyer

Cl

Pwdr.

Entry

Garage
22'-8" x 30'-8"
11'-4" Clg.

Sitting   AM Kitchen

Corner Fireplace

Master Bedroom
16'-3" x 31'-8"
Stepped Clg.

Outdoor Kitchen
13'-4" Clg.

WIC

Privacy Garden

Whirlpool

Master Foyer

Master Bath

Walk-In Shower

WIC

Ironing Station

Sauna

Wet Bar

Study
14'-3" x 18'-8"
Coffered Clg.

Exercise Room
9'-10" x 14'-0"
Vaulted Clg.

Arch

REAR ELEVATION

The Cardiff

© Sater Design Collection, Inc.

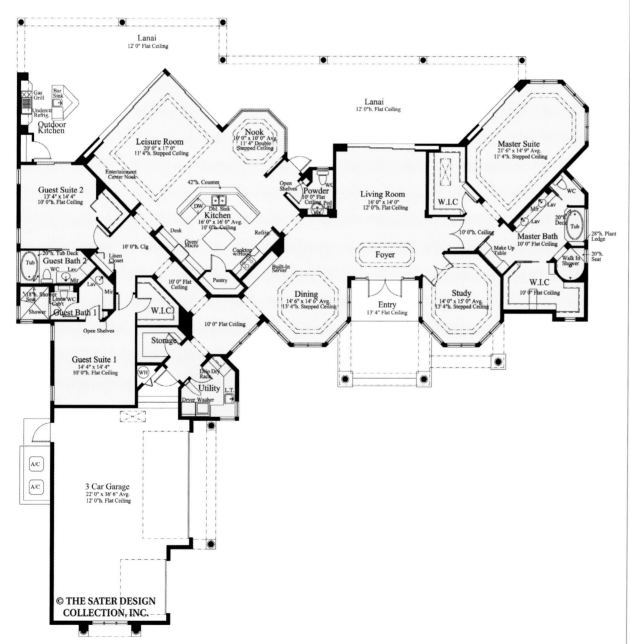

Lanai
12' 0" Flat Ceiling

Outdoor Kitchen
Gas Grill
Bar Sink
Undercn Refrig.

Leisure Room
20' 0" x 17' 0"
11' 4"h. Stepped Ceiling

Nook
10' 0" x 10' 0" Avg.
11' 4" Double Stepped Ceiling

Lanai
12' 0"h. Flat Ceiling

Master Suite
21' 6" x 14' 9" Avg.
11' 4"h. Stepped Ceiling

Guest Suite 2
13' 4" x 14' 4"
10' 0" Flat Ceiling

Entertainment Center Nook

42"h. Counter

Kitchen
16' 0" x 16' 0" Avg.
10' 0"h. Ceiling

Dbl. Sink
DW

Open Shelves

Powder
10' 0" Flat Ceiling Ped

WC

Living Room
16' 0" x 14' 0"
12' 0"h. Flat Ceiling

W.I.C

WC
Lav
Mr
Lav

Master Bath
10' 0" Flat Ceiling

Tub

28"h. Plant Ledge

Guest Bath 2
20"h. Tub Deck
WC Lav

Linen Closet

Desk

Oven/Micro

Refrig

10' 0" Clg

Cooktop w/Hood

Built-In Server

10' 0"h. Ceiling

Make Up Table

Walk In Shower
Walk In Shower
20"h. Seat

Shower Seat
Linen WC Cab't

Guest Bath 1

Mir

Pantry

W.I.C.
10' 0" Flat Ceiling

Open Shelves

Storage

Guest Suite 1
14' 4" x 14' 4"
10' 0"h. Flat Ceiling

WH

Dining
14' 6" x 14' 6" Avg.
13' 4"h. Stepped Ceiling

Foyer

Entry
13' 4" Flat Ceiling

Study
14' 4" x 15' 0" Avg.
13' 4"h. Stepped Ceiling

W.I.C
10' 0" Flat Ceiling

Drip Dry Rack

Utility

L.T.

Dryer Washer

A/C
A/C

3 Car Garage
22' 0" x 36' 6" Avg.
12' 0"h. Flat Ceiling

© THE SATER DESIGN COLLECTION, INC.

Photographed home may have been modified from the original construction documents.

SPECIFICATIONS:

Bedrooms: **3**

Baths: **3½**

Width: **101' 4"**

Depth: **106' 0"**

1st Floor: **3883** *sf*

Total Living: **3883** *sf*

Foundation: **Slab**

PLAN PRICING:

Vellum & PDF - **$2524**

PLAN NUMBER:

6750

Elegant detailing elevates the atmosphere of this elegant home. The formal rooms are located immediately off the foyer, while the casual living spaces of the dining nook and leisure room are further back in the plan. The gourmet kitchen links the spaces and boasts an eating bar, walk-in pantry and prep island. The master suite boasts an expansive bedroom, dual walk-in closets and a luxurious bathroom.

REAR ELEVATION

McKinney

© Sater Design Collection, Inc.

SPECIFICATIONS:

Bedrooms: **3**

Baths: **3½**

Width: **104' 4"**

Depth: **111' 0"**

1st Floor: **4302** *sf*

Total Living: **4302** *sf*

Foundation: **Slab**

PLAN PRICING:

Vellum & PDF - **$2796**

PLAN NUMBER:

6936

In the flowing, festive style of a Mediterranean manor, this majestic villa would make a "grand entrance" in even the most exclusive neighborhoods. The defining characteristic of its facade is a stately a pair of turrets, standing somewhat stoic and taciturn behind a grand carved and open entry, "upstaged" by a pair of decorative columns. Just beyond, a magnificent set of carved double doors beckons.

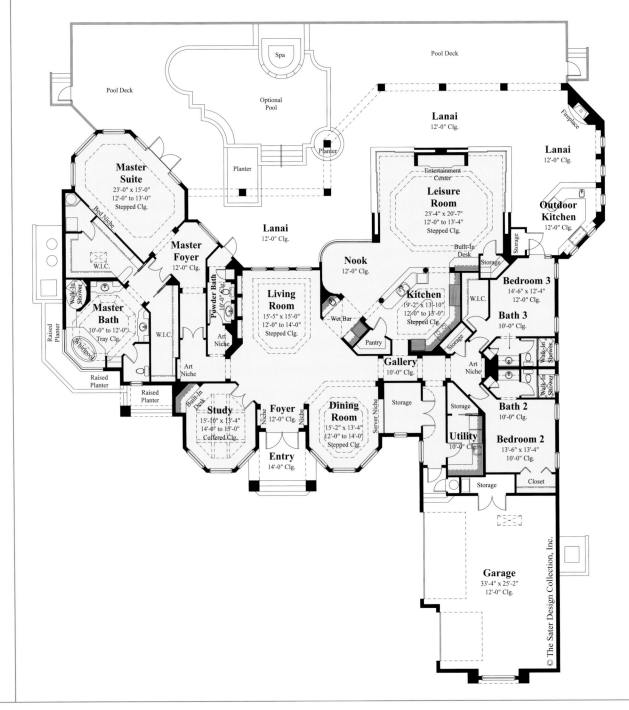

~ *Any plan can be customized to meet your needs, find out how by calling* **800-718-7526**. ~

REAR ELEVATION

Jasper Park

© Sater Design Collection, Inc.

Veranda
33'-0" x 15'-10" Avg.
12'-0" Clg.

Firepit

Vaulted Clg.

Outdoor Kitchen

Pool Bath

Leisure Room
20'-4" x 20'-0"
12'-0"-13'-0" Clg.

Veranda
12'-0" Clg.

Nook
7'-8" x 9'-6"
12'-0" Clg.

Wet Bar

Bath 2

WIC

Master Suite
15'-3" x 22'-0"
10'-0"-11'-0" Clg.

Arch

Kitchen
16'-2" x 16'-4"
12'-0"-12'-8" Clg.

Guest Suite 2
11'-10" x 13'-9"
10'-0" Clg.

W.I.C.
9'-0" x 16'-10"

Arch

Study
12'-2" x 12'-6"
10'-0"-11'-0" Clg.

Arch

Living Room
18'-0" x 22'-0"
12'-0"-13'-4" Clg.

Art Niche

Art Niche

Bath 1

Art Niche

Arch

Arch

Arch

Arch

Arch

Powder Bath

Art Niche

Foyer
13'-0" Clg.

Art Niche

Art Niche

Guest Suite 1
13'-8" x 12'-2"
10'-0" Clg.

Master Bath
10'-0" Clg.

Dining Room
12'-0" x 11'-2"
12'-0"-13'-0" Clg.

Cl

Arch

Entry
14'-0" Clg.

Utility
10'-0" Clg.

Privacy Garden

Walk-In Shower

Garage
22'-8" x 21'-10"
10'-6" Clg.

Garage
20'-0" x 14'-4"
10'-6" Clg.

© The Sater Design Collection, Inc.

SPECIFICATIONS:

Bedrooms: **3**

Full Baths: **3**

Half Baths: **2**

Width: **77' 0"**

Depth: **114' 5"**

1st Floor: **3674** *sf*

Total Living: **3674** *sf*

Foundation: **Slab**

PLAN PRICING:

Vellum & PDF - **$1837**

CAD - **$3307**

PLAN NUMBER:
6941

Architectural details inherent in Mediterranean design are carried throughout the home in the column- and corbel-supported openings to the dining room and a unique wall niche in the living room. Retreating glass walls open the study, living and leisure rooms to the outdoors where a meandering veranda includes a surprise: an octagonal gazebo with a stone fire pit in the center.

REAR ELEVATION

Monterchi

© Sater Design Collection, Inc.

SPECIFICATIONS:

Bedrooms: **3**

Baths: **3½**

Width: **58' 6"**

Depth: **107' 0"**

1ˢᵗ Floor: **2789** *sf*

2ⁿᵈ Floor: **859** *sf*

Total Living: **3648** *sf*

Foundation: **Slab**

PLAN PRICING:

Vellum & PDF - **$1824**

CAD - **$3284**

PLAN NUMBER:

6965

The Monterchi home plan is a modern Tuscan villa with stacked stone facade and brick arches. The two-story portico and foyer make a grand statement of luxury and richness. It features an entry courtyard that is overlooked by the first floor guest suite. Inside the foyer one is greeted by a wrought iron railed staircase and overlooking loft above. Directly beyond is the spacious great room with adjacent kitchen and dining space. All this overlooks a roomy veranda complete with outdoor kitchen.

FIRST FLOOR

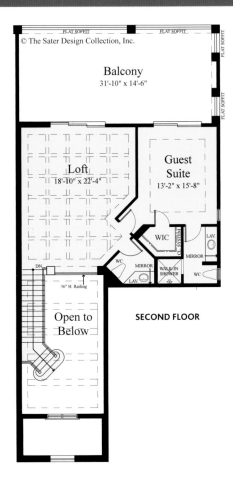

SECOND FLOOR

Not available for construction in Lee or Collier Counties, Florida.

REAR ELEVATION

Teodora

© Sater Design Collection, Inc.

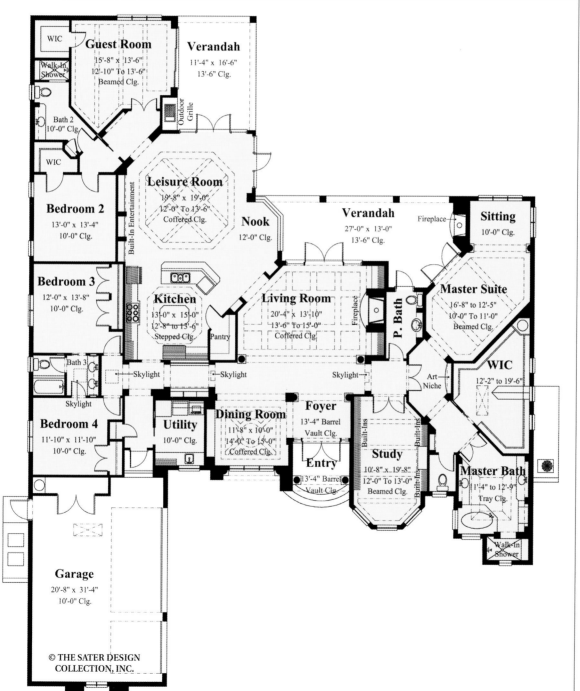

Floor plan rooms:

- **Guest Room** — 15'-8" x 13'-6", 12'-10" To 13'-6" Beamed Clg.
- WIC
- Walk-In Shower
- Bath 2 — 10'-0" Clg.
- WIC
- **Verandah** — 11'-4" x 16'-6", 13'-6" Clg.
- Outdoor Grille
- **Leisure Room** — 19'-8" x 19'-6", 12'-0" To 13'-6" Coffered Clg.
- Built-In Entertainment
- **Nook** — 12'-0" Clg.
- **Verandah** — 27'-0" x 13'-0", 13'-6" Clg.
- Fireplace
- **Sitting** — 10'-0" Clg.
- **Bedroom 2** — 13'-0" x 13'-4", 10'-0" Clg.
- **Bedroom 3** — 12'-0" x 13'-8", 10'-0" Clg.
- **Kitchen** — 13'-0" x 15'-0", 12'-8" to 13'-6" Stepped Clg.
- Pantry
- **Living Room** — 20'-4" x 13'-10", 13'-6" To 15'-0" Coffered Clg.
- Fireplace
- **P. Bath**
- **Master Suite** — 16'-8" to 12'-5", 10'-0" To 11'-0" Beamed Clg.
- **WIC** — 12'-2" to 19'-6"
- Art Niche
- Bath 3
- Skylight
- **Bedroom 4** — 11'-10" x 11'-10", 10'-0" Clg.
- **Utility** — 10'-0" Clg.
- **Dining Room** — 11'-8" x 10'-0", 14'-0" To 15'-0" Coffered Clg.
- **Foyer** — 13'-4" Barrel Vault Clg.
- **Entry** — 13'-4" Barrel Vault Clg.
- **Study** — 10'-8" x 19'-8", 12'-0" To 13'-0" Beamed Clg.
- Built-Ins
- **Master Bath** — 11'-4" to 12'-9" Tray Clg.
- Walk-In Shower
- **Garage** — 20'-8" x 31'-4", 10'-0" Clg.

© THE SATER DESIGN COLLECTION, INC.

SPECIFICATIONS:

Bedrooms: **5**

Baths: **3½**

Width: **80' 0"**

Depth: **104' 0"**

1st Floor: **3993** *sf*

Total Living: **3993** *sf*

Foundation: **Slab**

PLAN PRICING:

Vellum & PDF - **$2595**

CAD - **$4592**

PLAN NUMBER:

8066

The Teodora luxury home plan exhibits a European Spanish flair. A grand cupola, bay turret and a recessed arch entry adorn this Spanish-inspired home. The home boasts an impressive barrel-vaulted covered entry. Inside, rooms are embellished with fine details built-in cabinetry, fireplaces, and art niches. Columns and specialty ceilings define the interior spaces.

REAR ELEVATION

Madra

© Sater Design Collection, Inc.

SPECIFICATIONS:

Bedrooms: **5**

Baths: **4**

Width: **92' 0"**

Depth: **63' 0"**

1ˢᵗ Floor: **2628** *sf*

2ⁿᵈ Floor: **1320** *sf*

Total Living: **3948** *sf*

Foundation: **Slab**

PLAN PRICING:

Vellum & PDF - **$2566**

CAD - **$4540**

PLAN NUMBER:

6864

A wraparound entry portico is just the beginning to this plan of perfect symmetry. Inside, an unrestrained floor plan permits public and casual spaces to flex, with rooms that facilitate planned events as easily as they do family gatherings. Arches define the dining room and parlor, which complements an informal nook adjacent to the great room.

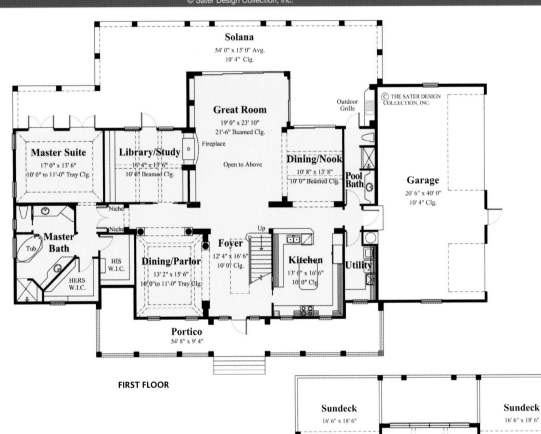

FIRST FLOOR

SECOND FLOOR

REAR ELEVATION

Tre Mori

© Sater Design Collection, Inc.

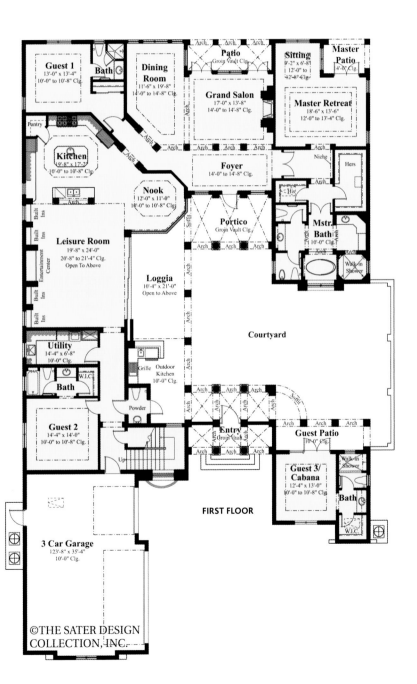

©THE SATER DESIGN COLLECTION, INC.

SECOND FLOOR

FIRST FLOOR

©THE SATER DESIGN COLLECTION, INC.

SPECIFICATIONS:

Bedrooms: **5**

Baths: **5½**

Width: **69' 10"**

Depth: **120' 0"**

1st Floor: **3683** *sf*

Cabana: **310** *sf*

2nd Floor: **563** *sf*

Total Living: **4556** *sf*

Foundation: **Slab**

PLAN PRICING:

Vellum & PDF - **$2961**

CAD - **$5239**

PLAN NUMBER:

8078

Past the groin-vaulted entry, an enchanting courtyard greets visitors in this Spanish-inspired villa. Beyond the foyer, the kitchen flows into the nook and leisure room, extending onto the loggia through retreating glass walls. Secluded guest suites include one upstairs with a private balcony and a detached, cabana-style retreat on the main level.

REAR ELEVATION

La Riviere

© Sater Design Collection, Inc.

Arched windows and dormers set off a rich blend of clapboard, stucco and stone with this New World villa. An open arrangement of the public zone secures panoramic views within each of the formal spaces. The living room boasts a sense of nature granted through a two-story bow window, framed by bay windows in the nook and master suite. On the upper level, a computer loft links the guest bedrooms and a step-down bonus room.

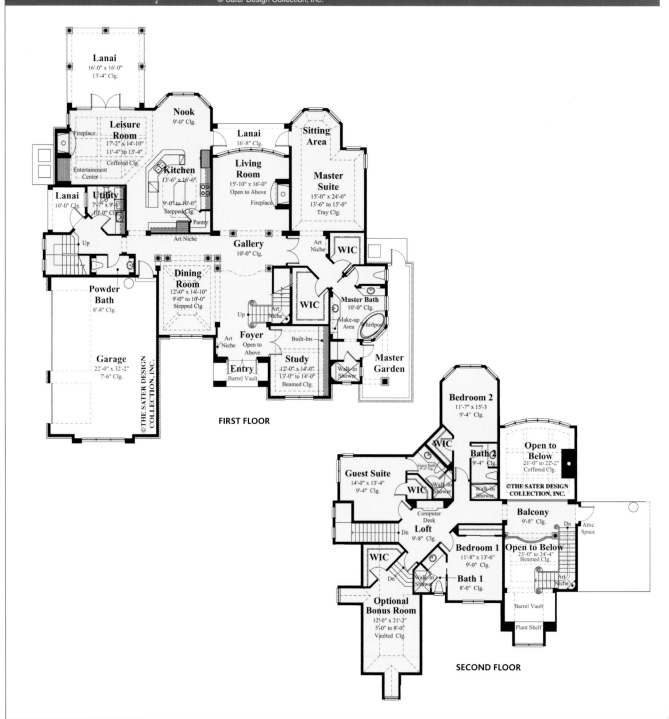

FIRST FLOOR

SECOND FLOOR

REAR ELEVATION

Mezzina

© Sater Design Collection, Inc.

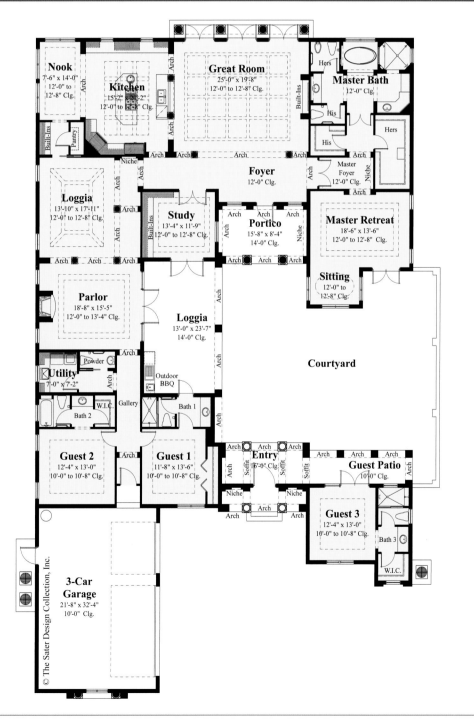

Nook
7'-6" x 14'-0"
12'-0" to
12'-8" Clg.

Kitchen
15'-2" x 12'-2"
12'-0" to 12'-8" Clg.

Great Room
25'-0" x 19'-8"
12'-0" to 12'-8" Clg.

Master Bath
12'-0" Clg.

Pantry

Built-Ins

Loggia
13'-10" x 17'-11"
12'-0" to 12'-8" Clg.

Study
13'-4" x 11'-9"
12'-0" to 12'-8" Clg.

Foyer
12'-0" Clg.

Portico
15'-8" x 8'-4"
14'-0" Clg.

Master Foyer
12'-0" Clg.

Master Retreat
18'-6" x 13'-6"
12'-0" to 12'-8" Clg.

Parlor
18'-8" x 15'-5"
12'-0" to 13'-4" Clg.

Loggia
13'-0" x 23'-7"
14'-0" Clg.

Sitting
12'-0" to
12'-8" Clg.

Courtyard

Powder

Utility
7'-0" x 7'-2"

Outdoor
BBQ

Gallery

W.I.C.

Bath 2

Bath 1

Guest 2
12'-4" x 13'-0"
10'-0" to 10'-8" Clg.

Guest 1
11'-8" x 13'-6"
10'-0" to 10'-8" Clg.

Entry
16'-0" Clg.

Guest Patio
10'-0" Clg.

Niche

Guest 3
12'-4" x 13'-0"
10'-0" to 10'-8" Clg.

Bath 3

W.I.C.

3-Car Garage
21'-8" x 32'-4"
10'-0" Clg.

© The Sater Design Collection, Inc.

SPECIFICATIONS:

Bedrooms: **4**

Baths: **4½**

Width: **69' 10"**

Depth: **120' 4"**

1st Floor: **4175** *sf*

Total Living: **4175** *sf*

Foundation: **Slab**

PLAN PRICING:

Vellum & PDF - **$2714**

CAD - **$4801**

PLAN NUMBER:

8073

This unique villa features private family and guest spaces with open connections to a spacious courtyard area. Past the portico, the foyer opens up to views beyond the grand salon's floor-to-ceiling windows. Nearby, the leisure room opens to the loggia and outdoor kitchen. A gallery leads to two secluded guest suites, while a detached guest suite provides even more privacy.

REAR ELEVATION

Kendrick

© Sater Design Collection, Inc.

SPECIFICATIONS:

Bedrooms: **5**

Baths: **3½**

Width: **71' 0"**

Depth: **72' 0"**

1st Floor: **2163** *sf*

2nd Floor: **1415** *sf*

Total Living: **3578** *sf*

Foundation: **Slab**

PLAN PRICING:

Vellum & PDF - **$1789**

CAD - **$3220**

PLAN NUMBER:

8050

A triplet of paneled doors leads through the foyer to a spectacular great room with unimpeded views of the rear property. Art niches and a massive hearth define one wall of the great room, and contradict an opposing series of flat soffits that open the space to the kitchen. To the right of the plan, the master wing sports a luxe bath. Upstairs, a balcony loft links four bedrooms and leads to the front deck.

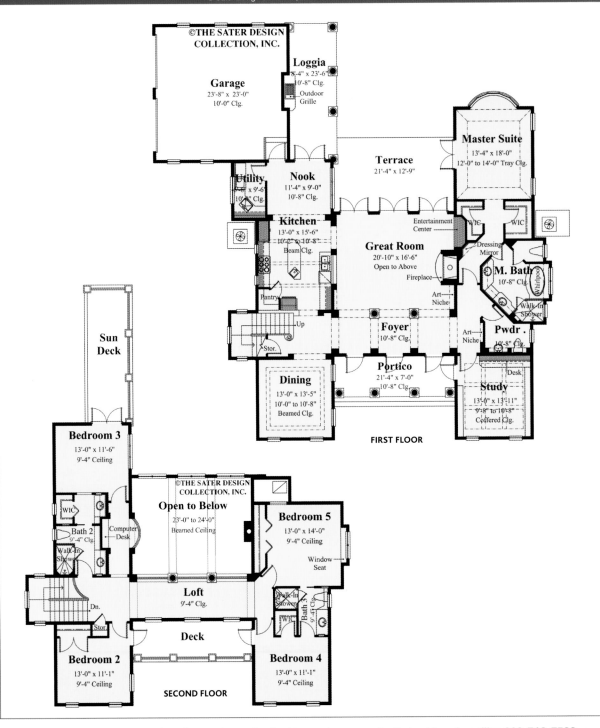

REAR ELEVATION

Plantation Pine Road

© Sater Design Collection, Inc.

Floor Plan Labels:

Guest Suite
12'-4" x 16'-0"

Lanai
12'-0" Clg.

Bath 4

Walk-In Shower

WIC

Fireplace

Outdoor Kitchen

Leisure
22'-0" x 22'-0"
12'-0"-14'-0"
Stepped Clg.

Enter. Center

Lanai
45'-0" x 9'-0"
10'-0" Clg.

Nook
12'-0" Clg.

Sitting

Master Suite
25'-0" x 15'-0"
10'-0"-12'-0"
Stepped Ceiling

Study
18'-8" x 11'-7"
14'-0"-15'-0"
Coffered Ceiling

Living Room
17'-0" x 15'-3"
14'-0"-15'-0"
Stepped Ceiling

Dining
11'-2" x 15'-3"
14'-0"-15'-0"
Stepped Ceiling

Kitchen
17'-2" x 13'-4"

Guest 1
12'-0" x 16'-0"
10'-0" Clg.

Arch

Art Niche

Gallery
12'-0" Clg.

Personal Valet

WIC

Pantry

Stepped Clg.

Walk-In Shower

Bath 1

WIC

Bath 2

WIC

Tub

Master Bath
10'-0" x 11'-0"
Stepped Ceiling

Foyer
14'-0"-15'-0"
Stepped Clg.

Gallery

Art Niche

Arch

Whirlpool

Private Garden

WIC

Exercise
10'-0" x 13'-4"
12'-0" Clg.

Entry

Bath 3
10'-0" Clg.

Computer Center

Guest 2
12'-0" x 13'-0"
10'-0" Clg.

Bonus Room
16'-8" x 17'-8"
Tray Clg.

Storage

DryAir Cabinet

Studio
10'-0" Clg.

Iron Station

SinkSpa

Duct W/D

Garage
23'-2" x 40'-1"
12'-0" Clg.

©THE SATER DESIGN COLLECTION, INC.

SPECIFICATIONS:

Bedrooms: **4**

Baths: **5**

Width: **88' 0"**

Depth: **133' 0"**

1st Floor: **4296** *sf*

Guest Suite: **330** *sf*

Total Living: **4626** *sf*

Foundation: **Slab**

PLAN PRICING:

Vellum & PDF - **$3007**

CAD - **$5320**

PLAN NUMBER:

6735

Focused around the outdoors, the main living areas have windows or doors taking advantage of the natural surroundings. Off the master suite are the exercise room and study with a coffered ceiling and built-in cabinetry. A large relaxing leisure room has a fireplace, a built-in entertainment center and a stepped ceiling. The other wing of the house has a bonus room computer center and an optional detached guest suite off the leisure room.

REAR ELEVATION

Beauchamp

© Sater Design Collection, Inc.

SPECIFICATIONS:

Bedrooms: **4**

Baths: **3½**

Width: **80' 8"**

Depth: **104' 8"**

1st Floor: **3790** *sf*

Total Living: **3790** *sf*

Foundation: **Slab**

PLAN PRICING:

Vellum & PDF - **$2464**

CAD - **$4359**

PLAN NUMBER:

8044

Dentils, rusticated pilasters, pediments and quoins set off a symmetrical facade. This facade calls up the aristocratic lines of 16th-century French renaissance villas. An ornamented pediment and a roofline balustrade framed by two chimneys indicate a later, Beaux Arts influence. The stunning mix of distinctive rugged stone and smooth stucco is reiterated throughout the interior.

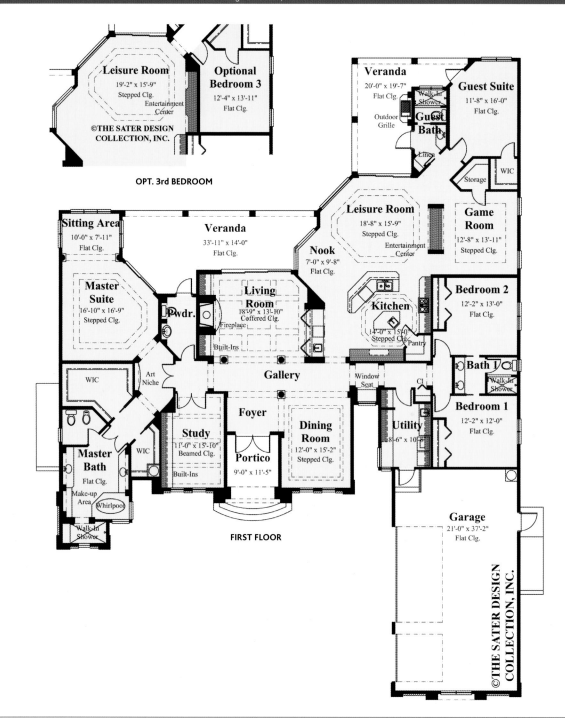

Leisure Room 19'-2" x 15'-9" Stepped Clg. Entertainment Center

Optional Bedroom 3 12'-4" x 13'-11" Flat Clg.

©THE SATER DESIGN COLLECTION, INC.

OPT. 3rd BEDROOM

Veranda 20'-0" x 19'-7" Flat Clg.

Outdoor Grille

Walk-In Shower

Guest Bath

Guest Suite 11'-8" x 16'-0" Flat Clg.

Linen

WIC

Storage

Sitting Area 10'-0" x 7'-11" Flat Clg.

Veranda 33'-11" x 14'-0" Flat Clg.

Leisure Room 18'-8" x 15'-9" Stepped Clg. Entertainment Center

Game Room 12'-8" x 13'-11" Stepped Clg.

Master Suite 16'-10" x 16'-9" Stepped Clg.

Nook 7'-0" x 9'-8" Flat Clg.

Living Room 18'-9" x 13'-10" Coffered Clg.

Kitchen 14'-0" x 15'-0" Stepped Clg.

Pantry

Bedroom 2 12'-2" x 13'-0" Flat Clg.

Pwdr.

Fireplace

Built-Ins

Bath 1

Walk-In Shower

WIC

Art Niche

Gallery

Window Seat

Cl.

Bedroom 1 12'-2" x 12'-0" Flat Clg.

Foyer

WIC

Study 11'-0" x 15'-10" Beamed Clg. Built-Ins

Dining Room 12'-0" x 15'-2" Stepped Clg.

Utility 8'-6" x 10'-0"

Master Bath Flat Clg.

Make-up Area

Whirlpool

Walk-In Shower

Portico 9'-0" x 11'-5"

FIRST FLOOR

Garage 21'-0" x 37'-2" Flat Clg.

©THE SATER DESIGN COLLECTION, INC.

REAR ELEVATION

Saint-Germain

© Sater Design Collection, Inc.

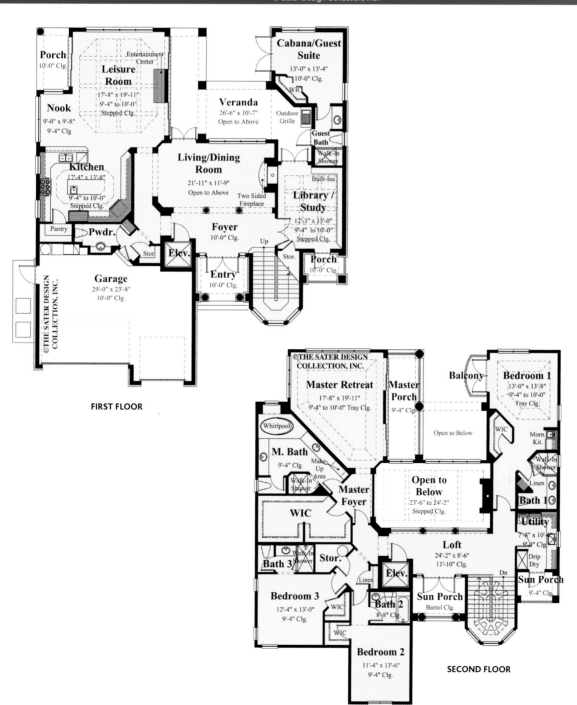

FIRST FLOOR

- Porch 10'-0" Clg.
- Leisure Room 17'-8" x 19'-11" 9'-4" to 10'-0" Stepped Clg.
- Entertainment Center
- Nook 9'-0" x 9'-8" 9'-4" Clg.
- Kitchen 17'-4" x 13'-8" 9'-4" to 10'-0" Stepped Clg.
- Pantry
- Pwdr.
- Stor.
- Elev.
- Garage 29'-0" x 23'-8" 10'-0" Clg.
- ©THE SATER DESIGN COLLECTION, INC.
- Cabana/Guest Suite 13'-0" x 13'-4" 10'-0" Clg.
- WIC
- Veranda 26'-6" x 10'-7" Open to Above
- Outdoor Grille
- Guest Bath
- Walk-In Shower
- Living/Dining Room 21'-11" x 11'-9" Open to Above
- Two Sided Fireplace
- Built-Ins
- Library / Study 12'-3" x 15'-0" 9'-4" to 10'-0" Stepped Clg.
- Foyer 10'-0" Clg.
- Entry 10'-0" Clg.
- Up
- Stor.
- Porch 10'-0" Clg.

SECOND FLOOR

- ©THE SATER DESIGN COLLECTION, INC.
- Master Retreat 17'-8" x 19'-11" 9'-4" to 10'-0" Tray Clg.
- Master Porch 9'-4" Clg.
- Balcony
- Bedroom 1 13'-0" x 13'-8" 9'-4" to 10'-0" Tray Clg.
- Whirlpool
- M. Bath 9'-4" Clg.
- Make Up Area
- Walk-In Shower
- Master Foyer
- Open to Below 23'-6" to 24'-2" Stepped Clg.
- WIC
- Linen
- Morn. Kit.
- Walk-In Shower
- Bath 1
- Linen
- Utility 7'-8" x 10'-4" 9'-4" Clg.
- Bath 3
- Walk-In Shower
- Stor.
- Elev.
- Loft 24'-2" x 8'-6" 11'-10" Clg.
- Bath 2 8'-8" Clg.
- Liner
- Sun Porch Barrel Clg.
- Dn
- Drip Dry
- Sun Porch 9'-4" Clg.
- Bedroom 3 12'-4" x 13'-0" 9'-4" Clg.
- WIC
- WIC
- Bedroom 2 11'-4" x 13'-6" 9'-4" Clg.

SPECIFICATIONS:

Bedrooms: **5**

Baths: **5½**

Width: **58' 0"**

Depth: **65' 0"**

1st Floor: **1995** sf

2nd Floor: **2165** sf

Total Living: **4160** sf

Foundation: **Slab**

PLAN PRICING:

Vellum & PDF - **$2705**

CAD - **$4784**

PLAN NUMBER:

8026

As steeped in artistry on the outside as it is state-of-the-art within, this dreamy villa blends bark-hued shingles with yellow brick and cream-white stucco. Mixing forms such as flared eaves, slump arches and a semi-hexagonal turret make this home one to be desired. Sculpted outdoor places lend definition and dignity to the elevation, reiterating a highly crafted interior. A convenient elevator complements the high glam staircase.

REAR ELEVATION

Gullane

© Sater Design Collection, Inc.

SPECIFICATIONS:

Bedrooms: **5**

Baths: **5½**

Width: **58' 0"**

Depth: **65' 0"**

1st Floor: **2164** *sf*

2nd Floor: **2312** *sf*

Total Living: **4476** *sf*

Foundation: **Slab**

PLAN PRICING:

Vellum & PDF - **$2909**

CAD - **$5147**

PLAN NUMBER:

8031

Rows of windows punctuate a stucco facade, which integrates classic lines with an oceanfront attitude. The spirit throughout the house is formal, yet extends a sense of welcome to guests. Open, public spaces are framed by columns and beamed ceilings, with floor-to-ceiling windows in the living room offering commanding views. Retreating glass walls integrate the common living space with the loggia.

FIRST FLOOR

SECOND FLOOR

~ Any plan can be customized to meet your needs, find out how by calling 800-718-7526. ~

REAR ELEVATION

Bartlett

© Sater Design Collection, Inc.

FIRST FLOOR

Verandah
31'-2" x 19'-8"
12'-6" Clg.

Leisure Room
16'-2" x 25'-2"
12'-0" to 13'-4" Clg.

Nook
10'-0" to 12'-0" Clg.

Kitchen
16'-1" x 21'-8"
9'-4" Clg.

Verandah
37'-0" x 12'-4"
10'-6" Clg.

Master Suite
17'-0" x 21'-1"
12'-0" to 14'-0"
Stepped Clg.

Living Room
18'-2" x 19'-2"
Open to Above

Study
11'-6" x 14'-6"
10'-0" Clg.

Utility
11'-6" x 8'-0"
10'-0" Clg.

Stor.

Desk

Pantry

2-Sided Fireplace

Built-Ins

WIC
6'-7" x 8'-8"

WIC
5'-0" x 14'-6"

Art Niche

Gallery

Foyer

Gallery

Art Niche

Stor.

Linen

Walk-In Shower

Pwdr.
10'-0" Clg.

Dining
14'-8" x 16'-4"
10'-0" Clg.

Entry

Up

Garage
22'-4" x 34'-8"
11'-8" Clg.

Master Bath
Vaulted Clg.

Whirlpool Tub

©THE SATER DESIGN COLLECTION, INC.

SECOND FLOOR

©THE SATER DESIGN COLLECTION, INC.

WIC

Balcony
12'-6" x 12'-4"

Balcony
16'-6" x 12'-4"

Bedroom 2
14'-11" x 16'-0"
9'-0" Clg.

Open to Below
Coffered Clg.

Bedroom 3
13'-0" x 14'-6"
9'-0" Clg.

Walk-In Shower

Walk-In Shower

Bath 2
9'-0" Clg.

Bath 3
9'-0" Clg.

WIC

WIC

Linen

Bedroom 4
14'-8" x 16'-4"
9'-0" Clg.

Balcony
9'-0" Clg.

Balcony
18'-8" x 5'-8"

Dn.

SPECIFICATIONS:

Bedrooms: **4**

Baths: **3½**

Width: **95' 0"**

Depth: **82' 8"**

1st Floor: **3588** *sf*

2nd Floor: **1287** *sf*

Total Living: **4875** *sf*

Foundation: **Basement**

PLAN PRICING:

Vellum & PDF - **$3900**

PLAN NUMBER:

8064

Hipped rooflines and a triplet of dormers provide contrast for the sculpted aspects of this Euro elevation: gables, turrets and an entry arcade. Interior vistas that extend beyond the walls of glass to the rear of the plan dominate the foyer and central living room. A shoes-off atmosphere prevails in the casual living zone, with French doors expanding the space to the verandah. Positioned to access the formal and informal rooms.

REAR ELEVATION

Aubrey

© Sater Design Collection, Inc.

SPECIFICATIONS:

Bedrooms: **4**

Baths: **3½**

Width: **83' 0"**

Depth: **71' 8"**

1st Floor: **2485** *sf*

2nd Floor: **1127** *sf*

Total Living: **3612** *sf*

Bonus Room: **368** *sf*

Foundation: **Slab**

PLAN PRICING:

Vellum & PDF - **$1806**

CAD - **$3251**

PLAN NUMBER:

8016

Wrought iron balustrades and sculpted masonry define a classic elevation that is anchored by a stunning side turret, twin dormers and Doric columns. Arches and columns frame the foyer and gallery, flanked by well-defined formal rooms. A spacious leisure room leads to the lanai, and brags a two-sided fireplace shared with a study. The opposing turret harbors a spiral staircase and a loft that links with the balcony and sleeping quarters.

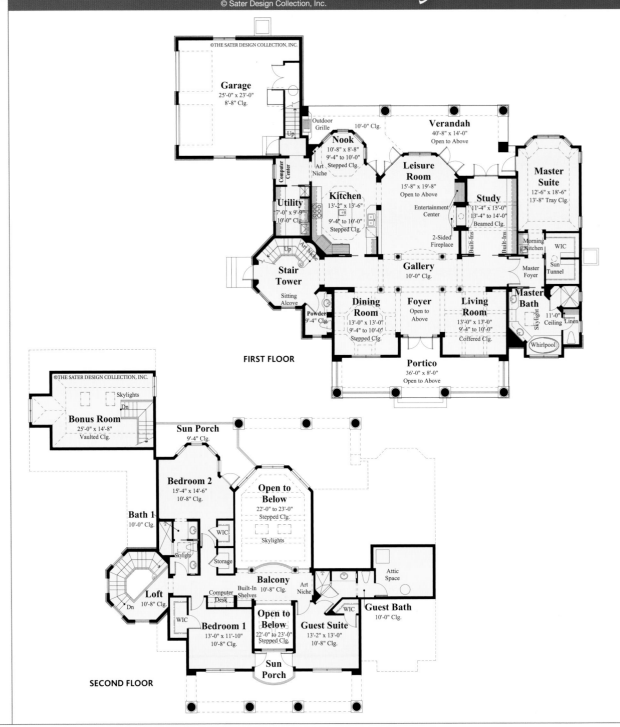

~ Any plan can be customized to meet your needs, find out how by calling 800-718-7526. ~

REAR ELEVATION

Solaine

© Sater Design Collection, Inc.

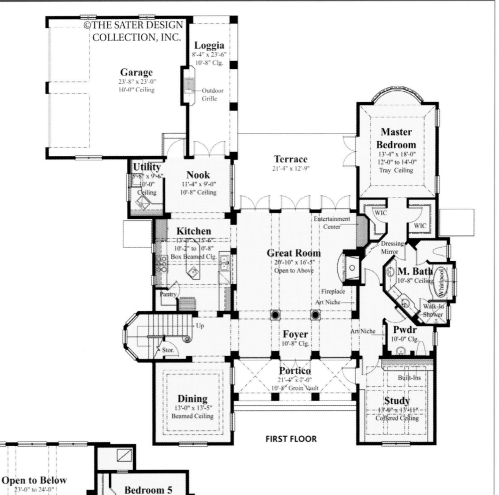

©THE SATER DESIGN COLLECTION, INC.

Loggia 8'-4" x 23'-6" 10'-8" Clg.

Garage 23'-8" x 23'-0" 10'-0" Ceiling

Outdoor Grille

Utility 5'-5" x 9'-6" 10'-0" Ceiling

Nook 11'-4" x 9'-0" 10'-8" Ceiling

Terrace 21'-4" x 12'-9"

Master Bedroom 13'-4" x 18'-0" 12'-0" to 14'-0" Tray Ceiling

Kitchen 13'-0" x 15'-6" 10'-2" to 9'-8" Box Beamed Clg.

Great Room 20'-10" x 16'-5" Open to Above

Entertainment Center

WIC

WIC

Dressing Mirror

M. Bath 10'-8" Ceiling

Whirlpool

Pantry

Fireplace

Art Niche

Walk-In Shower

Up

Stor.

Foyer 10'-8" Clg.

Art Niche

Pwdr 10'-0" Clg.

Sun Deck

Dining 13'-0" x 13'-5" Beamed Ceiling

Portico 21'-4" x 7'-0" 10'-8" Groin Vault

Built-Ins

Study 13'-0" x 13'-11" Coffered Ceiling

FIRST FLOOR

Bedroom 3 13'-0" x 11'-6" 9'-4" Ceiling

Bath 2 9'-4" Ceiling

Computer Desk

Open to Below 23'-0" to 24'-0" Beamed Ceiling

©THE SATER DESIGN COLLECTION, INC.

Bedroom 5 13'-0" x 14'-0" 9'-4" Ceiling

Window Seat

Dn.

Stor.

Loft 9'-4" Ceiling

Deck

WIC

Bath 3 9'-4" Ceiling

Bedroom 2 13'-0" x 11'-1" 9'-4" Ceiling

SECOND FLOOR

Bedroom 4 13'-0" x 11'-1" 9'-4" Ceiling

SPECIFICATIONS:

Bedrooms: **5**

Baths: **3½**

Width: **71' 0"**

Depth: **72' 0"**

1st Floor: **2163** *sf*

2nd Floor: **1415** *sf*

Total Living: **3578** *sf*

Foundation: **Slab**

PLAN PRICING:

Vellum & PDF - **$1789**

CAD - **$3220**

PLAN NUMBER:

8051

The Solaine home plan exhibits a lovely European French country style. The spacious floor plan design has 3578 square feet of living area. It features five bedrooms and three and 1/2 bathrooms. Rusticated columns and a balcony balustrade on this stately elevation suggest early 20th-Century influences. Yet the interior of the Solaine home plan is purely modern.

One Floor Plan 3 Different Looks!

While many of our floor plans are widely desired, certain elevation styles may not suit your locale or personal interests. On this page is one of our most popular floor plans with three distinct exterior elevations. Each exterior showcases a unique architectural style whether French Chateauesque, British Cottswald, or Italian/Mediterranean for your particular setting.

REAR ELEVATION

FEATURES:

- Fireplace
- Walk-in Pantry
- Main Floor Master
- His & Hers Closets
- Built-in Cabinetry
- Art Niches

The floor plan integrates a pleasing flow of interconnected spaces with out-of-this-world amenities and spectacular interior vistas granted by French doors and a bow window A gallery links the grand foyer with the formal rooms, including a private study, an open formal dining room and a palatial living room that leads outdoors. Built-ins and a massive fireplace anchor the leisure space, which boasts a wall of glass shared with the morning nook, and easy access to the veranda. Upper-level sleeping quarters are connected by a balcony hall that overlooks the foyer and living room.

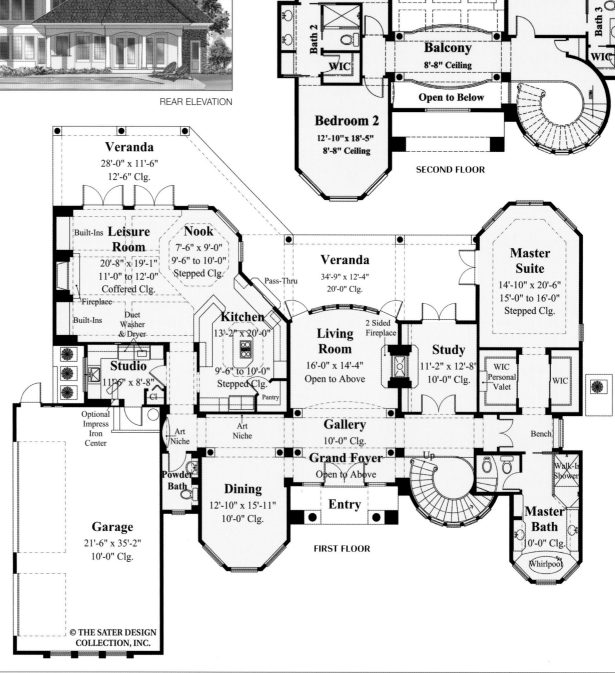

Royal Country Down

SPECIFICATIONS:

Bedrooms: **4**

Baths: **3½**

Width: **85' 0"**

Depth: **76' 8"**

1st Floor: **2829** *sf*

2nd Floor: **1127** *sf*

Total Living: **3956** *sf*

Foundation: **Slab**

PLAN PRICING:

Vellum & PDF - **$2571**

CAD - **$4549**

PLAN NUMBER:

8001

Clarissant

SPECIFICATIONS:

Bedrooms: **4**

Baths: **3½**

Width: **85' 0"**

Depth: **76' 8"**

1st Floor: **2829** *sf*

2nd Floor: **1127** *sf*

Total Living: **3956** *sf*

Foundation: **Slab**

PLAN PRICING:

Vellum & PDF - **$2571**

CAD - **$4549**

PLAN NUMBER:

8002

Fiddler's Creek

SPECIFICATIONS:

Bedrooms: **4**

Baths: **3½**

Width: **85' 0"**

Depth: **76' 2"**

1st Floor: **2841** *sf*

2nd Floor: **1052** *sf*

Total Living: **3893** *sf*

Foundation: **Slab**

PLAN PRICING:

Vellum & PDF - **$2530**

PLAN NUMBER:

6746

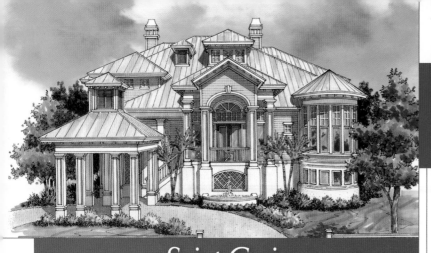

Saint Croix

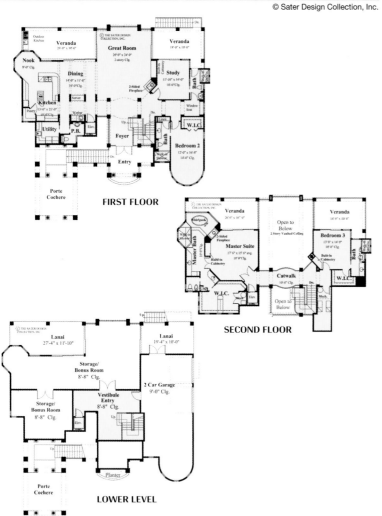

FIRST FLOOR

SECOND FLOOR

LOWER LEVEL

Anna Belle

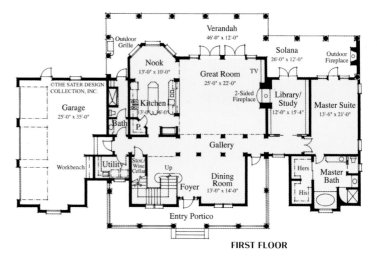

FIRST FLOOR

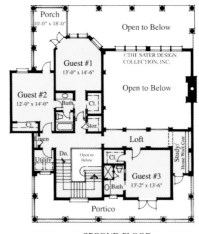

SECOND FLOOR

SPECIFICATIONS:

Bedrooms: **3**

Baths: **3½**

Width: **71' 0"**

Depth: **69' 0"**

1st Floor: **2391** *sf*

2nd Floor: **1539** *sf*

Lower Level: **429** *sf*

Total Living: **4359** *sf*

Foundation:
Island Basement

PLAN PRICING:

Vellum & PDF - **$2833**

PLAN NUMBER:
6822

SPECIFICATIONS:

Bedrooms: **4**

Baths: **4**

Width: **98' 0"**

Depth: **60' 0"**

1st Floor: **2716** *sf*

2nd Floor: **1195** *sf*

Total Living: **4091** *sf*

Foundation: **Crawl Space**

PLAN PRICING:

Vellum & PDF - **$2659**

CAD - **$4705**

PLAN NUMBER:
6782

Les Tourelles

© Sater Design Collection, Inc.

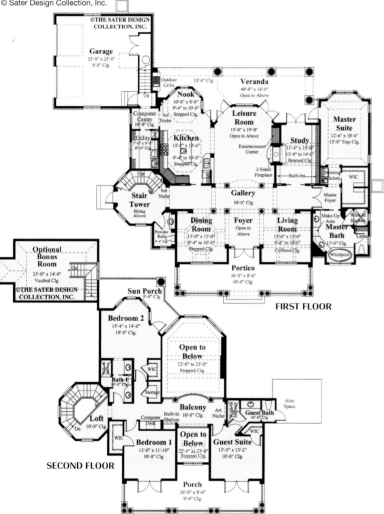

FIRST FLOOR

SECOND FLOOR

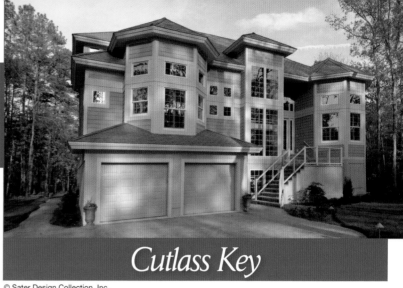

Cutlass Key

© Sater Design Collection, Inc.

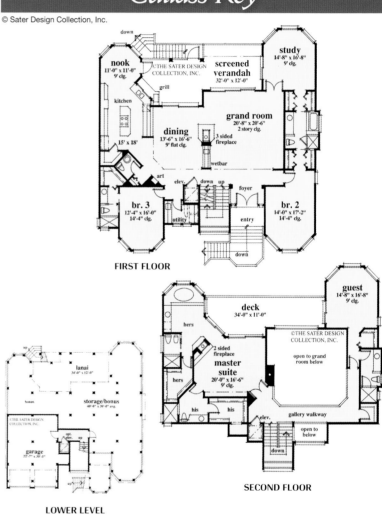

FIRST FLOOR

SECOND FLOOR

LOWER LEVEL

SPECIFICATIONS:
Bedrooms: **4**
Baths: **3½**
Width: **83' 0"**
Depth: **71' 8"**
1st Floor: **2485** sf
2nd Floor: **1127** sf
Total Living: **3612** sf
Opt. Bonus Room: **368** sf
Foundation: **Slab**

PLAN PRICING:
Vellum & PDF - **$1806**
CAD - **$3251**

PLAN NUMBER:
8017

SPECIFICATIONS:
Bedrooms: **4**
Baths: **5½**
Width: **61' 4"**
Depth: **62' 0"**
1st Floor: **2725** sf
2nd Floor: **1418** sf
Total Living: **4143** sf
Foundation:
Island Basement

PLAN PRICING:
Vellum & PDF - **$2693**
CAD - **$4764**

PLAN NUMBER:
6619

Small Luxury Collection

*These homes plans are **3499** square feet or less in living area.*

L uxury is not confined by size. All our home designs incorporate the same rich detailing and style one comes to expect from a Sater Design home plan. Innovative incorporation of outdoor areas expands the sense of space in our home designs. You'll find courtyards, verandas, solana's, balcony's and decks all add to this effect. Open flowing spaces are an even more effective in creating the smaller luxury home.

Peruse through these plans and you'll see that luxury living doesn't have to be large.

Avignon

REAR ELEVATION

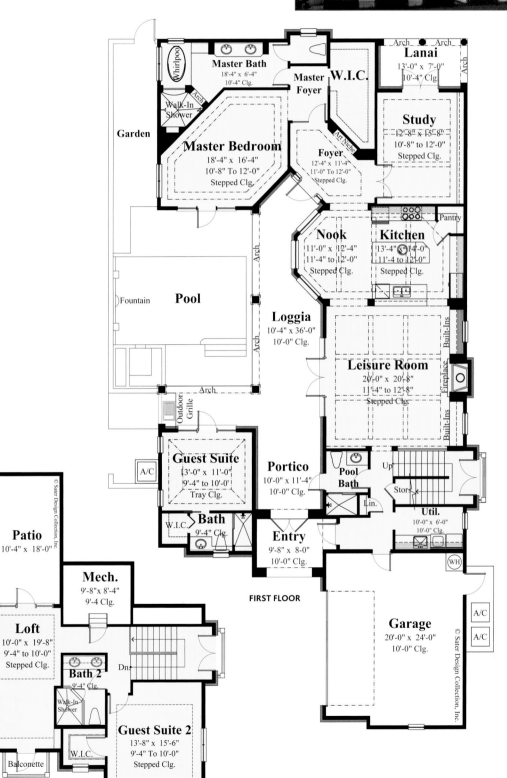

FIRST FLOOR

SECOND FLOOR

Photographed home may have been modified from the original construction documents.

© Sater Design Collection, Inc.

First Floor

- **Master Bath** 18'-4" x 6'-4", 10'-4" Clg.
- Whirlpool
- Walk-In Shower
- **Master Foyer**
- **W.I.C.**
- **Lanai** 13'-0" x 7'-0", 10'-4" Clg.
- Garden
- **Master Bedroom** 18'-4" x 16'-4", 10'-8" To 12'-0" Stepped Clg.
- **Foyer** 12'-4" x 11'-4", 11'-0" To 12'-0" Stepped Clg.
- **Study** 12'-8" x 15'-8", 10'-8" to 12'-0" Stepped Clg.
- **Nook** 11'-0" x 12'-4", 11'-4" to 12'-0" Stepped Clg.
- **Kitchen** 13'-4" x 14'-0", 11'-4" to 12'-0" Stepped Clg.
- Pantry
- **Pool**
- Fountain
- **Loggia** 10'-4" x 36'-0", 10'-0" Clg.
- **Leisure Room** 20'-0" x 20'-8", 11'-4" to 12'-8" Stepped Clg.
- Built-Ins / Fireplace
- Outdoor Grille
- **Guest Suite** 13'-0" x 11'-0", 9'-4" to 10'-0" Tray Clg.
- A/C
- **Portico** 10'-0" x 11'-4", 10'-0" Clg.
- **Pool Bath**
- Up / Stor.
- **Util.** 10'-0" x 6'-0", 10'-0" Clg.
- **Bath** 9'-4" Clg. / W.I.C.
- **Entry** 9'-8" x 8'-0", 10'-0" Clg.
- WH

Second Floor

- **Balcony** 13'-6" x 6'-0"
- **Patio** 10'-4" x 18'-0"
- **Mech.** 9'-8" x 8'-4", 9'-4 Clg.
- **Guest Suite 3** 13'-0" x 11'-0", 9'-4" To 10'-0" Tray Clg.
- **Loft** 10'-0" x 19'-8", 9'-4" to 10'-0" Stepped Clg.
- W.I.C. / **Bath 3** 9'-4" Clg. / Walk-In Shower
- **Bath 2** 9'-4" Clg.
- Dn.
- **Guest Suite 2** 13'-8" x 15'-6", 9'-4" To 10'-0" Stepped Clg.
- W.I.C.
- Balconette
- **Garage** 20'-0" x 24'-0", 10'-0" Clg.
- A/C

SPECIFICATIONS:

Bedrooms: **4**

Baths: **5**

Width: **45' 0"**

Depth: **97' 10"**

1st Floor: **2015** sf

2nd Floor: **848** sf

Cabana: **240** sf

Total Living: **3103** sf

Foundation: **Slab**

PLAN PRICING:

Vellum & PDF - **$1552**

CAD - **$2793**

PLAN NUMBER:
6769

This charming courtyard home features private, family and guest spaces filled with French Country design details and open connections to a central loggia with fountain pool. The great room has a boxed-beamed ceiling, fireplace, built-in cabinetry and retreating glass doors opening to the loggia. The second-level includes a loft, guest bedrooms and decks with courtyard views.

Mirella

Our Mirella home plan offers a distinct Mediterranean inspired exterior that is complemented by a soft contemporary interior. This combination yields elegance with a sophisticated yet relaxed lifestyle. This great room floor plan with enclosed Florida Room affords its owners an expansive living and entertaining space. It's large island kitchen is front and center to all activities in the home and is in close proximity to the garage via a family valet with built-ins to place those purses, keys and other in transit items. The ample size utility room is nearby as well.

The kitchen features a walk-in pantry and an adjacent optional dry bar. The master suite features a his/hers closet and bath with walk-in shower. The two guest suites are located off the foyer. One has a private bath and the other shares a bath with public areas, but can be easily incorporated for private use. A study is conveniently located off the home's great room.

Raised spa spills into pool below.

The master bath's dual lavatory vanity.

Spacious island kitchen with crisp white cabinets, marble counters and stainless steel hood vent lend to modern feel.

~ Any plan can be customized to meet your needs, find out how by calling 800-718-7526. ~

The Mirella's openness is wonderfully exhibited in these two photos of the great room, Florida Room and kitchen.

The Florida Room's fireplace with TV above is rooms centerpiece.

Guest bedroom 2 with bayed arched window.

Guest bedroom 3.

The master suite opens onto home's rear via sliding glass doors.

FLORIDA ROOM

View of great room in distance is foyer and island kitchen.

Master Suite
15'-4" x 16'-4"
10'-0" To 11'-0"
Stepped Clg.

Built-In

Fireplace w/ TV Above

Florida Room
34'-10" T15'-4" x
10'-0" o 11'-0"
Stepped Clg.

Built-In

W.I.C.

W.I.C.

Lin.

Dining Room
13'-0" x 12'-6"
10'-0" To 11'-0"
Stepped Clg.

Great Room
24'-8" x 20'-8"
10'-0" To 11'-0"
Stepped Clg.

M. Bath
12'-6" x 10'-6"
10'-0" Clg.

Walk-In Shower

Kitchen
13'-4" x 13'-0"
10'-0" Clg.

Dry Bar

Bedroom 3
12'-4" x 11'-10"
10'-0" Clg.

Garage 1
17'-10" x 21'-0"
10'-0" Clg.

P.

Study
11'-0" x 12'-8"
10'-0" Clg.

Foyer
9'-0" x 13'-0"
12'-" To 13'-0"
Stepped Clg.

Bath

Tub/ Shower

Utility
11'-4" x 7'-4"
10'-0" Clg.

Family Valet
5'-4" x 7'-0"
10'-0" Clg.

Bath

Walk-In Shower

Lin.

Portico
22'-0" x 6'-4"
14'-0" Clg.

Arch ● Arch

Arch

Garage 2
21'-0" x 22'-0"
10'-0" Clg.

Bedroom 2
14'-8" x 12'-0"
10'-0" Clg.

© THE SATER DESIGN COLLECTION, INC.

SPECIFICATIONS:

Bedrooms: **3**

Baths: **3**

Width: **72' 4"**

Depth: **82' 11"**

1st Floor: **3083** *sf*

Total Living: **3083** *sf*

Foundation: **Slab**

Exterior Wall: **8" Block**

PLAN PRICING:

Vellum & PDF - **$1542**

CAD - **$2775**

PLAN NUMBER:

6562

PLAN NAME:

Mirella

Not available for construction in Lee or Collier Counties, Florida.

Ferretti

With its terra-cotta-hued barrel roof tiles, limestone sheathed walls, stone accents and golden-hued stucco façade, this is a quintessential Tuscan-inspired home. Entering the courtyard through a pair of wrought iron gates, a loggia of stone-covered pillars and arched openings travels the length of the home. Myriad windows and glass doors grace the interior walls resulting in an instant and irrevocable synergy that connects the interior and exterior spaces.

To the left of the foyer, the master suite faces the pool and seemingly draws the outdoors inward. The library is located near the foyer and adjacent to the airy kitchen, dining and great room, which naturally transition outward onto the covered loggia and ensuing pool area. Facing the enclosed courtyard, two second-story guest suites share a common loft that opens up onto a covered balcony and pergola-shaded deck. Anchored on one side by a private guesthouse, a privacy wall encloses the courtyard, enhancing the home's oasis-like ambiance.

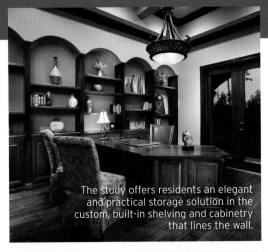

The study offers residents an elegant and practical storage solution in the custom, built-in shelving and cabinetry that lines the wall.

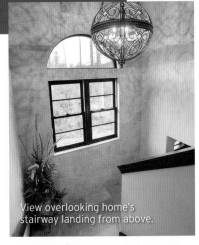

View overlooking home's stairway landing from above.

Spacious kitchen with it's large center island and extended breakfast bar, transitions easily into the great room.

Arched niches flank the coffer ceilinged great room's fireplace. The graceful wrought iron stair rail and landing add light and interest to the space.

A balcony accessed from the second-floor loft and third guest suite provides a quiet respite from a harried day to enjoy wide views of lush scenery.

A spa-like bath overlooks a side garden contained within the courtyard's privacy wall that spans the length of the home.

Adjacent to the dining room and kitchen, the great room, with its repeating arches, beamed coffered ceiling and wood mantel, ties together like a perfectly accessorized outfit.

A warming outdoor fireplace adjacent to the built-in grille and outdoor kitchen.

An expansive wall of glass-fronted doors connects the master suite to the courtyard.

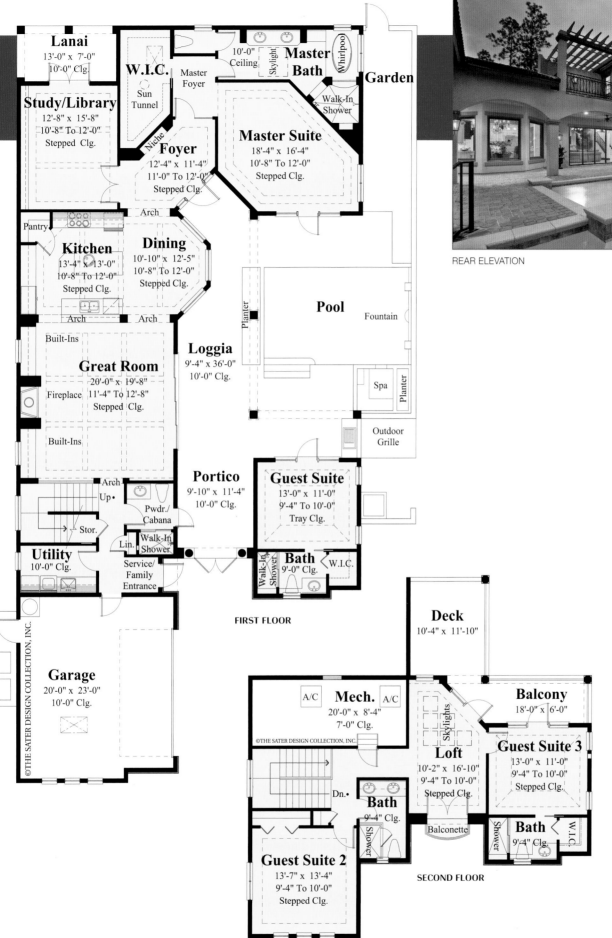

Lanai
13'-0" x 7'-0"
10'-0" Clg.

W.I.C.
Master Foyer

Master Foyer

10'-0" Ceiling
Skylight

Master Bath
Whirlpool

Garden

Study/Library
12'-8" x 15'-8"
10'-8" To 12'-0"
Stepped Clg.

Sun Tunnel

Niche

Walk-In Shower

Foyer
12'-4" x 11'-4"
11'-0" To 12'-0"
Stepped Clg.

Master Suite
18'-4" x 16'-4"
10'-8" To 12'-0"
Stepped Clg.

Arch

Pantry

Kitchen
13'-4" x 13'-0"
10'-8" To 12'-0"
Stepped Clg.

Dining
10'-10" x 12'-5"
10'-8" To 12'-0"
Stepped Clg.

Arch

Arch

Planter

Pool
Fountain

Built-Ins

Great Room
20'-0" x 19'-8"
11'-4" To 12'-8"
Stepped Clg.

Fireplace

Built-Ins

Loggia
9'-4" x 36'-0"
10'-0" Clg.

Planter

Spa

Planter

Outdoor Grille

Arch

Up

Portico
9'-10" x 11'-4"
10'-0" Clg.

Guest Suite
13'-0" x 11'-0"
9'-4" To 10'-0"
Tray Clg.

Pwdr./ Cabana

Stor.

Utility
10'-0" Clg.

Lin.

Walk-In Shower

Service/ Family Entrance

Walk-In Shower

Bath
9'-0" Clg.

W.I.C.

FIRST FLOOR

Garage
20'-0" x 23'-0"
10'-0" Clg.

Photographed home may have been modified from the original construction documents.

© THE SATER DESIGN COLLECTION, INC.

© Sater Design Collection, Inc.

REAR ELEVATION

Deck
10'-4" x 11'-10"

A/C

Mech.
20'-0" x 8'-4"
7'-0" Clg.

A/C

Balcony
18'-0" x 6'-0"

Skylights

©THE SATER DESIGN COLLECTION, INC.

Dn.

Loft
10'-2" x 16'-10"
9'-4" To 10'-0"
Stepped Clg.

Guest Suite 3
13'-0" x 11'-0"
9'-4" To 10'-0"
Stepped Clg.

Shower

Bath
9'-4" Clg.

Shower

Bath
9'-4" Clg.

W.I.C.

Balconette

Guest Suite 2
13'-7" x 13'-4"
9'-4" To 10'-0"
Stepped Clg.

SECOND FLOOR

SPECIFICATIONS:

Bedrooms: **4**

Baths: **5**

Width: **45' 0"**

Depth: **95' 8"**

1ˢᵗ Floor: **2254** *sf*

2ⁿᵈ Floor: **777** *sf*

Total Living: **3031** *sf*

Foundation: **Slab**

Exterior Wall: **2x6 Wood**

PLAN PRICING:

Vellum & PDF - **$1516**

CAD - **$2728**

PLAN NUMBER:

6786

PLAN NAME:

Ferretti

Arabella

Aurora Award Winner!

The Arabella's Old World Tuscan styling is unmistakable, from it's stone walled entry courtyard with bougainvillea draped trellis and wrought iron gateway, to the towering circular entry portico. This 3,433 square foot living area home plan features three bedrooms and three and a half baths. Upon entering the home's expansive coffer ceilinged foyer, one is invited to the formal dining room with its French doors that open onto another small side courtyard. Stepping through the foyer, one enters into the great room with kitchen and nook. This spacious area overlooks the veranda and views beyond.

The master suite is accessed off the foyer and features his and hers closet, as well as a third closet for storing winter clothes or perhaps maybe house those special shoes and handbags. The master bath has a walk-in shower and whirlpool tub. The master suite itself includes a sitting area and overlooks the veranda.

Rounding out the home's spaces is a roomy study which overlooks the front courtyard and is accessed via double doors. The two guest suites each have walk-in closets and private baths and look out onto adjacent patio or courtyards. The conveniently located powder bath and ample utility room complete this well appointed and thoughtfully laid out floor plan.

Formal dining room with coffered ceiling and mirrored recesses lend to it's drama.

The kitchen features a walk-in pantry and stone cooktop hood and is open to the casual nook that overlooks the veranda.

Home's great room/kitchen with foyer and entry door visible in distance.

ABOVE: The study opens onto front courtyard.

RIGHT: The great room opens onto veranda through pocketing glass sliding door.

The master bath features a dramatic, freestanding tub, dual vanities, and a walk-in shower.

The veranda's outdoor fireplace with TV above.

The great room's dramatic built-ins.

This luxurious master suite has a sitting area that overlooks the veranda and view beyond. It is highlighted by a stepped tray ceiling.

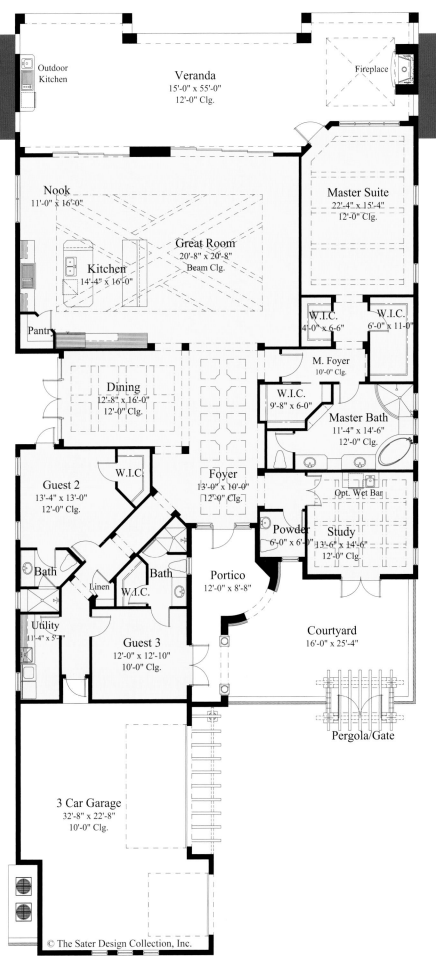

Veranda
15'-0" x 55'-0"
12'-0" Clg.

Outdoor Kitchen

Fireplace

Nook
11'-0" x 16'-0"

Master Suite
22'-4" x 15'-4"
12'-0" Clg.

Great Room
20'-8" x 20'-8"
Beam Clg.

Kitchen
14'-4" x 16'-0"

Pantry

W.I.C.
4'-0" x 6'-6"

W.I.C.
6'-0" x 11'-0"

M. Foyer
10'-0" Clg.

W.I.C.
9'-8" x 6'-0"

Dining
12'-8" x 16'-0"
12'-0" Clg.

Master Bath
11'-4" x 14'-6"
12'-0" Clg.

Guest 2
13'-4" x 13'-0"
12'-0" Clg.

W.I.C.

Foyer
13'-0" x 10'-0"
12'-0" Clg.

Opt. Wet Bar

Bath

Linen

W.I.C.

Bath

Powder
6'-0" x 6'-0"

Study
13'-6" x 14'-6"
12'-0" Clg.

Portico
12'-0" x 8'-8"

Utility
11'-4" x 5'-1"

Guest 3
12'-0" x 12'-10"
10'-0" Clg.

Courtyard
16'-0" x 25'-4"

Pergola/Gate

3 Car Garage
32'-8" x 22'-8"
10'-0" Clg.

© The Sater Design Collection, Inc.

REAR ELEVATION

SPECIFICATIONS:

Bedrooms: **3**

Baths: **3½**

Width: **55' 0"**

Depth: **124' 8"**

1st Floor: **3433** *sf*

Total Living: **3433** *sf*

Foundation: **Slab**

Exterior Wall: **8" Block**

PLAN PRICING:

Vellum & PDF - **$1717**

CAD - **$3090**

PLAN NUMBER:
6799

PLAN NAME:
Arabella

Not available for construction in Lee or Collier Counties, Florida.

Wulfert Point

ARDA Award Winner!

The Wulfert Point draws inspiration from many European styles, represented in the exterior's stucco façade and the rich architectural detailing of this truly unique home. All about the views, this house positions every common room to at least have a glimpse of, if not be fully oriented toward, its natural surroundings.

Fountains, planters and covered porches merge with windows, French doors and an open floor plan to blend indoor and outdoor living. The ornate spa and lap pool fulfill the needs of relaxation and exercise at home.

The second level is reserved for the private bedrooms and bathrooms and includes the master suite and two secondary bedrooms. The master retreat features large walk-in closets and a self-contained master bath. This level boasts its own wraparound covered porch accessible from two bedrooms (including the master) and the hall.

Downstairs, the gourmet kitchen incorporates a step-saving design and services the great room through a pass-thru, while the large central island serves as a prep area as well as a place for quick meals.

The bonus room/ guest suite performs as a self-sufficient studio apartment or distinctly separate home office. The separate entrance grants it independence from the house proper.

The bayed dining room is open to the great room beyond.

Home's stairway landing.

Boasting copious counter space as well as a large work island, this kitchen is suitable for cooks of all skill levels.

The spacious great room interacts easily with both the kitchen and dining room, while providing breathtaking views of the scenery to the rear of the property. Three sets of French doors open onto the covered porch.

Tuscan columns line the covered porch that provides vistas as well as respite from the sun. It also offers a range of possibilities from entertaining guests to enjoying a quiet moment alone.

The spacious master bathroom features a glass enclosed, walk-in shower, plentiful cabinets, dual vanities and steps leading up to a bathtub. Windows allow natural light to permeate the space.

With multiple French doors the scenery is always close at hand in the master suite located on the second floor.

This view-oriented design features a wraparound porch, bountiful windows, multiple sets of French doors and outdoor living spaces.

Side loggia off of great room.

~ *Any plan can be customized to meet your needs, find out how by calling* **800-718-7526**. ~

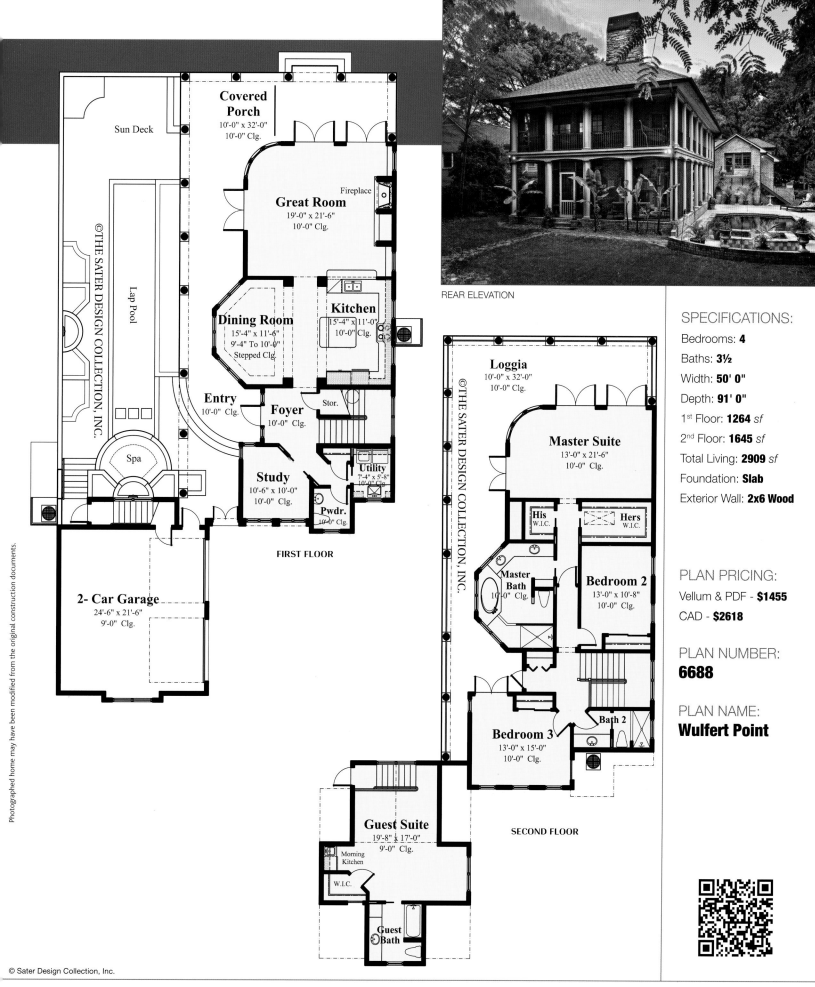

Sun Deck

Covered Porch
10'-0" x 32'-0"
10'-0" Clg.

Lap Pool

Great Room
19'-0" x 21'-6"
10'-0" Clg.

Fireplace

©THE SATER DESIGN COLLECTION, INC.

Kitchen
15'-4" x 11'-0"
10'-0" Clg.

Dining Room
15'-4" x 11'-6"
9'-4" To 10'-0"
Stepped Clg.

Entry
10'-0" Clg.

Foyer
10'-0" Clg.

Stor.

Spa

Study
10'-6" x 10'-0"
10'-0" Clg.

Utility
7'-4" x 5'-8"
10'-0" Clg.

Pwdr.
10'-0" Clg.

FIRST FLOOR

2- Car Garage
24'-6" x 21'-6"
9'-0" Clg.

REAR ELEVATION

Loggia
10'-0" x 32'-0"
10'-0" Clg.

Master Suite
13'-0" x 21'-6"
10'-0" Clg.

©THE SATER DESIGN COLLECTION, INC.

His
W.I.C.

Hers
W.I.C.

Master Bath
10'-0" Clg.

Bedroom 2
13'-0" x 10'-8"
10'-0" Clg.

Bedroom 3
13'-0" x 15'-0"
10'-0" Clg.

Bath 2

SECOND FLOOR

Guest Suite
19'-8" x 17'-0"
9'-0" Clg.

Morning Kitchen

W.I.C.

Guest Bath

SPECIFICATIONS:

Bedrooms: **4**

Baths: **3½**

Width: **50' 0"**

Depth: **91' 0"**

1st Floor: **1264** *sf*

2nd Floor: **1645** *sf*

Total Living: **2909** *sf*

Foundation: **Slab**

Exterior Wall: **2x6 Wood**

PLAN PRICING:

Vellum & PDF - **$1455**

CAD - **$2618**

PLAN NUMBER:
6688

PLAN NAME:
Wulfert Point

Caprina

Repeating arches and rope columns, along with the matching arched transom windows express the Mediterranean sensibility that is found throughout the home. An elegant façade enhances every streetscape. Art niches provide opportunities to showcase decorative accents throughout the home.

Formal rooms are front and center once inside the home, where a wet bar offers drinks to those enjoying the elevated atmosphere of the formal living and dining rooms. French doors provide access to the lanai.

Just beyond the wet bar lies a more casual living space, encompassing a gourmet kitchen with a spacious island, angled eating bar and walk-in pantry, as well as a casual dining nook and leisure room with built-in entertainment center. The nook enjoys views of the pool through a mitered glass bay window. Retreating walls of glass seamlessly transition the leisure room to the covered lanai outdoors, which offers a fireplace and built-in grille.

The master suite consumes the entire left side of the home with a host of amenities to pamper the owners. Two secondary bedrooms inside share a Jack-and-Jill bath, but each boasts a walk-in closet and access to the side lanai. Reserved for special guests, a separate guest suite is secluded from the home to the rear of the plan.

View from dinning room overlooks wet bar and leisure room beyond.

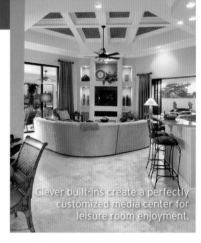

Clever built-ins create a perfectly customized media center for leisure room enjoyment.

An art niche provides the perfect display space near the kitchen, which resides under a detailed coffered ceiling.

Wainscoting's elegance imparts the formal living and dining rooms with the perfect environment for the finest of occasions.

REAR ELEVATION

Guest Suite
13'-0" x 16'-2"
10'-0" Clg.

Lanai
28'-8" x 27'-0"
10'-8" Clg.

Walk-In Shower

Outdoor Grille

Guest Bath
10'-0" Clg.

Master Suite
13'-4" x 20'-8"
10'-0" to 11'-0"
Stepped Clg.

Leisure Room
20'-6" x 18'-6"
10'-8" to 11'-8"
Coffered Clg.

Entertainment Center

Lanai
17'-0" x 12'-11"
10'-8" Clg.

WIC

WIC

Art Niche

Nook
10'-0" x 11'-5"
10'-8" Clg.

Lanai
11'-3" x 46'-0"
10'-8" Clg.

Kitchen
18'-0" x 15'-3"
10'-8" Clg.

Fireplace

Wet Bar

Art Niche

Pantry

M. Bath
10'-0" Clg.

Whirlpool

Living Room
11'-6" x 14'-4"
12'-4" to 13'-4"
Coffered Clg.

Foyer
13'-4" Clg.

Dining
11'-8" x 14'-4"
12'-4" to 13'-4"
Stepped Clg.

Pwdr.
10'-0" Clg.

WIC

Bedroom 2
12'-0" x 12'-6"
10'-0" Clg.

Walk-In Shower

Linen

Entry
13'-4" Clg.

Bath 2
10'-0" Clg.

Utility
8'-6" x 8'-0"
10'-0" Clg.

WIC

Bedroom 3
13'-6" x 14'-10"
10'-0" Clg.

Garage
23'-0" x 32'-10"
11'-4" Clg.

© THE SATER DESIGN COLLECTION, INC.

SPECIFICATIONS:

Bedrooms: **4**

Baths: **3½**

Width: **74' 8"**

Depth: **118' 0"**

1st Floor: **3271** *sf*

Total Living: **3271** *sf*

Foundation: **Slab**

Exterior Wall: **2x6 Wood**

PLAN PRICING:

Vellum & PDF - **$1636**

CAD - **$2944**

PLAN NUMBER:

8052

PLAN NAME:

Caprina

San Sebastian

The influence of the Spanish vernacular is abundantly evident in this remarkable Mediterranean-style villa. Arches, corbels, wrought iron elements and mustard-colored stucco all evoke a feeling of serenity and sunshine. That tranquil aura continues inside the double entry doors, where the foyer offers views of an elegant living room – a space expanded and warmed by a stepped ceiling, Mediterranean-influenced fireplace and sliding glass doors to the lanai. A striking dining room and customized study sit conveniently on either side of the entry at the front of the home, and a powder room is tucked neatly in the foyer.

The master suite extends along the entire right side of the home. The master bedroom has a stepped ceiling, oversized walk-in closet, a welcoming foyer and French doors to the lanai. The generous and tastefully appointed bath includes an L-shaped privacy garden viewed from a corner-set garden tub.

The living areas are designed in convenient relationship to each other and to the outdoors, making family leisure time as well as large-scale parties both efficient and fun. A fully appointed guest suite and two more bedrooms offer exceedingly comfortable accommodations for family and out-of-town friends, and the lanai is a perfect place for a frolic in the pool or an early-evening cocktail.

Leisure room and breakfast nook are conjoined to create an informal and highly functional common zone. Zero-corner sliding glass doors add yet another dimension by stylishly incorporating the exterior landscape.

Ergonomically designed, this gourmet kitchen is ultra-efficient - everything required is well within the chef's reach including state-of-the-art appliances.

Arches, columns and stepped ceilings create a cathedral-like serenity throughout the entire interior, including this formal living area.

REAR ELEVATION

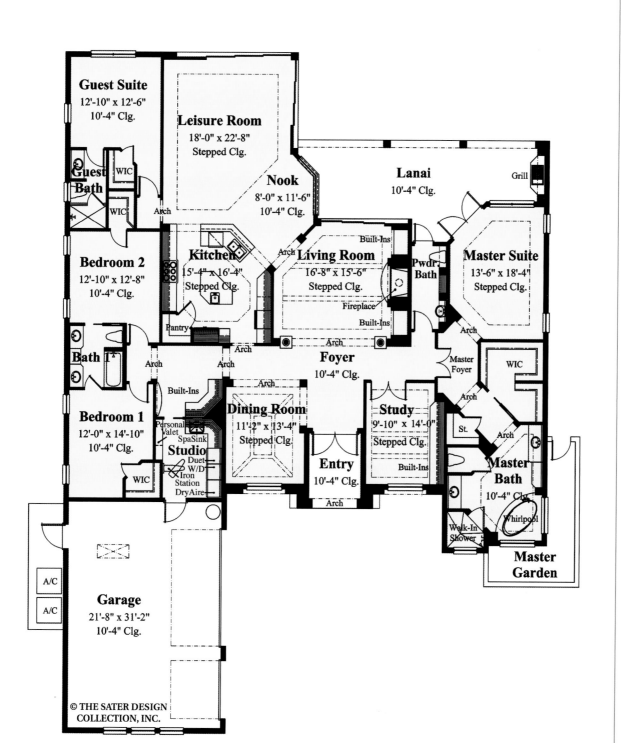

Guest Suite
12'-10" x 12'-6"
10'-4" Clg.

Guest Bath

WIC

WIC

Leisure Room
18'-0" x 22'-8"
Stepped Clg.

Nook
8'-0" x 11'-6"
10'-4" Clg.

Lanai
10'-4" Clg.

Grill

Arch

Bedroom 2
12'-10" x 12'-8"
10'-4" Clg.

Kitchen
15'-4" x 16'-4"
Stepped Clg.

Pantry

Arch

Living Room
16'-8" x 15'-6"
Stepped Clg.

Built-Ins

Pwdr. Bath

Master Suite
13'-6" x 18'-4"
Stepped Clg.

Fireplace

Built-Ins

Arch

Bath 1

Built-Ins

Arch

Arch

Foyer
10'-4" Clg.

Arch

Master Foyer

WIC

Arch

St.

Arch

Bedroom 1
12'-0" x 14'-10"
10'-4" Clg.

Personal Valet
SpaSink

Studio
Duet W/D
Iron Station
DryAire

WIC

Dining Room
11'-2" x 13'-4"
Stepped Clg.

Study
9'-10" x 14'-0"
Stepped Clg.

Built-Ins

Master Bath
10'-4" Clg.

Whirlpool

Entry
10'-4" Clg.

Arch

Walk-In Shower

Master Garden

A/C

A/C

Garage
21'-8" x 31'-2"
10'-4" Clg.

© THE SATER DESIGN
COLLECTION, INC.

SPECIFICATIONS:

Bedrooms: **4**

Baths: **3½**

Width: **68' 8"**

Depth: **93' 8"**

1st Floor: **3433** *sf*

Total Living: **3433** *sf*

Foundation: **Slab**

Exterior Wall: **8" Block**

PLAN PRICING:

Vellum & PDF - **$1717**

CAD - **$3090**

PLAN NUMBER:

6945

PLAN NAME:

San Sebastian

Melito

This luxury Mediterranean narrow courtyard home creates a private sanctuary to enjoy the outdoors. An airy atmosphere is created because the master suite, great room, dining room, and guest rooms are all open to the porch. The great room and kitchen enjoy coffered ceilings, while the master suite offers a stepped ceiling. The kitchen has plenty of counter space, including a center island. Offering little luxuries, the master suite has his and her closets, a dual vanity, walk-in closet and shower, and a whirlpool tub. The master suite is on the opposite side of the house from the guest rooms to offer privacy. The cabana and its private bathroom are disconnected from the house, which makes it a perfect guest retreat. The second floor showcases a generous loft, an extra bedroom and bathroom, and petite deck.

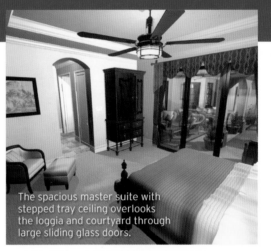

The spacious master suite with stepped tray ceiling overlooks the loggia and courtyard through large sliding glass doors.

The master bath features a double vanity, arched soffit and whirlpool tub for relaxation.

Vaulted ceilings with hewn wood beams extend the length of the open kitchen/great room space. The arched entertainment niche and island kitchen are but, a few of this homes many features.

~ Any plan can be customized to meet your needs, find out how by calling 800-718-7526. ~

The wrap-around loggia overlooks the courtyard and optional pool.

LOGGIA AND COURTYARD

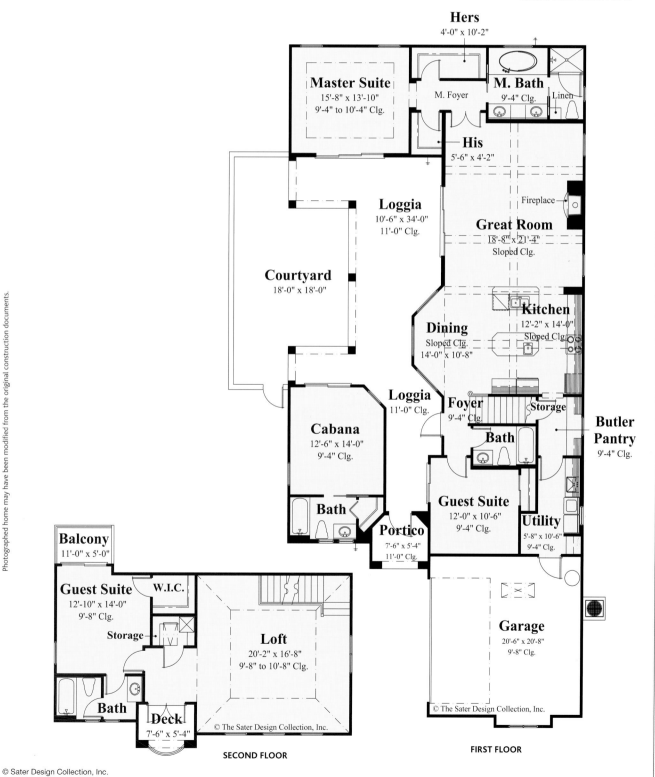

Hers
4'-0" x 10'-2"

Master Suite
15'-8" x 13'-10"
9'-4" to 10'-4" Clg.

M. Bath
9'-4" Clg.

M. Foyer

Linen

His
5'-6" x 4'-2"

Loggia
10'-6" x 34'-0"
11'-0" Clg.

Fireplace

Great Room
18'-8" x 21'-4"
Sloped Clg.

Courtyard
18'-0" x 18'-0"

Kitchen
12'-2" x 14'-0"
Sloped Clg.

Dining
Sloped Clg.
14'-0" x 10'-8"

Loggia
11'-0" Clg.

Foyer
9'-4" Clg.

Storage

Cabana
12'-6" x 14'-0"
9'-4" Clg.

Butler Pantry
9'-4" Clg.

Bath

Bath

Guest Suite
12'-0" x 10'-6"
9'-4" Clg.

Utility
5'-8" x 10'-6"
9'-4" Clg.

Portico
7'-6" x 5'-4"
11'-0" Clg.

© The Sater Design Collection, Inc.

FIRST FLOOR

Balcony
11'-0" x 5'-0"

Guest Suite
12'-10" x 14'-0"
9'-8" Clg.

W.I.C.

Storage

Bath

Deck
7'-6" x 5'-4"

Loft
20'-2" x 16'-8"
9'-8" to 10'-8" Clg.

Garage
20'-6" x 20'-8"
9'-8" Clg.

© The Sater Design Collection, Inc.

SECOND FLOOR

SPECIFICATIONS:

Bedrooms: **4**

Baths: **4**

Width: **40' 0"**

Depth: **89' 0"**

1st Floor: **1664** *sf*

2nd Floor: **749** *sf*

Total Living: **2676** *sf*

Cabana: **263** *sf*

Foundation: **Slab**

Exterior Wall: **2x6 Wood**

PLAN PRICING:

Vellum & PDF - **$1338**

CAD - **$2408**

PLAN NUMBER:
6555

PLAN NAME:
Melito

Not available for construction in Horry or Georgetown Counties, South Carolina.

The marble surround and classic mantle create an easy focal point for the great room, while arched transom windows heighten views.

Aruba Bay

An elevated covered entry, cloud white trim and varied rooflines give lots of personality to this charming coastal cottage. Creative room placement in an unrestricted floor plan make the Aruba Bay ultra-livable as a year-round or vacation home. Packed with functional and aesthetic details like a smart great room/dining room/kitchen design to multiple decks and porches, the home invites fun, relaxation and memory making. Entertaining is a breeze in a large, airy dining room just steps from the kitchen and great room. An oversized window and glass door to one of the main level's three porches connect the space with the outdoors. Dinner guests can retire to either the great room's fireplace or enjoy the evening air, just steps away on the nearby porch.

At the end of the evening, the master retreat offers a quiet place to relax. A private deck and spa-like bath create a restful haven. Upstairs, a loft overlooks the great room and connects two guest bedrooms. On the lower level, a large bonus area offers many design options.

A large, airy dining room is just steps from the kitchen and great room.

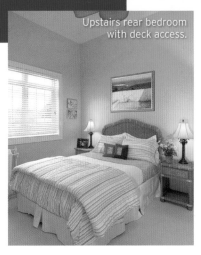

Upstairs rear bedroom with deck access.

The kitchen offers lots of storage and serving space with its deep, curved counter and a long wall of cabinetry culminating in a corner pantry. Open to the dining and great rooms, it's the home's center stage.

*~ Any plan can be customized to meet your needs, find out how by calling **800-718-7526**. ~*

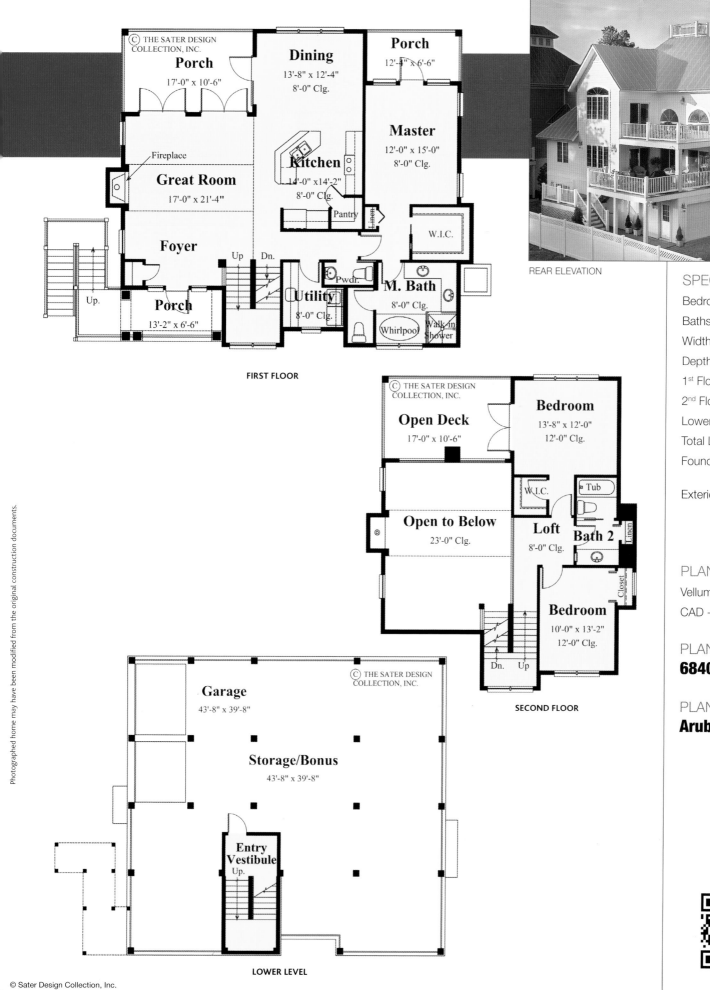

FIRST FLOOR

Porch
17'-0" x 10'-6"

Dining
13'-8" x 12'-4"
8'-0" Clg.

Porch
12'-4" x 6'-6"

Fireplace

Great Room
17'-0" x 21'-4"

Kitchen
14'-0" x 14'-2"
8'-0" Clg.

Master
12'-0" x 15'-0"
8'-0" Clg.

Pantry

Linen

Foyer

W.I.C.

Up. Dn.

Up.

Porch
13'-2" x 6'-6"

Pwdr.

Utility
8'-0" Clg.

M. Bath
8'-0" Clg.

Whirlpool

Walk in Shower

FIRST FLOOR

REAR ELEVATION

SECOND FLOOR

Open Deck
17'-0" x 10'-6"

Bedroom
13'-8" x 12'-0"
12'-0" Clg.

W.I.C.

Tub

Open to Below
23'-0" Clg.

Loft
8'-0" Clg.

Bath 2

Linen

Bedroom
10'-0" x 13'-2"
12'-0" Clg.

Dn. Up

Closet

SECOND FLOOR

LOWER LEVEL

Garage
43'-8" x 39'-8"

Storage/Bonus
43'-8" x 39'-8"

Entry Vestibule
Up.

LOWER LEVEL

SPECIFICATIONS:

Bedrooms: **3**

Baths: **2½**

Width: **44' 0"**

Depth: **40' 0"**

1st Floor: **1342** sf

2nd Floor: **511** sf

Lower Level: **33** sf

Total Living: **1886** sf

Foundation: **Island Basement**

Exterior Wall: **2x6 Wood**

PLAN PRICING:

Vellum & PDF - **$943**

CAD - **$1697**

PLAN NUMBER:

6840

PLAN NAME:

Aruba Bay

Maxina

It was Andrea Palladio who, over four hundred and fifty years ago, conceived of adapting the pediment and columns of Greek architecture to private residents. Nowhere are his ideas more beautifully adapted to modern day needs than in the Maxina, a simple yet elegant floor plan designed for great views, fabulous entertaining and seamless indoor-outdoor living.

From the welcoming front portico, the foyer opens onto a generously sized great room featuring one wall of built-ins for family collectibles and media components and another wall of disappearing glass that extends this great leisure space onto the full-length lanai. The kitchen offers a center cook top island, serving bar facing the leisure room, and plenty of cabinets and countertops. Retreating glass walls expand the breakfast nook to the lanai's outdoor kitchen and fireplace.

The entire left side of the home is allocated to the master suite, which boasts three walk-in closets and a corner walk-in shower hidden behind a magnificent angled garden tub. To the far right of the home are two guest bedrooms. Each has its own walk-in closet and full bath.

This leisure room has beautifully crafted built-ins and a stepped ceiling

Guests seated at this formal dining room table are treated to a view of the night sky through a splendid arch top window.

The "common zone" created by the nook, kitchen and leisure room, provides ample entertaining space.

Master bath with double vanity and island tub with walk-in shower.

REAR ELEVATION

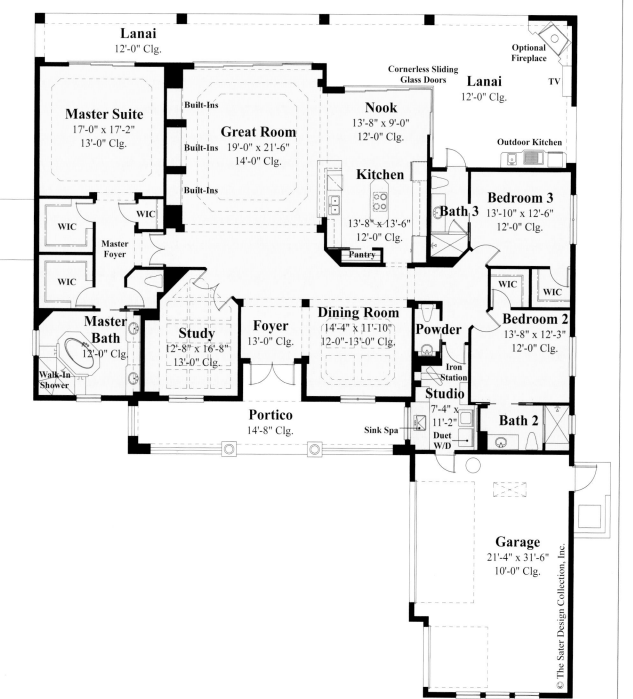

Lanai
12'-0" Clg.

Optional Fireplace

Cornerless Sliding Glass Doors

Lanai
12'-0" Clg.

TV

Master Suite
17'-0" x 17'-2"
13'-0" Clg.

Built-Ins

Great Room
19'-0" x 21'-6"
14'-0" Clg.

Built-Ins

Built-Ins

Nook
13'-8" x 9'-0"
12'-0" Clg.

Outdoor Kitchen

Kitchen
13'-8" x 13'-6"
12'-0" Clg.

WIC

WIC

Master Foyer

WIC

Pantry

Bath 3

Bedroom 3
13'-10" x 12'-6"
12'-0" Clg.

WIC

WIC

Master Bath
12'-0" Clg.

Study
12'-8" x 16'-8"
13'-0" Clg.

Foyer
13'-0" Clg.

Dining Room
14'-4" x 11'-10"
12'-0"-13'-0" Clg.

Powder

Iron Station

Bedroom 2
13'-8" x 12'-3"
12'-0" Clg.

Walk-In Shower

Studio
7'-4" x 11'-2"

Bath 2

Portico
14'-8" Clg.

Sink Spa

Duet W/D

Garage
21'-4" x 31'-6"
10'-0" Clg.

SPECIFICATIONS:

Bedrooms: **3**

Baths: **3½**

Width: **74' 0"**

Depth: **90' 2"**

1ST Floor: **3104** *sf*

Total Living: **3104** *sf*

Foundation: **Slab**

Exterior Wall: **8" Block**

PLAN PRICING:

Vellum & PDF - **$1552**

CAD - **$2794**

PLAN NUMBER:

6944

PLAN NAME:

Maxina

Not available for construction in Lee or Collier Counties, Florida.

Loft overlooking great room with fireplace below.

Nicholas Park

The Nicholas Park is something entirely different: It's a home designed to showcase the outdoors in just about every room you find yourself in.

The handsome, striking façade of this design warmly welcomes you into a soaring foyer where you can see directly through the expansive great room and out to one of the home's multiple rear porch areas. From the open gourmet kitchen, the living area cascades from the dining room out to the porch to the master suite and back to the great room again, with the elegant touches of arches, French doors and transoms found along the way.

The second-floor's generous loft and two spacious bedrooms with private porches provide views of the great room below and the outdoors beyond. Multiple doors and walls of glass on the home's backside provide even more opportunities for extravagant views and outdoor living.

An elaborate entry porch with bold columns sets off this chic villa. The open arrangement of the two-story great room, gallery kitchen and casual dining area creates a natural gathering spot for all to enjoy. Multiple sets of French doors provide seamless connections with the outdoors. The gallery hall leads to the private master suite and upstairs, two ample guest bedrooms have tray ceilings and open to the rear observation deck.

The master suite has multiple windows and French doors which access a sizable outdoor porch.

An impressive master bath features a tray ceiling accented with crown moulding.

The kitchen features an arched pass-thru to the great room and a casual wraparound eating bar.

Porch
30'-10"- 12'-8"
10 Clg.

Dining
12'-0" x 11'-4"
10'-0" Clg.

Great Room
16'-4" x 18'-0"
19'-4" - 20'-0" Clg.
Fireplace

Kitchen
12'-2" x 13'-4"
10'-0" Clg.

Master Suite
13'-0" x 16'-0"
9'-0" - 10'-0" Clg.

Entertainment Center

Niche

Linen

Ref.

Master Bath
10'-0" Clg.

Walk-in Shower

Whirlpool

WIC

Powder
10'-0" clg.

Linen

Utility

Foyer
9'-10" clg.

FIRST FLOOR

Porch
12'-0" clg.

REAR ELEVATION

SPECIFICATIONS:

Bedrooms: **3**

Baths: **3½**

Width: **44' 0"**

Depth: **49' 0"**

1st Floor: **1510** sf

2nd Floor: **864** sf

Total Living: **2374** sf

Foundation: **Island Basement**

Exterior Wall: **2x6 Wood**

PLAN PRICING:

Vellum & PDF - **$1187**

CAD - **$2137**

PLAN NUMBER:

6804

PLAN NAME:

Nicholas Park

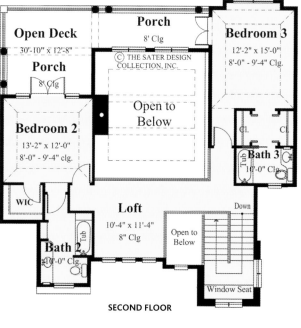

Open Deck
30'-10" x 12'-8"

Porch
8' Clg

Porch
8' Clg

Porch
8' Clg

Bedroom 3
12'-2" x 15'-0"
8'-0" - 9'-4" Clg.

Open to Below

Bedroom 2
13'-2" x 12'-0"
8'-0" - 9'-4" clg.

WIC

Cl.

Cl.

Bath 3
10'-0" Clg.

Tub

Loft
10'-4" x 11'-4"
8" Clg

Down

Bath 2
10'-0" Clg.

Tub

Open to Below

Window Seat

SECOND FLOOR

Lower Porch
30' 0" x 7' 2"

Storage/Bonus

Garage
24'-0" x 25'-6"

Storage

UP

LOWER LEVEL

Bergantino

ARDA Award Winner!

This mid-sized European plan lives large with a wealth of well-appointed indoor and outdoor living space. A triple arch entry, cupola and carved eave brackets set the atmosphere that is continued inside the home with multiple columns and rich, beamed ceilings.

An elegant foyer welcomes guests to the home, while the grand room's windows and French doors provide views of the amenity-rich courtyard. The solana hosts a spacious outdoor kitchen and fireplace beneath a distinctive tray ceiling.

The airy kitchen boasts a roomy island and is open to the casual dining nook and leisure room, but also offers easy access to the formal living and dining rooms. Built-ins throughout the home, such as the family valet near the rear-loading garage and the entertainment center in the leisure room, and utility, storage space add enduring value to the home.

An expansive master retreat offers the owners a luxe master bath with his-and-hers sinks as well as a central spa tub. An elegant art niche foyer features the perfect place to set the mood for relaxation. The suite also boasts a walk-in closet built for two and access to the covered loggia and courtyard through French doors.

Leisure room with kitchen and nook beyond.

Formal dining room with tray ceiling.

Wide countertops offer plenty of prep space and the island offers a prep sink

A wonderful outdoor living space offers an outdoor kitchen and fireplace.

REAR ELEVATION

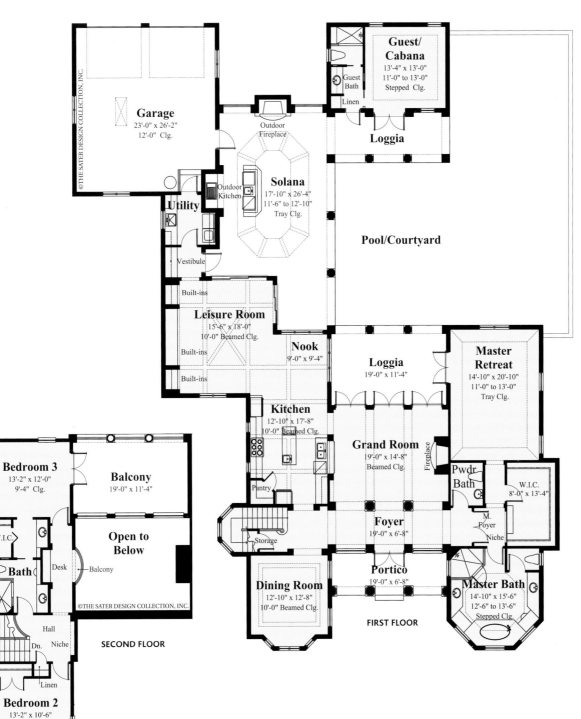

Garage
23'-0" x 26'-2"
12'-0" Clg.

©THE SATER DESIGN COLLECTION, INC.

Guest/ Cabana
13'-4" x 13'-0"
11'-0" to 13'-0"
Stepped Clg.

Guest Bath

Linen

Loggia

Outdoor Fireplace

Utility

Outdoor Kitchen

Solana
17'-10" x 26'-4"
11'-6" to 12'-10"
Tray Clg.

Vestibule

Pool/Courtyard

Built-ins

Leisure Room
15'-6" x 18'-0"
10'-0" Beamed Clg.

Built-ins

Nook
9'-0" x 9'-4"

Built-ins

Loggia
19'-0" x 11'-4"

Master Retreat
14'-10" x 20'-10"
11'-0" to 13'-0"
Tray Clg.

Kitchen
12'-10" x 17'-8"
10'-0" Beamed Clg.

Grand Room
19'-0" x 14'-8"
Beamed Clg.

Fireplace

Pantry

Pwdr Bath

W.I.C.
8'-0" x 13'-4"

Photographed home may have been modified from the original construction documents.

Bedroom 3
13'-2" x 12'-0"
9'-4" Clg.

Balcony
19'-0" x 11'-4"

W.I.C.

Bath

Desk

Balcony

Open to Below

©THE SATER DESIGN COLLECTION, INC.

M. Foyer

Niche

Foyer
19'-0" x 6'-8"

Storage

Portico
19'-0" x 6'-8"

Dining Room
12'-10" x 12'-8"
10'-0" Beamed Clg.

Master Bath
14'-10" x 15'-6"
12'-6" to 13'-6"
Stepped Clg.

FIRST FLOOR

Hall

Dn. Niche

SECOND FLOOR

Linen

Bedroom 2
13'-2" x 10'-6"
9'-4" Clg.

© Sater Design Collection, Inc.

SPECIFICATIONS:

Bedrooms: **4**

Baths: **3½**

Width: **80' 8"**

Depth: **100' 0"**

1st Floor: **2474** *sf*

2nd Floor: **668** *sf*

Total Living: **3142** *sf*

Foundation: **Slab**

Exterior Wall: **8" Block**

PLAN PRICING:

Vellum & PDF - **$1571**

PLAN NUMBER:
8079

PLAN NAME:
Bergantino

REAR ELEVATION

Kinsey

© Sater Design Collection, Inc.

SPECIFICATIONS:

Bedrooms: **3**

Baths: **2½**

Width: **65' 0"**

Depth: **84' 0"**

1st Floor: **2907** *sf*

Total Living: **2907** *sf*

Foundation: **Slab**

PLAN PRICING:

Vellum & PDF - **$1454**

CAD - **$2616**

PLAN NUMBER:

6756

This home uniquely blends a triple arched entry with a stucco and banded detail to give it a southern traditional feel. Inside the home, the open floor plan allows the formal spaces to feel grand while allowing the outdoors in. Corner pocket sliding glass doors at the living room open completely and let the lanai become part of the home.

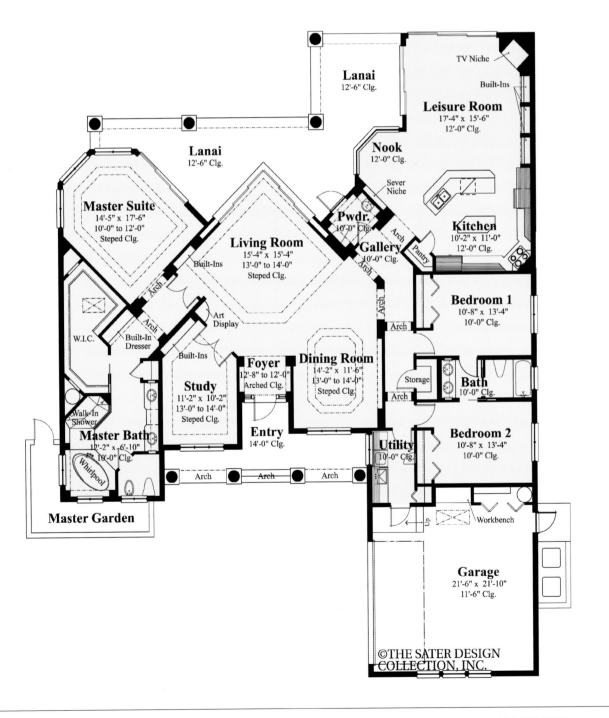

~ Any plan can be customized to meet your needs, find out how by calling 800-718-7526. ~

REAR ELEVATION

Deauville

© Sater Design Collection, Inc.

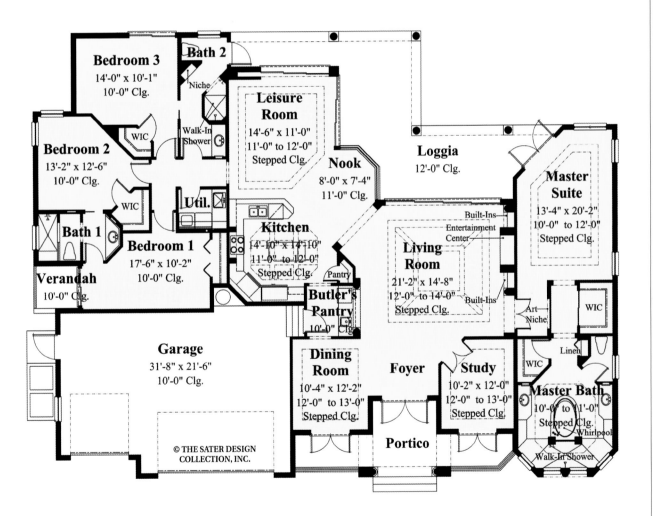

Bedroom 3
14'-0" x 10'-1"
10'-0" Clg.

Bath 2

Niche

Walk-In
Shower

WIC

Leisure
Room
14'-6" x 11'-0"
11'-0" to 12'-0"
Stepped Clg.

Nook
8'-0" x 7'-4"
11'-0" Clg.

Loggia
12'-0" Clg.

Master
Suite
13'-4" x 20'-2"
10'-0" to 12'-0"
Stepped Clg.

Bedroom 2
13'-2" x 12'-6"
10'-0" Clg.

WIC

Util.

Kitchen
14'-10" x 14'-10"
11'-0" to 12'-0"
Stepped Clg.

Pantry

Built-Ins

Entertainment
Center

Living
Room
21'-2" x 14'-8"
12'-0" to 14'-0"
Stepped Clg.

Built-Ins

WIC

Bath 1

Bedroom 1
17'-6" x 10'-2"
10'-0" Clg.

Butler's
Pantry
10'-0" Clg.

Art
Niche

WIC

Linen

Verandah
10'-0" Clg.

Garage
31'-8" x 21'-6"
10'-0" Clg.

Dining
Room
10'-4" x 12'-2"
12'-0" to 13'-0"
Stepped Clg.

Foyer

Study
10'-2" x 12'-0"
12'-0" to 13'-0"
Stepped Clg.

Master Bath
10'-0" to 11'-0"
Stepped Clg.   Whirlpool

Walk-In Shower

Portico

© THE SATER DESIGN
COLLECTION, INC.

Photographed home may have been modified from the original construction documents.

SPECIFICATIONS:

Bedrooms: **4**

Baths: **3**

Width: **80' 10"**

Depth: **59' 10"**

1st Floor: **2908** *sf*

Total Living: **2908** *sf*

Foundation: **Slab**

PLAN PRICING:

Vellum & PDF - **$1454**

CAD - **$2617**

PLAN NUMBER:

6778

Repeating arches line the portico entry of this Italianate-style home. Just past the foyer, the living room features a built-in entertainment center and retreating glass walls to the loggia. A spacious butler's pantry connects the formal dining room to the gourmet-caliber kitchen. Nearby, a family-friendly leisure room opens to the loggia, making indoor/outdoor entertaining easy.

REAR ELEVATION

Santa Rosa

© Sater Design Collection, Inc.

SPECIFICATIONS:

Bedrooms: **3**

Baths: **2**

Width: **48' 0"**

Depth: **48' 0"**

1st Floor: **1383** *sf*

2nd Floor: **595** *sf*

Total Living: **1978** *sf*

Foundation: **Island Basement**

PLAN PRICING:

Vellum & PDF - **$989**

CAD - **$1780**

PLAN NUMBER:

6808

This charming cottage evokes a bygone era with fresh white shutters and periwinkle blue siding, yet features the best modern conveniences in an impressive floor plan. The home's vibrant interior emphasizes a central fireplace, high ceilings that rise to an open balcony and a wall of windows that illuminate the living areas with views.

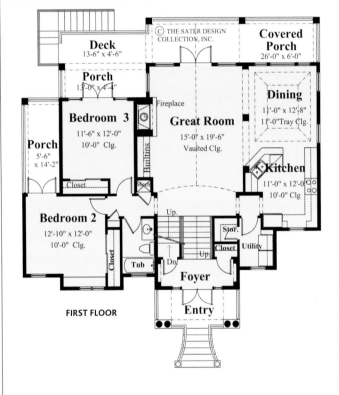

FIRST FLOOR

SECOND FLOOR

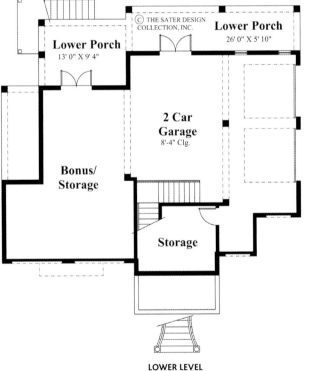

LOWER LEVEL

Photographed home may have been modified from the original construction documents.

REAR ELEVATION

Governor's Club Way

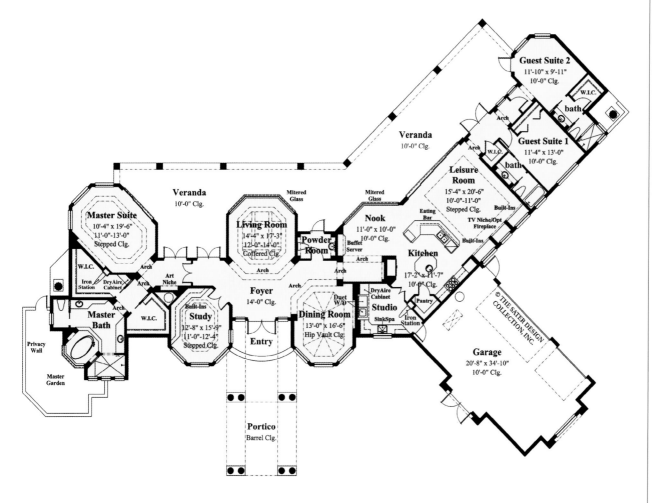

Master Suite
10'-4" x 19'-6"
11'-0"-13'-0"
Stepped Clg.

Veranda
10'-0" Clg.

Living Room
14'4" x 17'-3"
12'-0"-14'-0"
Coffered Clg.

Mitered Glass

Mitered Glass

Veranda
10'-0" Clg.

Guest Suite 2
11'-10" x 9'-11"
10'-0" Clg.

W.I.C.

bath

Guest Suite 1
11'-4" x 13'-0"
10'-0" Clg.

W.I.C.

bath

Arch

Leisure Room
15'-4" x 20'-6"
10'-0"-11'-0"
Stepped Clg.

Built-Ins

TV Niche/Opt Fireplace

Built-Ins

Eating Bar

Nook
11'-0" x 10'-0"
10'-0" Clg.

Powder Room

Buffet Server

Kitchen
17'-2" x 11'-7"
10'-0" Clg.

Pantry

Iron Station

W.I.C.

Iron Station

DryAire Cabinet

Arch

Art Niche

Foyer
14'-0" Clg.

Arch

DryAire Cabinet

Duct W/D

Studio

Sink Spa

Master Bath

W.I.C.

Built-Ins

Study
12'-8" x 15'-9"
11'-0"-12'-4"
Stepped Clg.

Dining Room
13'-0" x 16'-6"
Hip Vault Clg.

Entry

Privacy Wall

Master Garden

Garage
20'-8" x 34'-10"
10'-0" Clg.

© THE SATER DESIGN COLLECTION, INC.

Portico
Barrel Clg.

SPECIFICATIONS:

Bedrooms: **3**

Baths: **3½**

Width: **121' 5"**

Depth: **96' 2"**

1st Floor: **3398** *sf*

Total Living: **3398** *sf*

Foundation: **Slab**

PLAN PRICING:

Vellum & PDF - **$1699**

CAD - **$3058**

PLAN NUMBER:

6674

This custom-feel ranch provides an expansive layout that opens to outdoor views and creates two distinctive wings — one for the private master retreat and another for family living spaces and guest bedrooms. Inside, arches lead down the gallery toward the family area of the home. This area focuses around a spacious leisure room that features a wall of built-ins and a space for an optional fireplace.

REAR ELEVATION

© Sater Design Collection, Inc.

Lexington

SPECIFICATIONS:

Bedrooms: **3**

Baths: **2**

Width: **80' 6"**

Depth: **66' 6"**

1st Floor: **2454** sf

Total Living: **2454** sf

Opt. Bonus Room: **256** sf

Foundation: **Crawl Space**

PLAN PRICING:

Vellum & PDF - **$1227**

CAD - **$2209**

PLAN NUMBER:

7065

The picturesque porch, lined with columns and arches, sets off decorative shutters and dormers. The substantial great room features a coffered ceiling, built-ins and open access to the kitchen and dining rooms. The great room and study share a double-sided fireplace, and both rooms boast French door access to the rear porch — as does the sizeable master suite. Lexington also features a luxurious master bath, bonus room and more.

ARDA Award Winner!

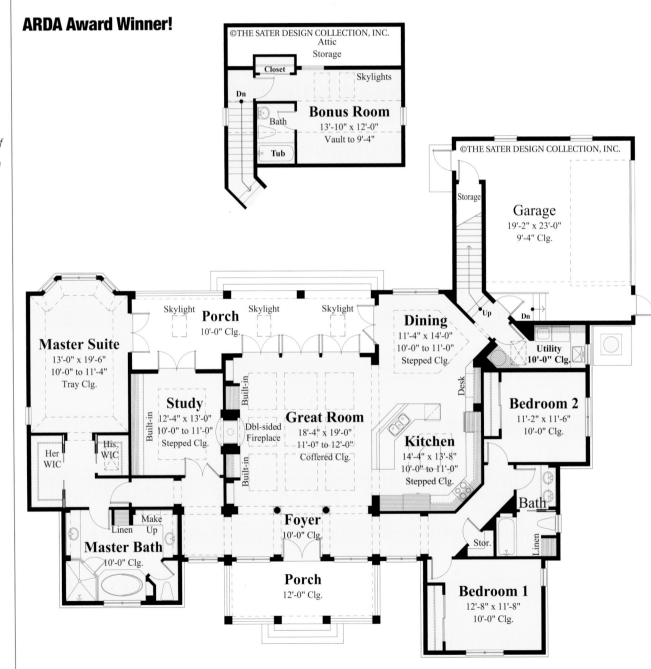

REAR ELEVATION

Bainbridge

© Sater Design Collection, Inc.

ARDA Award Winner!

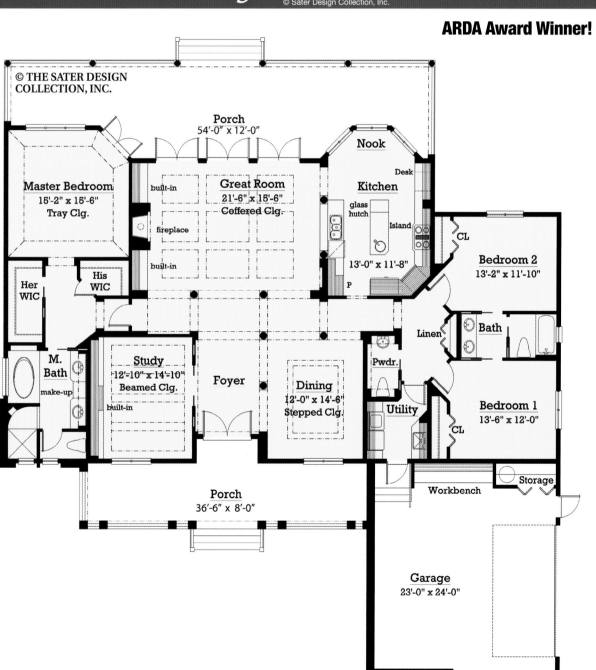

© THE SATER DESIGN COLLECTION, INC.

Porch
54'-0" x 12'-0"

Nook

Master Bedroom
15'-2" x 15'-6"
Tray Clg.

built-in

Great Room
21'-6" x 15'-6"
Coffered Clg.

Kitchen

Desk

glass
hutch

Island

13'-0" x 11'-8"

fireplace

built-in

CL

Bedroom 2
13'-2" x 11'-10"

Her
WIC

His
WIC

Linen

Bath

M.
Bath

make-up

Study
12'-10" x 14'-10"
Beamed Clg.

built-in

Foyer

Dining
12'-0" x 14'-6"
Stepped Clg.

Pwdr.

Utility

Bedroom 1
13'-6" x 12'-0"

CL

Workbench

Storage

Porch
36'-6" x 8'-0"

Garage
23'-0" x 24'-0"

SPECIFICATIONS:

Bedrooms: **3**

Baths: **2½**

Width: **70' 6"**

Depth: **76' 6"**

1st Floor: **2555** *sf*

Total Living: **2555** *sf*

Foundation: **Crawl Space**

PLAN PRICING:

Vellum & PDF - **$1278**

CAD - **$2300**

PLAN NUMBER:

7051

Indulge a love of details with lovely artistic balustrades and patterned trim work. It has a large dining, kitchen and great room divided by columns. Three sets of French doors open the great room to the back porch; another set is found in the impressive master bedroom. This split-floor plan affords easy privacy for both the master suite and two secondary bedrooms.

REAR ELEVATION

Turnberry Lane

SPECIFICATIONS:

Bedrooms: **3**

Baths: **3**

Width: **70' 0"**

Depth: **98' 0"**

1st Floor: **2794** *sf*

Total Living: **2794** *sf*

Foundation: **Slab**

PLAN PRICING:

Vellum & PDF - **$1397**

CAD - **$2515**

PLAN NUMBER:

6602

Decorative columns, circle-head windows and a double-arched entryway add curb appeal to this view-oriented design. Inside the foyer, a mitered glass window provides open views. The formal living and dining rooms are straight ahead, with a unique buffet server connecting the rooms.

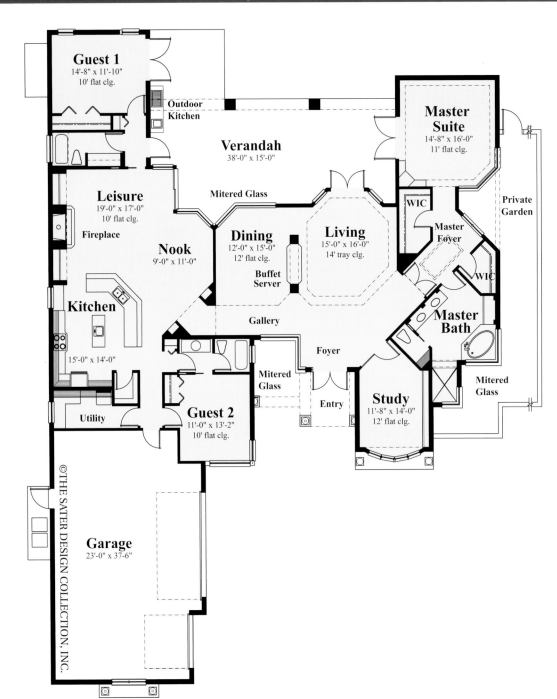

Photographed home may have been modified from the original construction documents.

©THE SATER DESIGN COLLECTION, INC.

REAR ELEVATION

Mission Hills

© Sater Design Collection, Inc.

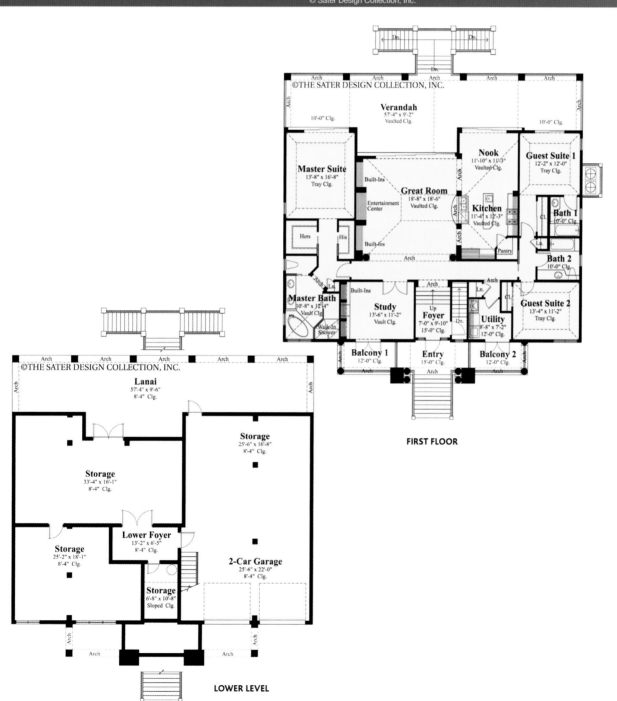

FIRST FLOOR

LOWER LEVEL

Photographed home may have been modified from the original construction documents.

SPECIFICATIONS:

Bedrooms: **3**

Baths: **3**

Width: **60' 0"**

Depth: **60' 0"**

1st Floor: **2350** *sf*

Total Living: **2350** *sf*

Foundation: **Island Basement**

PLAN PRICING:

Vellum & PDF - **$1175**

CAD - **$2115**

PLAN NUMBER:
6845

This enticing European villa boasts an Italian charm and a distinctly Mediterranean feel. Inside, the foyer steps led up to the formal living areas. Vaulted ceilings create a sense of spaciousness throughout the home, and enhance the interior vistas provided by the central great room, which overlooks the rear deck. The island kitchen is conveniently open to a breakfast nook.

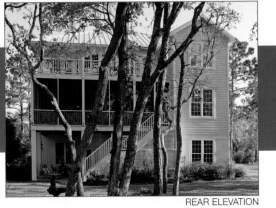

REAR ELEVATION

Carmel Bay

© Sater Design Collection, Inc.

SPECIFICATIONS:

Bedrooms: **3**

Baths: **3**

Width: **46' 0"**

Depth: **51' 0"**

1st Floor: **1551** *sf*

2nd Floor: **983** *sf*

Total Living: **2534** *sf*

Foundation: **Island Basement**

PLAN PRICING:

Vellum & PDF - **$1267**

CAD - **$2281**

PLAN NUMBER:

6810

The foyer announces an open arrangement of casual space and formal rooms. French doors lead to a quiet study or parlor, which features a wall of built-in shelves and an arched window that views the front property. Built-ins frame the fireplace in the great room, providing an anchor for the wall of glass that creates a connection with the outdoors.

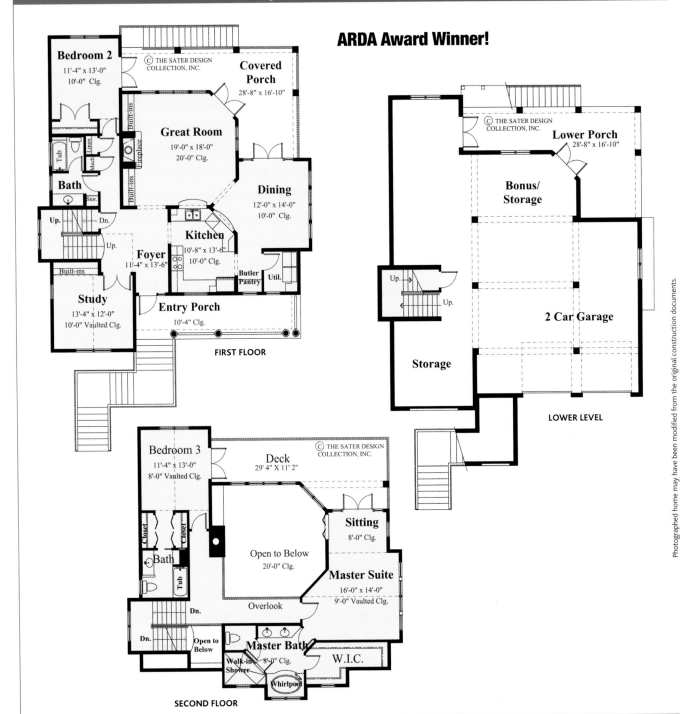

ARDA Award Winner!

Photographed home may have been modified from the original construction documents.

REAR ELEVATION

Hammock Grove

© Sater Design Collection, Inc.

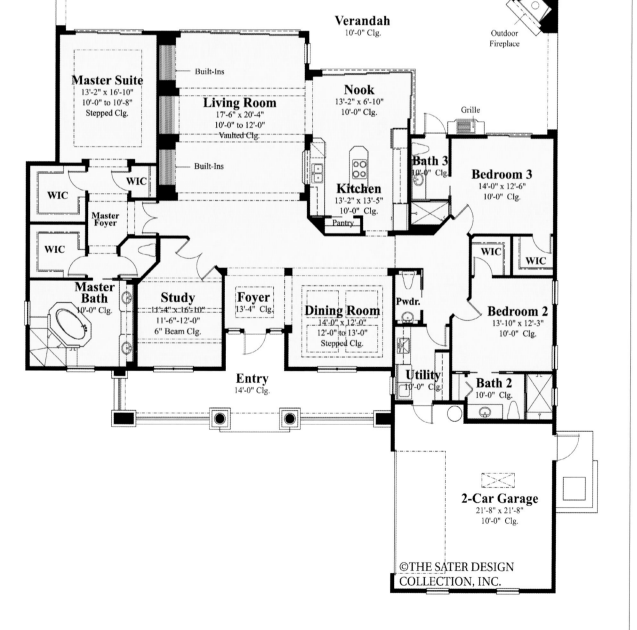

Verandah
10'-0" Clg.

Outdoor Fireplace

Master Suite
13'-2" x 16'-10"
10'-0" to 10'-8"
Stepped Clg.

Built-Ins

Living Room
17'-6" x 20'-4"
10'-0" to 12'-0"
Vaulted Clg.

Nook
13'-2" x 6'-10"
10'-0" Clg.

Grille

WIC

Built-Ins

WIC

Bath 3
10'-0" Clg.

Bedroom 3
14'-0" x 12'-6"
10'-0" Clg.

Master Foyer

Kitchen
13'-2" x 13'-5"
10'-0" Clg.

Pantry

WIC

WIC

WIC

WIC

Master Bath
10'-0" Clg.

Study
11'-4" x 16'-10"
11'-6"-12'-0"
6" Beam Clg.

Foyer
13'-4" Clg.

Dining Room
14'-0" x 12'-0"
12'-0" to 13'-0"
Stepped Clg.

Pwdr.

Bedroom 2
13'-10" x 12'-3"
10'-0" Clg.

Entry
14'-0" Clg.

Utility
10'-0" Clg.

Bath 2
10'-0" Clg.

2-Car Garage
21'-8" x 21'-8"
10'-0" Clg.

©THE SATER DESIGN
COLLECTION, INC.

SPECIFICATIONS:

Bedrooms: **3**

Baths: **3½**

Width: **72' 0"**

Depth: **80' 0"**

1st Floor: **2888** *sf*

Total Living: **2888** *sf*

Foundation: **Slab**

PLAN PRICING:

Vellum & PDF - **$1444**

CAD - **$2599**

PLAN NUMBER:
6780

A gracious front porch invites all into this creative three bedroom, three bath home filled with Old-World craftsmanship, expansive windows, varied ceiling treatments and a grand verandah with an outdoor fireplace. The spacious great room boasts built-in cabinetry, vaulted ceilings and flows into the nook and kitchen area.

Casina Rossa

© Sater Design Collection, Inc.

SPECIFICATIONS:

Bedrooms: **3**

Baths: **2½**

Width: **62' 10"**

Depth: **73' 6"**

1st Floor: **2192** *sf*

Total Living: **2192** *sf*

Foundation: **Slab**

PLAN PRICING:

Vellum & PDF - **$1096**

CAD - **$1972**

PLAN NUMBER:

8071

Columns, stucco and rough-hewn stone embellish the facade of this charming Tuscan villa. Inside, a beamed ceiling contributes a sense of spaciousness to the heart of the home, while walls of glass draw the outdoors inside. Varied ceiling treatments and sculpted arches define the wide-open interior, permitting flexibility as well as great views. The great room is anchored by a massive fireplace flanked by built-in shelves.

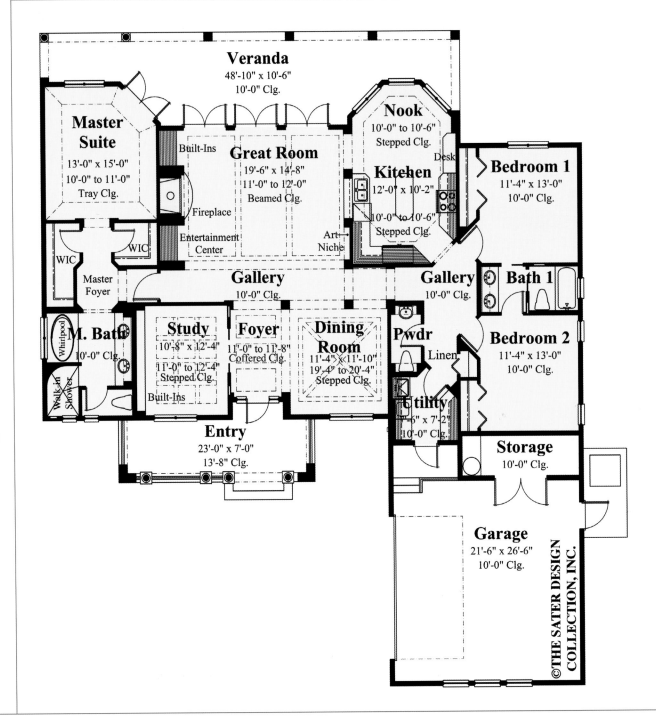

Veranda
48'-10" x 10'-6"
10'-0" Clg.

Master Suite
13'-0" x 15'-0"
10'-0" to 11'-0"
Tray Clg.

Built-Ins

Great Room
19'-6" x 14'-8"
11'-0" to 12'-2"
Beamed Clg.

Nook
10'-0" to 10'-6"
Stepped Clg.

Desk

Kitchen
12'-0" x 10'-2"
10'-0" to 10'-6"
Stepped Clg.

Bedroom 1
11'-4" x 13'-0"
10'-0" Clg.

Fireplace

Entertainment Center

Art Niche

WIC

WIC

Master Foyer

Gallery
10'-0" Clg.

Gallery
10'-0" Clg.

Bath 1

Whirlpool

M. Bath
10'-0" Clg.

Study
10'-8" x 12'-4"
11'-0" to 12'-4"
Stepped Clg.

Built-Ins

Foyer
11'-0" to 11'-8"
Coffered Clg.

Dining Room
11'-4" x 11'-10"
19'-4" to 20'-4"
Stepped Clg.

Pwdr

Linen

Bedroom 2
11'-4" x 13'-0"
10'-0" Clg.

Walk-in Shower

Utility
7'-6" x 7'-2"
10'-0" Clg.

Storage
10'-0" Clg.

Entry
23'-0" x 7'-0"
13'-8" Clg.

Garage
21'-6" x 26'-6"
10'-0" Clg.

© THE SATER DESIGN COLLECTION, INC.

REAR ELEVATION

Les Anges

© Sater Design Collection, Inc.

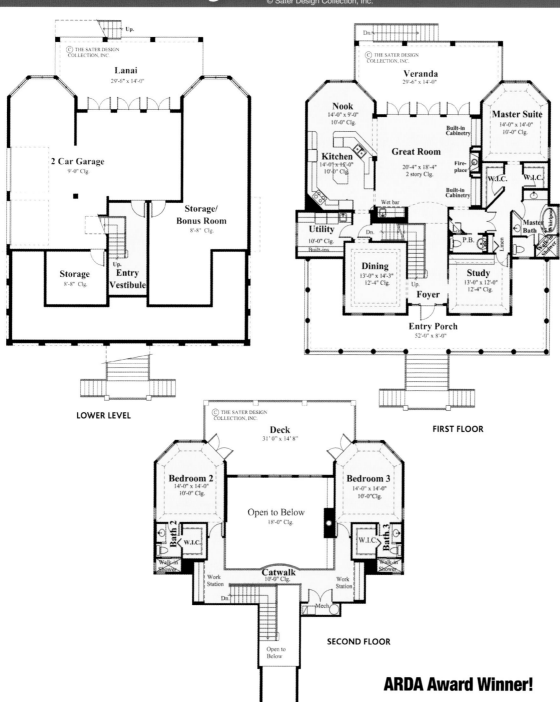

Lanai
29'-6" x 14'-0"

2 Car Garage
9'-0" Clg.

Storage/Bonus Room
8'-8" Clg.

Storage
8'-8" Clg.

Up. Entry Vestibule

LOWER LEVEL

Veranda
29'-6" x 14'-0"

Nook
14'-0" x 9'-0"
10'-0" Clg.

Master Suite
14'-0" x 14'-0"
10'-0" Clg.

Kitchen
14'-0" x 15'-0"
10'-0" Clg.

Great Room
20'-4" x 18'-4"
2 story Clg.

Built-in Cabinetry

Fireplace

Built-in Cabinetry

W.I.C.

W.I.C.

Wet bar

Utility
10'-0" Clg.
Built-ins

Dn.

P.B.

Master Bath

Linen

Walk-in Shower

Whirlpool

Dining
13'-0" x 14'-3"
12'-4" Clg.

Foyer

Study
13'-0" x 12'-0"
12'-4" Clg.

Up.

Entry Porch
52'-0" x 8'-0"

FIRST FLOOR

Deck
31'-0" x 14'-8"

Bedroom 2
14'-0" x 14'-0"
10'-0" Clg.

Bedroom 3
14'-0" x 14'-0"
10'-0"Clg.

Open to Below
18'-0" Clg.

Bath 2

W.I.C.

W.I.C.

Bath 3

Walk-in Shower

Walk-in Shower

Work Station

Work Station

Catwalk
10'-0" Clg.

Dn.

Mech.

Open to Below

SECOND FLOOR

ARDA Award Winner!

SPECIFICATIONS:

Bedrooms: **3**

Baths: **3½**

Width: **56' 0"**

Depth: **64' 0"**

1st Floor: **2146** *sf*

2nd Floor: **952** *sf*

Lower Level: **187** *sf*

Total Living: **3285** *sf*

Foundation: **Island Basement**

PLAN PRICING:

Vellum & PDF - **$1643**

CAD - **$2957**

PLAN NUMBER:
6825

An inviting wraparound porch and additional outdoor spaces extend the living area of this charming cottage. Built-in cabinetry, a massive fireplace and a host of French doors highlight the central living space, which also features a wet bar. The well-designed kitchen includes a sunny breakfast nook, center island, plenty of storage and easy access to the formal dining room.

REAR ELEVATION

Wentworth Trail

© Sater Design Collection, Inc.

SPECIFICATIONS:

Bedrooms: **3**

Baths: **3½**

Width: **67' 0"**

Depth: **102' 0"**

1st Floor: **2894** *sf*

2nd Floor: **568** *sf*

Total Living: **3462** *sf*

Foundation: **Slab**

PLAN PRICING:

Vellum & PDF - **$1731**

CAD - **$3116**

PLAN NUMBER:

6653

The elegance of brick and stucco give the exterior a feel of warmth while setting it apart from other homes in your area. Custom amenities and touches are the key to this livable home. The mixture of clean, simple styles makes it adaptable for any area. The exciting flow of the plan allows the rear of the home to look out to the yard.

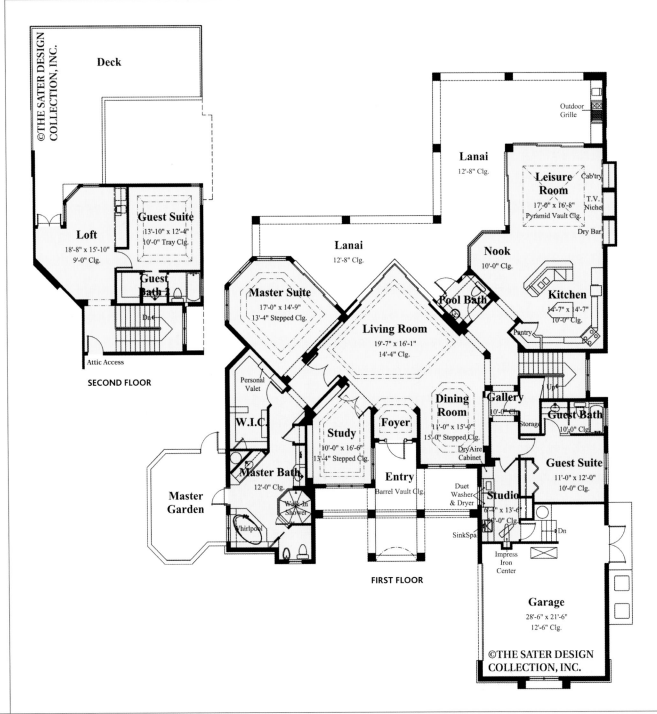

~ *Any plan can be customized to meet your needs, find out how by calling* **800-718-7526**. ~

REAR ELEVATION

Prairie Pine Court

© Sater Design Collection, Inc.

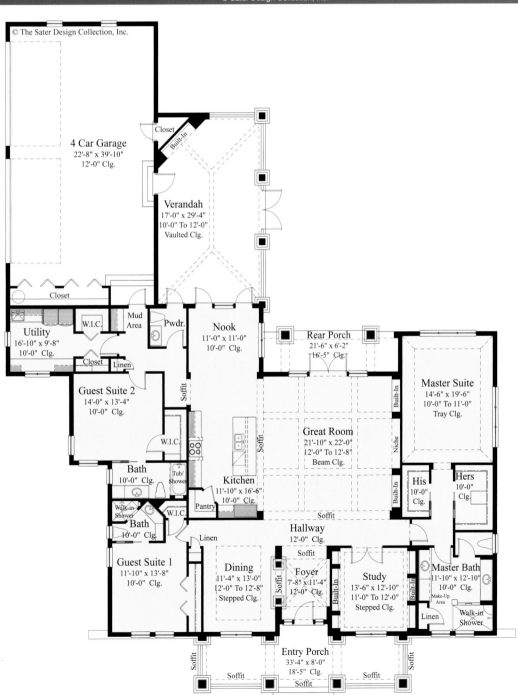

© The Sater Design Collection, Inc.

4 Car Garage
22'-8" x 39'-10"
12'-0" Clg.

Closet

Closet

Verandah
17'-0" x 29'-4"
10'-0" To 12'-0"
Vaulted Clg.

Utility
16'-10" x 9'-8"
10'-0" Clg.

W.I.C.

Closet

Mud Area

Pwdr.

Linen

Nook
11'-0" x 11'-0"
10'-0" Clg.

Rear Porch
21'-6" x 6'-2"
16'-5" Clg.

Master Suite
14'-6" x 19'-6"
10'-0" To 11'-0"
Tray Clg.

Guest Suite 2
14'-0" x 13'-4"
10'-0" Clg.

Soffit

W.I.C.

Great Room
21'-10" x 22'-0"
12'-0" To 12'-8"
Beam Clg.

Built-In

Niche

Bath
10'-0" Clg.

Tub/Shower

Kitchen
11'-10" x 16'-6"
10'-0" Clg.

Soffit

His
10'-0" Clg.

Hers
10'-0" Clg.

Walk-in Shower

Bath
10'-0" Clg.

W.I.C.

Pantry

Soffit

Hallway
12'-0" Clg.

Built-In

Linen

Guest Suite 1
11'-10" x 13'-8"
10'-0" Clg.

Dining
11'-4" x 13'-0"
12'-0" To 12'-8"
Stepped Clg.

Soffit

Foyer
7'-8" x 11'-4"
12'-0" Clg.

Study
13'-6" x 12'-10"
11'-0" To 12'-0"
Stepped Clg.

Built-In

Master Bath
11'-10" x 12'-10"
10'-0" Clg.

Make-Up Area

Linen

Walk-in Shower

Soffit

Entry Porch
33'-4" x 8'-0"
18'-5" Clg.

Soffit

Soffit

Soffit

Soffit

Soffit

Not available for construction in Lee County, Florida.

SPECIFICATIONS:

Bedrooms: **3**

Baths: **3½**

Width: **78' 0"**

Depth: **102' 8"**

1st Floor: **3108** *sf*

Total Living: **3108** *sf*

Foundation: **Slab**

PLAN PRICING:

Vellum & PDF - **$1554**

CAD - **$2797**

PLAN NUMBER:
7083

Our Prairie Pine Court home plan is a modern translation of a Prairie styled farmhouse. This is evident by its hipped rooflines. The Prairie Pine Court has broad, bracketed eaves and an entry porch supported by stone pilasters and square tapered columns. Cement fiber siding with the bold continuous cornice emphasizes the strong horizontal plains of the prairie. The rear garage de-emphasizes the auto and celebrates the home.

REAR ELEVATION

Toscana

© Sater Design Collection, Inc.

SPECIFICATIONS:

Bedrooms: **3**

Baths: **2**

Width: **64' 10"**

Depth: **55' 2"**

1st Floor: **2331** *sf*

Total Living: **2331** *sf*

Foundation: **Slab**

PLAN PRICING:

Vellum & PDF - **$1166**

CAD - **$2098**

PLAN NUMBER:

6758

Its grand facade with characteristic turrets and majestic open entry gives way to an interior that is spacious, casual and ideal for entertaining. A graceful arch creates an inviting transition into the dining room, where a pair of arch-top windows offers sunset views. A delightful tile-front fireplace with coffered mantle serves as an art niche, the centerpiece of an airy great room made even more spacious by retreating glass doors.

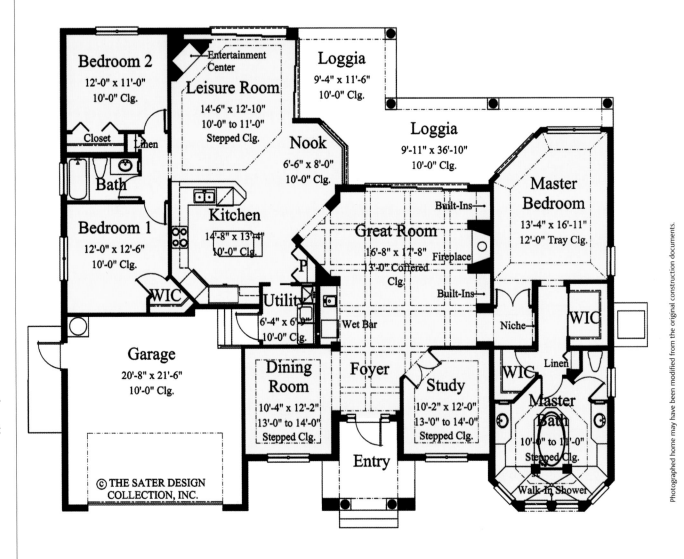

Bedroom 2
12'-0" x 11'-0"
10'-0" Clg.

Closet

Linen

Bath

Bedroom 1
12'-0" x 12'-6"
10'-0" Clg.

WIC

Entertainment Center

Leisure Room
14'-6" x 12'-10"
10'-0" to 11'-0"
Stepped Clg.

Kitchen
14'-8" x 13'-4"
10'-0" Clg.

Nook
6'-6" x 8'-0"
10'-0" Clg.

Loggia
9'-4" x 11'-6"
10'-0" Clg.

Loggia
9'-11" x 36'-10"
10'-0" Clg.

Built-Ins

Great Room
16'-8" x 17'-8"
13'-0" Coffered Clg.

Fireplace

Built-Ins

Master Bedroom
13'-4" x 16'-11"
12'-0" Tray Clg.

Niche

WIC

WIC

Linen

Utility
6'-4" x 6'-9"
10'-0" Clg.

Wet Bar

Garage
20'-8" x 21'-6"
10'-0" Clg.

Dining Room
10'-4" x 12'-2"
13'-0" to 14'-0"
Stepped Clg.

Foyer

Study
10'-2" x 12'-0"
13'-0" to 14'-0"
Stepped Clg.

Master Bath
10'-0" to 11'-0"
Stepped Clg.

Walk-In Shower

Entry

© THE SATER DESIGN COLLECTION, INC.

Photographed home may have been modified from the original construction documents.

~ *Any plan can be customized to meet your needs, find out how by calling* 800-718-7526. ~

REAR ELEVATION

Isabel

© Sater Design Collection, Inc.

FIRST FLOOR

Lanai
12'-0" Clg.

Guest
Bath

Outdoor
Kitchen

Leisure
Room
17'-4" x 22'-11"
12'-0" - 14'-0"
Vaulted Clg.

Guest
Suite
12'-5" x 17'-8"
10'-0" - 11'-0"
Stepped Clg.

Lanai
12'-0" Clg.

Fireplace

Nook
12'-0" Clg.

Master Suite
16'-2" x 21'-10"
10'-0" - 12'-0"
Stepped Clg.

Living Room
18'-8" x 19'-1"
12'-0" - 14'-0"
Stepped Clg.

Kitchen
16'-0" x 14'-6"
11'-0" - 12'-0"
Stepped Clg.

Pantry

Atrium

Fountain

WIC

WIC

Study
13'-0" x 13'-0"
12'-0" - 13'-0"
Stepped Clg.

Foyer

Dining
13'-0" x 13'-0"
12'-0" - 13'-0"
Stepped Clg.

Bath 2

Bedroom 2
16'-6" x 11'-6"
10'-0" Clg.

Master
Bath
10'-0" Clg.

Entry

Utility

UP

CL.

WIC

Privacy
Garden

Porte-Cochere

Garage
22'-8" x 32'-10"
9'-0" Clg. AFF

© The Sater Design
Collection, Inc.

OPTIONAL BONUS ROOM

Dwn.

Bonus
Room
23'-3" x 19'-10"
Vaulted Ceiling

WIC

Storage

© The Sater Design
Collection, Inc.

Photographed home may have been modified from the original construction documents.

SPECIFICATIONS:

Bedrooms: **3**

Baths: **3**

Width: **88' 4"**

Depth: **104' 4"**

1st Floor: **3273** *sf*

Total Living: **3273** *sf*

Opt. Bonus Room: **467** *sf*

Foundation: **Slab**

PLAN PRICING:

Vellum & PDF - **$1637**

PLAN NUMBER:

6938

An impressive porte-cochere distinguishes Isabel from the street-scape. Octagonal and diamond-shaped rooms are connected in an open floor plan, yet distinguished by elegant ceiling treatments and columns. Walls of glass grant endless views in every room. A side atrium with a fountain provides a unique outdoor living space.

Manchester

© Sater Design Collection, Inc.

Gavello

© Sater Design Collection, Inc.

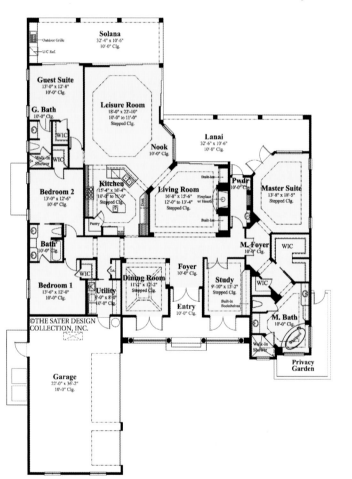

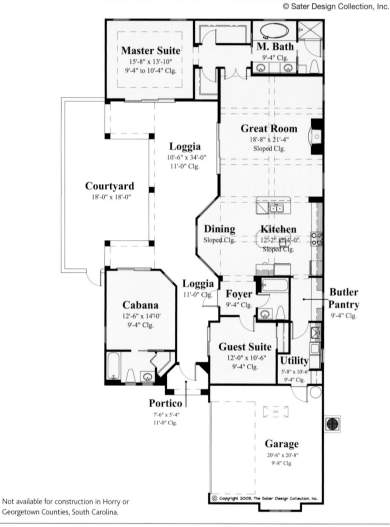

Photographed home may have been modified from the original construction documents.

Not available for construction in Horry or Georgetown Counties, South Carolina.

SPECIFICATIONS:

Bedrooms: **4**

Baths: **3**

Width: **68' 8"**

Depth: **106' 0"**

1st Floor: **3331** sf

Total Living: **3331** sf

FOUNDATION:

Slab

PLAN PRICING:

Vellum & PDF - **$1666**

CAD - **$2998**

PLAN NUMBER:

7080

SPECIFICATIONS:

Bedrooms: **3**

Baths: **3**

Width: **40' 0"**

Depth: **89' 0"**

1st Floor: **1629** sf

Cabana: **263** sf

Total Living: **1892** sf

FOUNDATION:

Slab

PLAN PRICING:

Vellum & PDF - **$946**

CAD - **$1703**

PLAN NUMBER:

6553

~ Any plan can be customized to meet your needs, find out how by calling 800-718-7526. ~

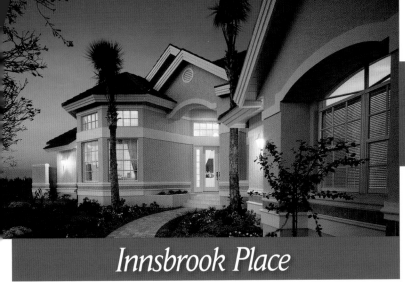

Innsbrook Place

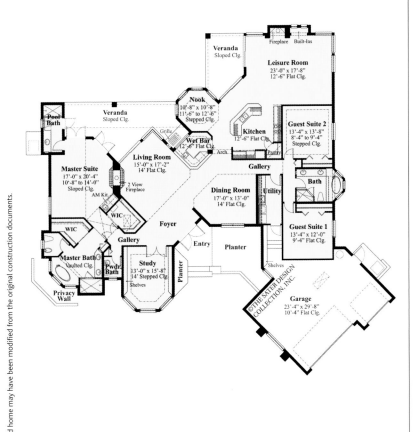

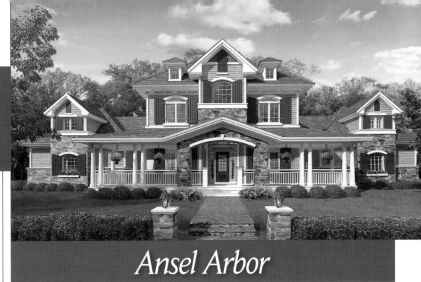

Ansel Arbor

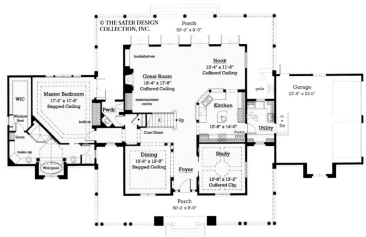

FIRST FLOOR

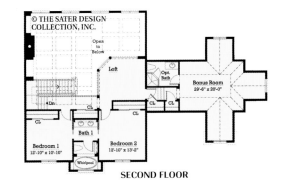

SECOND FLOOR

Photographed home may have been modified from the original construction documents.

SPECIFICATIONS:

Bedrooms: **3**

Baths: **3½**

Width: **95' 0"**

Depth: **88' 8"**

1st Floor: **3477** *sf*

Total Living: **3477** *sf*

FOUNDATION:

Slab

PLAN PRICING:

Vellum & PDF - **$1739**

CAD - **$3129**

PLAN NUMBER:

6634

SPECIFICATIONS:

Bedrooms: **3**

Baths: **2½**

Width: **98' 0"**

Depth: **56' 0"**

1st Floor: **2151** *sf*

2nd Floor: **738** *sf*

Total Living: **2889** *sf*

Opt. Bonus Room: **534** *sf*

FOUNDATION:

Crawl Space

PLAN PRICING:

Vellum & PDF - **$1445**

CAD - **$2600**

PLAN NUMBER:

7023

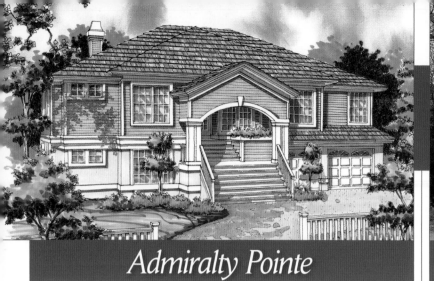

Admiralty Pointe

© Sater Design Collection, Inc.

Montego Bay

© Sater Design Collection, Inc.

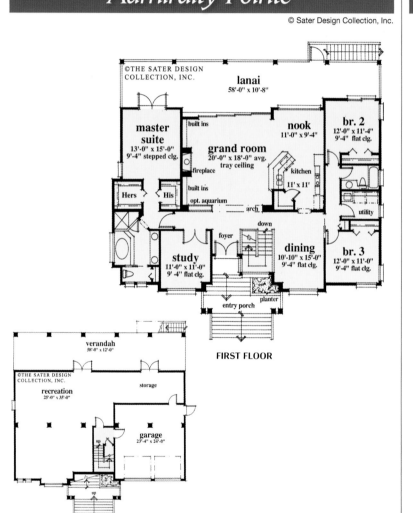

©THE SATER DESIGN COLLECTION, INC.

lanai
58'-0" x 10'-8"

master suite
13'-0" x 15'-0"
9'-4" stepped clg.

built ins

grand room
20'-0" x 18'-0" avg.
tray ceiling

fireplace

built ins

Hers   His

opt. aquarium

arch

study
11'-0" x 11'-0"
9'-4" flat clg.

foyer

down

nook
11'-0" x 9'-4"

kitchen
11' x 11'

dining
10'-10" x 15'-0"
9'-4" flat clg.

br. 2
12'-0" x 11'-4"
9'-4" flat clg.

utility

br. 3
12'-0" x 11'-0"
9'-4" flat clg.

entry porch   planter

FIRST FLOOR

©THE SATER DESIGN COLLECTION, INC.

verandah
58'-0" x 12'-0"

storage

recreation
25'-0" x 35'-0"

up

garage
23'-4" x 24'-0"

up

LOWER LEVEL

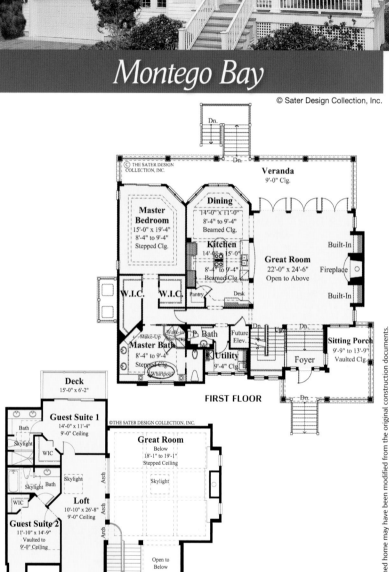

©THE SATER DESIGN COLLECTION, INC.

Veranda
9'-0" Clg.

Master Bedroom
15'-0" x 19'-4"
8'-4" to 9'-4"
Stepped Clg.

Dining
14'-0" x 11'-0"
8'-4" to 9'-4"
Beamed Clg.

Kitchen
14'-0" x 15'-0"
8'-4" to 9'-4"
Beamed Clg.

Great Room
22'-0" x 24'-6"
Open to Above

Built-In

Fireplace

Built-In

W.I.C.   W.I.C.   pantry   Desk

Walk-In Shower

Master Bath
8'-4" to 9'-4"
Stepped Clg.

Make-Up

Bath

Future Elev.

Whirlpool

Utility
9'-4"

Dn.

Dn.

Sitting Porch
9'-9" to 13'-9"
Vaulted Clg.

Foyer

FIRST FLOOR

Dn.

Deck
15'-0" x 6'-2"

Bath

Skylight

WIC

Guest Suite 1
14'-0" x 11'-4"
9'-0" Ceiling

Skylight

Bath

WIC

Guest Suite 2
11'-10" x 14'-9"
Vaulted to
9'-0" Ceiling

Skylight

Loft
10'-10" x 26'-8"
9'-0" Ceiling

Arch

Arch

Arch

Great Room
Below
18'-1" to 19'-1"
Stepped Ceiling

Skylight

Open to
Below

©THE SATER DESIGN COLLECTION, INC.

SECOND FLOOR

Photographed home may have been modified from the original construction documents.

SPECIFICATIONS:

Bedrooms: **3**

Baths: **2**

Width: **59' 8"**

Depth: **54' 0"**

1ˢᵗ Floor: **2190** sf

Total Living: **2190** sf

FOUNDATION:

Slab

PLAN PRICING:

Vellum & PDF - **$1095**

PLAN NUMBER:

6622

SPECIFICATIONS:

Bedrooms: **3**

Baths: **3½**

Width: **58' 0"**

Depth: **54' 0"**

1ˢᵗ Floor: **2118** sf

2ⁿᵈ Floor: **929** sf

Lower Level: **281** sf

Total Living: **3328** sf

FOUNDATION:

Island Basement

PLAN PRICING:

Vellum & PDF - **$1664**

CAD - **$2995**

PLAN NUMBER:

6800

Bartolini

© Sater Design Collection, Inc.

ARDA Award Winner!

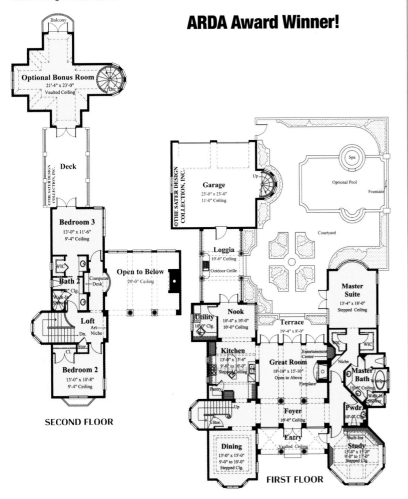

SECOND FLOOR

FIRST FLOOR

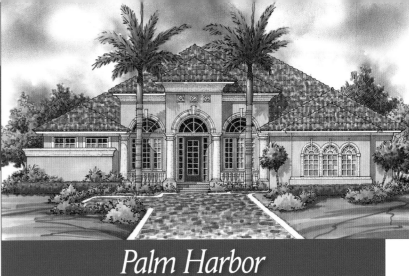

Palm Harbor

© Sater Design Collection, Inc.

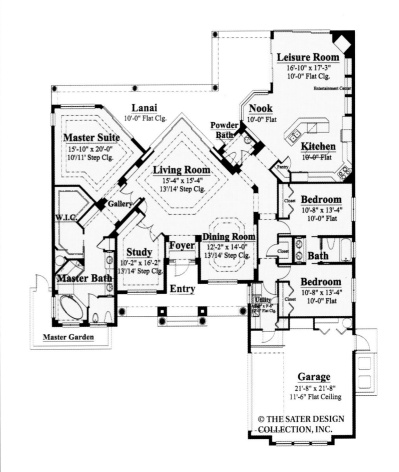

© THE SATER DESIGN COLLECTION, INC.

SPECIFICATIONS:

Bedrooms: **3**

Baths: **2½**

Width: **60' 6"**

Depth: **94' 0"**

1st Floor: **2084** sf

2nd Floor: **648** sf

Total Living: **2732** sf

Opt. Bonus Room: **364** sf

FOUNDATION:

Slab

PLAN PRICING:

Vellum & PDF - **$1366**

CAD - **$2459**

PLAN NUMBER:

8022

SPECIFICATIONS:

Bedrooms: **3**

Baths: **2½**

Width: **65' 0"**

Depth: **85' 4"**

1st Floor: **2823** sf

Total Living: **2823** sf

FOUNDATION:

Slab

PLAN PRICING:

Vellum & PDF - **$1412**

CAD - **$2541**

PLAN NUMBER:

6727

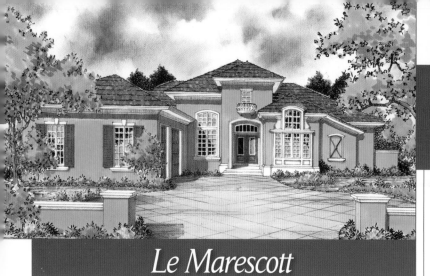

Le Marescott

© Sater Design Collection, Inc.

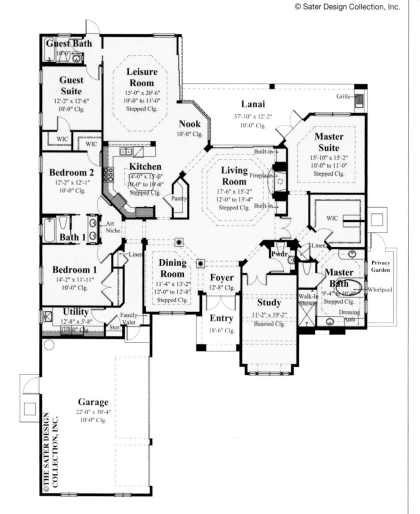

Guest Bath

Guest Suite
12'-2" x 12'-6"
10'-0" Clg.

Leisure Room
15'-0" x 20'-6"
10'-0" to 11'-0"
Stepped Clg.

Nook
10'-0" Clg.

Lanai
37'-10" x 12'-2"
10'-0" Clg.

Grille

WIC   WIC

Bedroom 2
12'-2" x 12'-1"
10'-0" Clg.

Kitchen
14'-0" x 15'-0"
18'-0" to 10'-8"
Stepped Clg.

Pantry

Living Room
17'-6" x 15'-2"
12'-0" to 13'-4"
Stepped Clg.

Fireplace

Built-in

Master Suite
15'-10" x 15'-2"
10'-0" to 11'-0"
Stepped Clg.

Built-in

WIC

Art Niche

Bath 1

Bedroom 1
14'-2" x 11'-11"
10'-0" Clg.

Linen

Dining Room
11'-4" x 13'-2"
12'-0" to 12'-8"
Stepped Clg.

Foyer
12'-8" Clg.

Pwdr.

Linen

Master Bath
9'-4" to 10'-0"
Stepped Clg.

Privacy Garden

Whirlpool

Utility
12'-8" x 5'-8"
10'-0" Clg.

Family Valet

Stor.

Entry
18'-6" Clg.

Study
11'-2" x 19'-2"
Beamed Clg.

Walk-In Shower

Dressing Area

Garage
22'-0" x 30'-4"
10'-0" Clg.

©THE SATER DESIGN COLLECTION, INC.

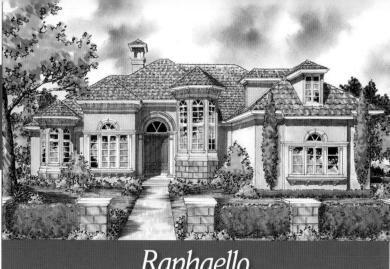

Raphaello

© Sater Design Collection, Inc.

Lanai
26'-0" x 15'-10"
10'-0" Clg.

Master Suite
13'-8" x 21'-2"
12'-0" to 13'-0"
Stepped Clg.

Bath 1

Great Room
21'-3" x 17'-8"
Vaulted w/
Beamed Clg.

Nook
9'-0" to 10'-0"
Stepped Clg.

Fireplace

Entertainment Center

Built-In Shelves

Dining Room
11'-10" x 12'-8"
9'-0" to 10'-0"
Coffered Clg.

Kitchen
13'-0" x 13'-9"

WIC   WIC

Foyer
18'-8" to 19'-8"
Stepped Clg.

Gallery
10'-0" Clg.

Utility
6'-8" x 9'-2"
10'-0" Clg.

Master Bath
12'-0" Clg.

Study
15'-4" x 15'-4"
16'-4" to 17'-4"
Beamed Clg.

Entry
18'-8" Clg.

Pwdr.

Storage

Up

Garage
21'-0" x 25'-4"
10'-0" Clg.

Whirlpool

©THE SATER DESIGN COLLECTION, INC.

FIRST FLOOR

©THE Sater DESIGN COLLECTION, INC.

Deck
26'-6" x 15'-10"

Bedroom 1
13'-0" x 14'-6"
9'-4" to 10'-4"
Tray Clg.

Bedroom 2
12'-2" x 14'-4"
10'-0" Clg.

Bath 2
10'-0" Clg.

WIC

Loft
10'-0" Clg.

Desk

Niche

Dn.

Bonus Bath

Optional Bonus Room
16'-6" x 19'-2"
Vaulted to
20'-8" Clg.

SECOND FLOOR

SPECIFICATIONS:

Bedrooms: **4**
Baths: **3½**
Width: **67' 0"**
Depth: **90' 8"**
1st Floor: **3166** sf
Total Living: **3166** sf

FOUNDATION:

Slab

PLAN PRICING:

Vellum & PDF - **$1583**
CAD - **$2849**

PLAN NUMBER:

8060

SPECIFICATIONS:

Bedrooms: **3**
Baths: **3½**
Width: **72' 0"**
Depth: **68' 3"**
1st Floor: **2250** sf
2nd Floor: **663** sf
Total Living: **2913** sf
Opt. Bonus Room: **351** sf

FOUNDATION:

Slab

PLAN PRICING:

Vellum & PDF - **$1457**
CAD - **$2622**

PLAN NUMBER:

8037

~ *Any plan can be customized to meet your needs, find out how by calling* **800-718-7526**. ~

Christabel

© Sater Design Collection, Inc.

Santa Trinita

© Sater Design Collection, Inc.

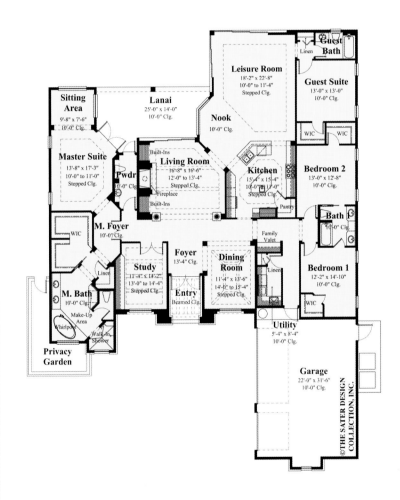

SPECIFICATIONS:

Bedrooms: **4**

Baths: **3½**

Width: **74' 8"**

Depth: **118' 0"**

1st Floor: **3271** sf

Total Living: **3271** sf

FOUNDATION:

Slab

PLAN PRICING:

Vellum & PDF - **$1636**

CAD - **$2944**

PLAN NUMBER:

8053

SPECIFICATIONS:

Bedrooms: **4**

Baths: **3½**

Width: **68' 8"**

Depth: **91' 8"**

1st Floor: **3497** sf

Total Living: **3497** sf

FOUNDATION:

Slab

PLAN PRICING:

Vellum & PDF - **$1749**

CAD - **$3147**

PLAN NUMBER:

8063

Brittany

© Sater Design Collection, Inc.

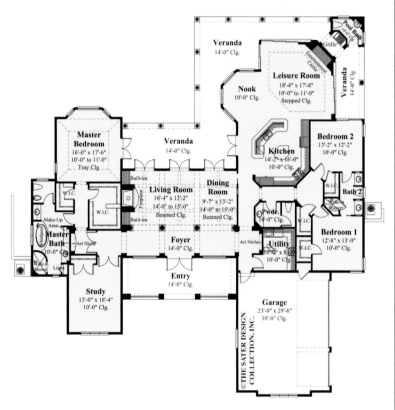

Berkley

© Sater Design Collection, Inc.

FIRST FLOOR

SECOND FLOOR

SPECIFICATIONS:

Bedrooms: **3**

Full Baths: **2**

Half Baths: **2**

Width: **84' 0"**

Depth: **92' 0"**

1st Floor: **3343** sf

Total Living: **3343** sf

FOUNDATION:

Slab

PLAN PRICING:

Vellum & PDF - **$1672**

CAD - **$3009**

PLAN NUMBER:

8040

SPECIFICATIONS:

Bedrooms: **4**

Baths: **3½**

Width: **91' 0"**

Depth: **52' 8"**

1st Floor: **2219** sf

2nd Floor: **1085** sf

Total Living: **3304** sf

Opt. Bonus Room: **404** sf

FOUNDATION:

Slab

PLAN PRICING:

Vellum & PDF - **$1652**

CAD - **$2974**

PLAN NUMBER:

8006

Jasmine Lane

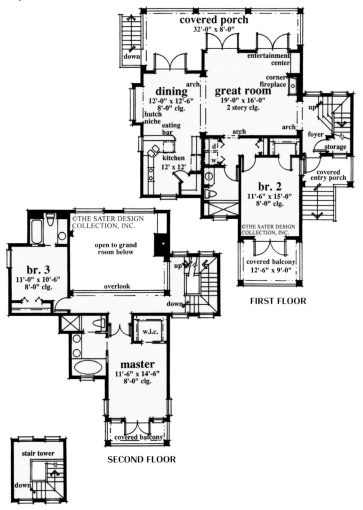

FIRST FLOOR

SECOND FLOOR

Nassau Cove

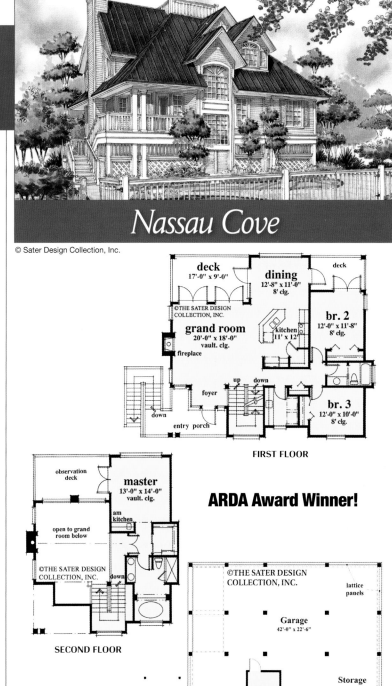

FIRST FLOOR

ARDA Award Winner!

SECOND FLOOR

LOWER LEVEL

SPECIFICATIONS:

Bedrooms: **3**

Baths: **3**

Width: **43' 8"**

Depth: **53' 6"**

1st Floor: **1007** sf

2nd Floor: **869** sf

Total Living: **1876** sf

FOUNDATION:

Crawl Space

PLAN PRICING:

Vellum & PDF - **$938**

CAD - **$1688**

PLAN NUMBER:

6680

SPECIFICATIONS:

Bedrooms: **3**

Baths: **2**

Width: **44' 0"**

Depth: **40' 0"**

1st Floor: **1342** sf

2nd Floor: **511** sf

Lower Level: **33** sf

Total Living: **1886** sf

FOUNDATION:

Island Basement

PLAN PRICING:

Vellum & PDF - **$943**

PLAN NUMBER:

6654

Ascott

© Sater Design Collection, Inc.

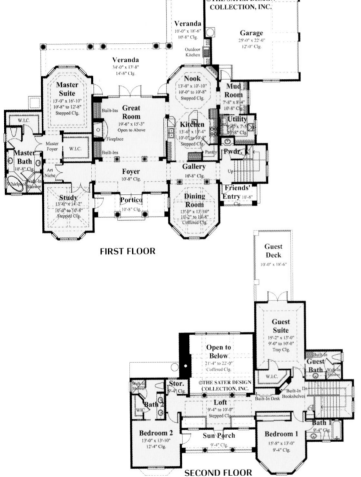

FIRST FLOOR

SECOND FLOOR

Newberry

© Sater Design Collection, Inc.

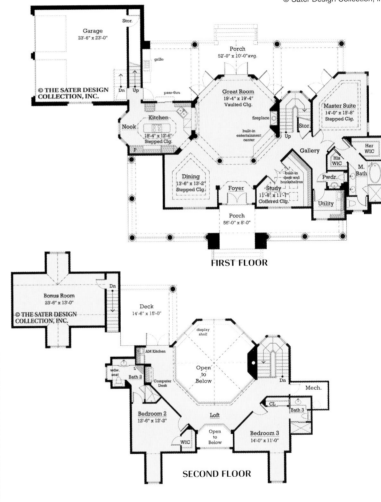

FIRST FLOOR

SECOND FLOOR

SPECIFICATIONS:

Bedrooms: **4**
Baths: **4½**
Width: **80' 0"**
Depth: **63' 9"**
1st Floor: **2226** sf
2nd Floor: **1248** sf
Total Living: **3474** sf

FOUNDATION:

Slab

PLAN PRICING:

Vellum & PDF - **$1737**

PLAN NUMBER:

8019

SPECIFICATIONS:

Bedrooms: **3**
Baths: **3½**
Width: **90' 6"**
Depth: **61' 0"**
1st Floor: **1853** sf
2nd Floor: **955** sf
Total Living: **2808** sf
Opt. Bonus Room: **424** sf

FOUNDATION:

Slab

PLAN PRICING:

Vellum & PDF - **$975**
CAD - **$1595**

PLAN NUMBER:

7059

Salcito

FIRST FLOOR

SECOND FLOOR

Alexandre

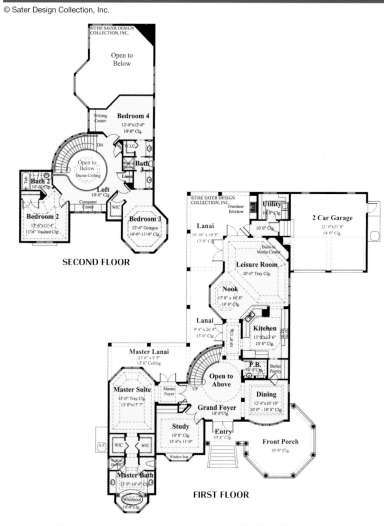

SECOND FLOOR

FIRST FLOOR

SPECIFICATIONS:

Bedrooms: **4**

Baths: **4½**

Width: **45' 0"**

Depth: **94' 0"**

1st Floor: **2087** sf

2nd Floor: **1099** sf

Cabana: **272** sf

Total Living: **3458** sf

FOUNDATION:

Slab

PLAN PRICING:

Vellum & PDF - **$1729**

CAD - **$3112**

PLAN NUMBER:

6787

SPECIFICATIONS:

Bedrooms: **4**

Baths: **3½**

Width: **74' 0"**

Depth: **88' 0"**

1st Floor: **2083** sf

2nd Floor: **1013** sf

Total Living: **3096** sf

FOUNDATION:

Crawl Space

PLAN PRICING:

Vellum & PDF - **$1548**

CAD - **$2786**

PLAN NUMBER:

6849

Bellini

© Sater Design Collection, Inc.

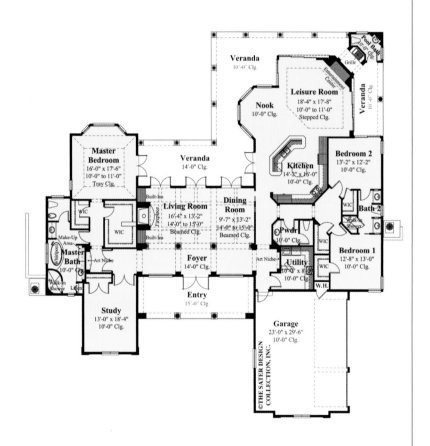

Torrey Pines Way

© Sater Design Collection, Inc.

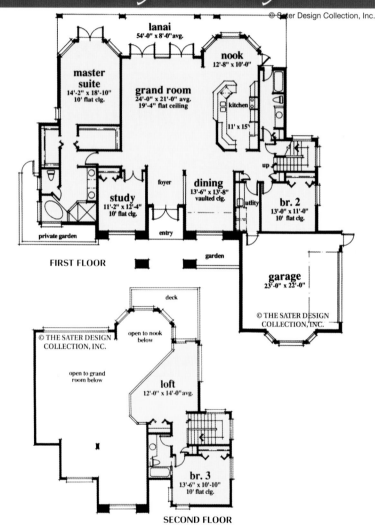

SPECIFICATIONS:

Bedrooms: **3**

Full Baths: **2**

Half Baths: **2**

Width: **84' 0"**

Depth: **92' 2"**

1st Floor: **3343** *sf*

Total Living: **3343** *sf*

FOUNDATION:

Slab

PLAN PRICING:

Vellum & PDF - **$1672**

CAD - **$3009**

PLAN NUMBER:

8042

SPECIFICATIONS:

Bedrooms: **3**

Baths: **3**

Width: **72' 8"**

Depth: **72' 0"**

1st Floor: **2461** *sf*

2nd Floor: **520** *sf*

Total Living: **2981** *sf*

FOUNDATION:

Slab

PLAN PRICING:

Vellum & PDF - **$1491**

CAD - **$2683**

PLAN NUMBER:

6608

Spring Hill Lane

© Sater Design Collection, Inc.

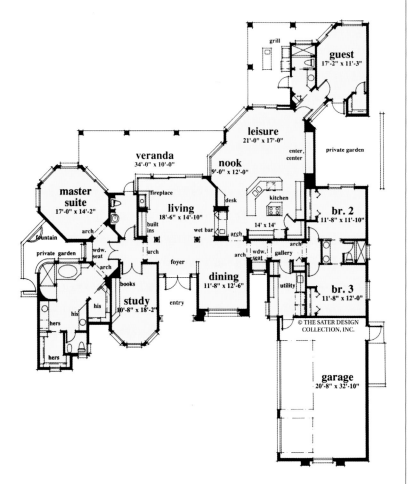

SPECIFICATIONS:

Bedrooms: **4**

Baths: **3½**

Width: **80' 0"**

Depth: **103' 8"**

1st Floor: **3301** sf

Total Living: **3301** sf

FOUNDATION:

Slab

PLAN PRICING:

Vellum & PDF - **$1651**

PLAN NUMBER:

6661

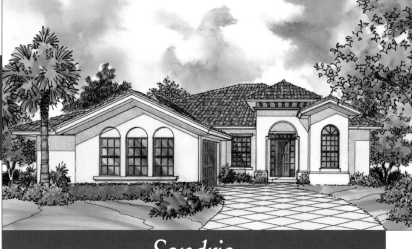

Sondrio

© Sater Design Collection, Inc.

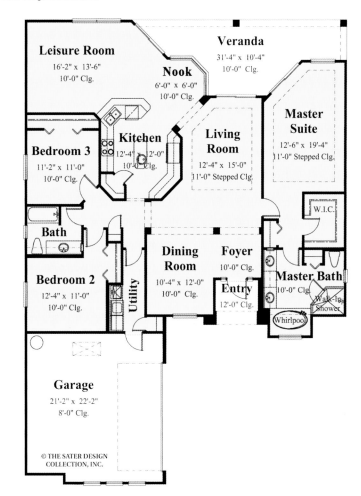

SPECIFICATIONS:

Bedrooms: **3**

Baths: **2**

Width: **50' 0"**

Depth: **69' 4"**

1st Floor: **2010** sf

Total Living: **2010** sf

FOUNDATION:

Slab

PLAN PRICING:

Vellum & PDF - **$1005**

CAD - **$1809**

PLAN NUMBER:

6511

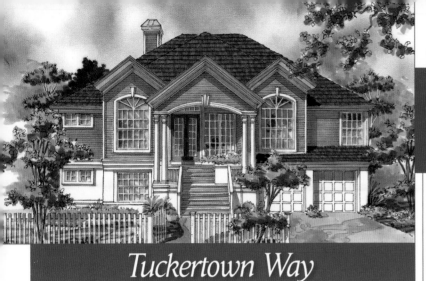

Tuckertown Way

© Sater Design Collection, Inc.

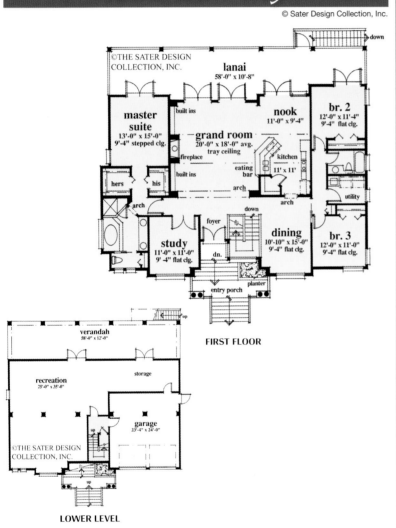

FIRST FLOOR

LOWER LEVEL

Montserrat

© Sater Design Collection, Inc.

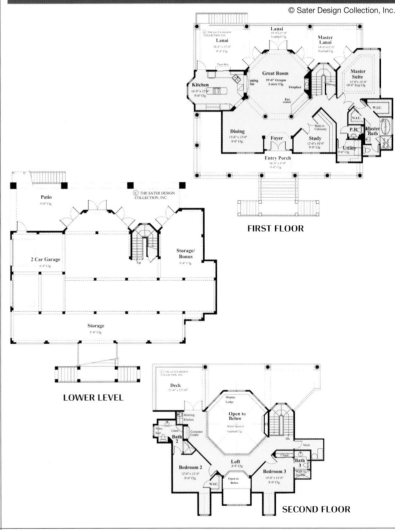

FIRST FLOOR

LOWER LEVEL

SECOND FLOOR

SPECIFICATIONS:

Bedrooms: **3**

Baths: **2**

Width: **59' 8"**

Depth: **54' 0"**

1st Floor: **2190** *sf*

Total Living: **2190** *sf*

FOUNDATION:

Island Basement

PLAN PRICING:

Vellum & PDF - **$1095**

CAD - **$1971**

PLAN NUMBER:
6692

SPECIFICATIONS:

Bedrooms: **3**

Baths: **3½**

Width: **66' 0"**

Depth: **50' 0"**

1st Floor: **1855** *sf*

2nd Floor: **901** *sf*

Total Living: **2756** *sf*

Lower Level: **1010** *sf*

FOUNDATION:

Island Basement

PLAN PRICING:

Vellum & PDF - **$1378**

CAD - **$2480**

PLAN NUMBER:
6858

Galleon Bay

© Sater Design Collection, Inc.

FIRST FLOOR

SECOND FLOOR

LOWER LEVEL

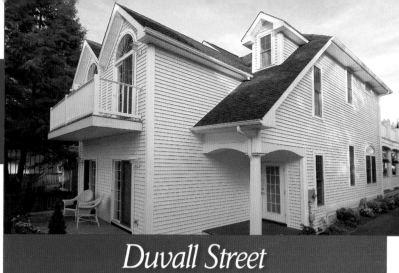

Duvall Street

© Sater Design Collection, Inc.

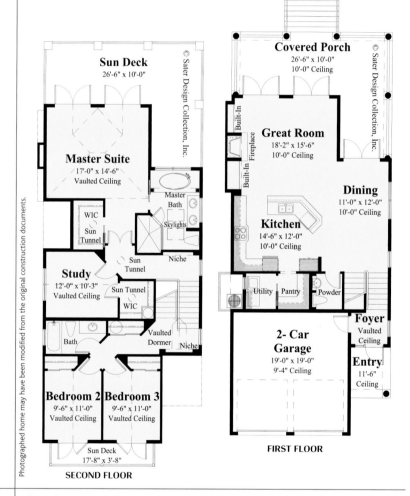

FIRST FLOOR

SECOND FLOOR

Photographed home may have been modified from the original construction documents.

SPECIFICATIONS:

Bedrooms: **3**

Baths: **3½**

Width: **64' 0"**

Depth: **45' 0"**

1st Floor: **2174** sf

2nd Floor: **827** sf

Lower Level: **119** sf

Total Living: **3120** sf

Bonus Room: **960** sf

FOUNDATION:

Island Basement

PLAN PRICING:

Vellum & PDF - **$1560**

CAD - **$2808**

PLAN NUMBER:

6620

SPECIFICATIONS:

Bedrooms: **3**

Baths: **2½**

Width: **27' 6"**

Depth: **64' 0"**

1st Floor: **878** sf

2nd Floor: **1245** sf

Total Living: **2123** sf

FOUNDATION:

Crawl Space

PLAN PRICING:

Vellum & PDF - **$1062**

PLAN NUMBER:

6701

Saint Basque

© Sater Design Collection, Inc.

Biltmore Trace

© Sater Design Collection, Inc.

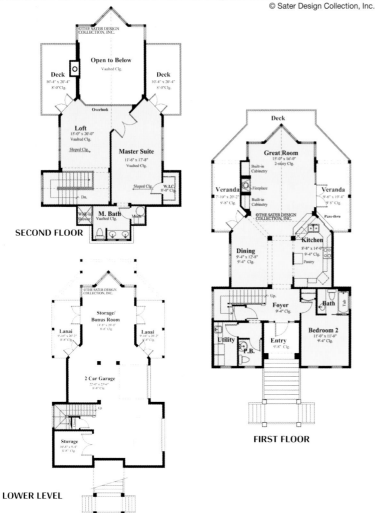

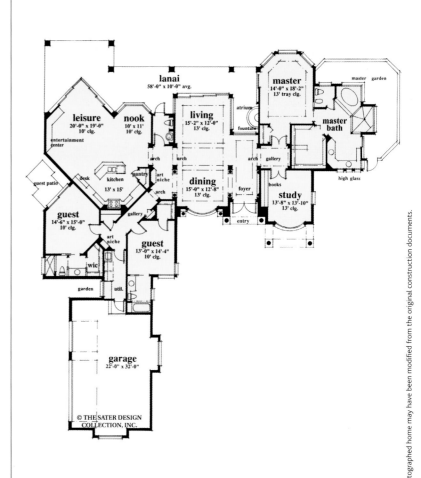

SPECIFICATIONS:
Bedrooms: **2**
Baths: **2½**
Width: **32' 0"**
Depth: **57' 0"**
1st Floor: **1143** sf
2nd Floor: **651** sf
Total Living: **1794** sf
Lower Level: **1200** sf

FOUNDATION:
Island Basement

PLAN PRICING:
Vellum & PDF - **$897**
CAD - **$1615**

PLAN NUMBER:
6851

SPECIFICATIONS:
Bedrooms: **3**
Baths: **3½**
Width: **90' 0"**
Depth: **105' 0"**
1st Floor: **3244** sf
Total Living: **3244** sf

FOUNDATION:
Slab

PLAN PRICING:
Vellum & PDF - **$1622**

PLAN NUMBER:
6657

~ Any plan can be customized to meet your needs, find out how by calling 800-718-7526. ~

Porta Rosa

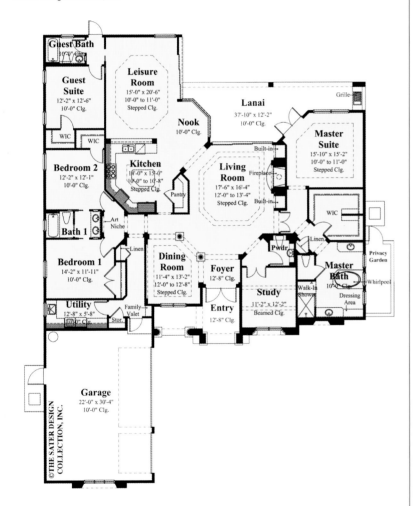

Southhampton Bay

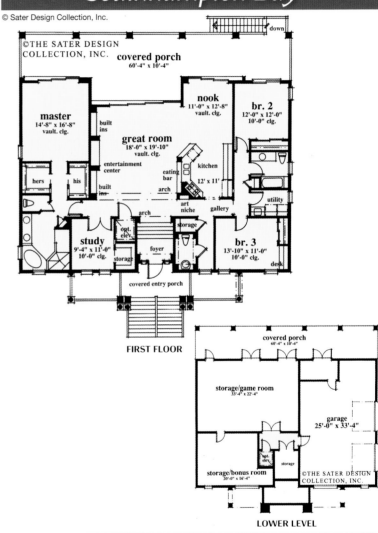

FIRST FLOOR

LOWER LEVEL

SPECIFICATIONS:

Bedrooms: **4**

Baths: **3½**

Width: **67' 0"**

Depth: **91' 8"**

1st Floor: **3166** *sf*

Total Living: **3166** *sf*

FOUNDATION:

Slab

PLAN PRICING:

Vellum & PDF - **$1583**

CAD - **$2849**

PLAN NUMBER:

8058

SPECIFICATIONS:

Bedrooms: **3**

Baths: **2½**

Width: **60' 4"**

Depth: **59' 4"**

1st Floor: **2385** *sf*

Lower Level: **80** *sf*

Total Living: **2465** *sf*

FOUNDATION:

Island Basement

PLAN PRICING:

Vellum & PDF - **$1233**

CAD - **$2219**

PLAN NUMBER:

6684

~ *Any plan can be customized to meet your needs, find out how by calling 800-718-7526.* ~

WHAT'S IN A SET OF plans?

A set of plans is a collection of drawings that show the important structural components and how the home should be built. Architectural and construction terms are complex. If you have further questions about these terms, ask your builder or visit our glossary online at www.saterdesign.com.

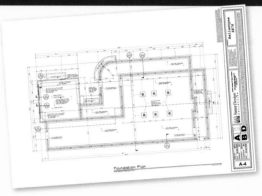

COVER SHEET, INDEX & SITE PLAN — The cover sheet features an elevation of the exterior of the house that shows approximately how the home will look when built. The index lists the order of the drawings included, with page numbers for easy reference. The site plan is a scaled footprint of the house to help determine how the home will be placed on the building site.

FOUNDATION LAYOUT PLAN — This sheet provides a fully dimensioned and noted foundation layout, including references to footings, pads and support walls. For plans with a basement, additional walls and columns may be shown. Basement plans come with a floor framing layout which may be included in this section of the floor framing section, depending on the plan. Actual structural information should be obtained by a locally licensed engineer for your specific site location.

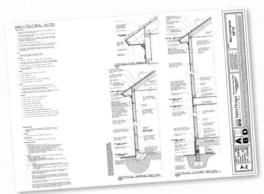

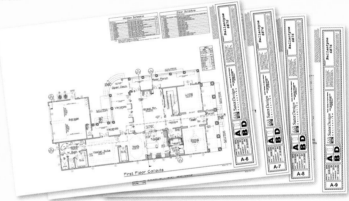

WALL SECTION & NOTES — This section shows section cuts of the exterior wall from the roof down through the foundation. These wall sections specify the home's construction and building materials. They also show the number of stories, type of foundation and the construction of the walls. Roofing materials, insulation, floor framing, wall finishes and elevation heights are all shown and referenced.

DETAILED FLOOR PLAN — This section provides detailed drawings and descriptions of all the elements that will be included on each floor of the home. The home's exterior footprint, openings and interior rooms are carefully dimensioned. Important features are noted including built-ins, niches and appliances. All doors and windows are identified. Typically this section also includes the square footage information.

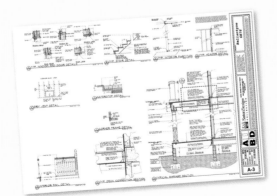

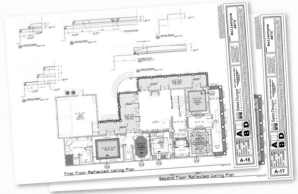

TYPICAL DETAILS & NOTES — This section addresses all the facets and details you will want to include in your home, with the exception of local building code requirements. Architectural and structural elements are detailed, including: window and door components, railings, balusters, wood stairs and headers, interior walls, interior partitions, concrete steps and footings (if applicable).

REFLECTED CEILING PLAN — One of Sater home's most distinguishable features is the highly detailed ceiling treatments. This section shows ceiling heights and treatments. It also shows the details, profiles and finishes of the ceiling treatments. Arches and soffits are also specified in this section.

bonus:

GREEN SOLUTIONS GUIDE — Guide designed to help make decisions about the level of green building you wish to implement in the construction of your home.

MATERIALS LIST — A Guide to assist in pricing and construction of a Sater home.

electronic plans:

Our plans are also available in an electronic format, supplied on a CD-ROM. All of the features explained below are included on this disk.

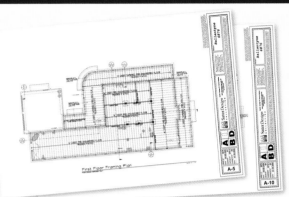

FLOOR FRAMING PLANS — Homes with a basement or crawl space will have a floor framing plan for the first floor. Multi-story homes will have floor framing plans for upper floors as well. The floor framing plans provide structural information such as the joist location, spacing and direction, as well as the floor heights and stair openings.

CROSS SECTION & DETAILS — This section will illustrate the important changes in the floor, ceiling and roof heights or the relationship of different floors to one another. Interior elements of rooms and areas, such as columns, arches, headers and soffits, are also discernible and easier to visualize in a cross section.

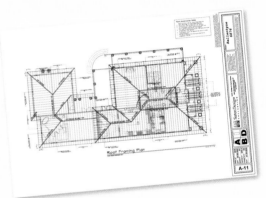

ROOF PLAN — The overall layout and necessary details for roof design are provided in this section. If trusses are used, we suggest using a local truss manufacturer to design your roof trusses to comply with your local codes and regulations.

INTERIOR ELEVATIONS — These elevations show the specific details and design of the kitchen, bathrooms, utility rooms, fireplaces, bookcases, built-in units and other special interior features. The interior elevations vary based on the complexity of the home.

EXTERIOR ELEVATIONS — Elevations are drawings that show how the finished home will approximately look. In this section, elevations of the front, rear and left and right sides of the home are shown. Exterior materials, details and heights are noted on these drawings.

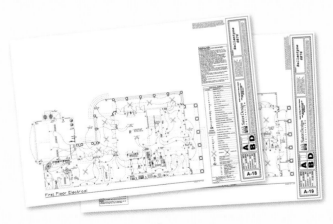

ELECTRICAL PLAN — This section shows an electrical plan that will enhance functionality and highlight the unique architectural features of the home.

QUICK TURNAROUND

If you place your order before 3:00 P.M. eastern time, we can usually have your plans to you the next business day. Some restrictions may apply. We cannot ship to a post office box, so please be prepared to supply us with a physical street address.

OUR EXCHANGE POLICY

We do not accept returns because each set of plans or disk is generated just for you at the time of your order. However, if you should find that the plan you purchased does not meet your needs, we do permit exchanges requested within sixty days of the date of purchase. At the time of exchange, you will be charged a processing fee of 20% of the total of your original order plus the difference in price between the plans (if applicable) and the cost to ship the new plans to you.

WHAT FORMAT OF PLANS SHOULD I GET?

Our plans are available in three formats: PDF plan sets, a reproducible vellum set and an electronic version on a disk. Most people select a format based on the changes they will make to their plan.

PDF plan sets are the fastest, most convenient way to get going. With a PDF file you can obtain the necessary copies (up to twenty) at your local print shop. This saves you shipping costs and time.

Vellum is a special type of paper that can be erased for small changes, such as moving kitchen appliances, or enlarging a shower. You will receive one set of plans on the special paper with permission to make up to twenty copies for the construction process.

Most customers, and engineers, prefer the electronic version of the plans. The AutoCAD file facilitates major modifications and dimensional changes. You will receive one disk with permission to make up to twenty copies for the construction process.

LOCAL BUILDING CODES AND ZONING REQUIREMENTS

Our plans are designed to meet or exceed the International Residential Code. Because of the great differences in geography and climate, each state, county and municipality has its own building codes and zoning requirements. Your plan may need to be modified to comply with local requirements regarding snow loads, energy codes, soil and seismic conditions and a wide range of other matters. Prior to using plans ordered from us, we strongly advise that you consult a local building official.

ARCHITECTURAL AND/OR ENGINEERING REVIEW

Some cities and states require a licensed architect or engineer to review and approve any set of building documents prior to permitting. These cities and states want to ensure that the proposed new home will be code compliant, zoning compliant, safe, and structurally sound. Often, this architect or engineer will have to create additional structural drawings to be submitted for permitting. You can learn if this will be necessary in your area from a local building official.

DISCLAIMER

We have put substantial care and effort into the creation of our house plans. We authorize the use of our plans on the express condition that you strictly comply with all local building codes, zoning requirements and other applicable laws, regulations and ordinances. However, because we cannot provide on-site consultation, supervision or control over the actual construction and because of the great variance in local building requirements, building practices and soil, seismic, weather and other conditions, WE CANNOT MAKE ANY WARRANTY, EXPRESS OR IMPLIED, WITH RESPECT TO THE CONTENT OR USE OF OUR PLANS, INCLUDING, BUT IS NOT LIMITED TO, ANY WARRANTY OF MARKETABILITY OR OF FITNESS FOR A PARTICULAR PURPOSE. Please note that floor plans included in this magazine are not construction documents and are subject to change. Renderings are an artist's concept only.

from Sater Design Collection, Inc.

1-800-718-7526
www.saterdesign.com

what is a license?

**CONSIDERATIONS IN ORDERING
A SATER DESIGN PLAN.**

PRINT LICENSE

This license is issued in the form of a single vellum set of plan prints. The licensee is entitled to customize and build one time only.

ELECTRONIC LICENSE

This license is issued in the form of an electronic (AutoCAD or PDF) files. The licensee is entitled to customize and build one time only.

HOW TO ORDER

**ORDER BY PHONE
1-800-718-7526**

ORDER ONLINE
www.saterdesign.com

SATER DESIGN COLLECTION
25241 Elementary Way, Suite 102
Bonita Springs, FL 34135

WHAT SETS A SATER PLAN APART?

In order to ensure that your home is built to look just as spectacular as the homes shown in this magazine, we have created highly detailed construction drawings. Our plans are the ultimate guide to building the home of your dreams. Some of the features that you'll find in Sater plans, but not other plans, are:

	SATER	OTHERS
Extensive Interior Elevations *Interior design-quality drawings, showing highly detailed elevations of architectural built-ins and cabinetry*	YES	NO
Detailed Materials List *To assist the owner and builder with estimating building costs (Some offer this for a fee, but with us it's free!)*	YES	NO
Reflected Ceiling Plans *With detailed sections of the numerous ceiling and soffit designs*	YES	NO
Separate Electrical Plans *Carefully designed lighting plans that contemplate your family's use and enjoyment*	YES	NO
Green Brochure *To help you make decisions about implementing green building practices in your home's construction .*	YES	NO
Unparalleled Customer Support *Our dedicated staff is committed to helping you in the decision process*	YES	NO

PLAN CUSTOMIZATION SERVICES

If you want to tweak the plan to better suit you and your family, we certainly understand and hope you'll let us make the changes for you. That way we can ensure that the plan with the changes is just as beautiful as the plan before the changes and that all changes are properly made. Call 1-800-718-7526 to speak with a customer service representative about your needs, we're happy to help!

We DO NOT sell photography shown in this book for any purpose.
Prices of plans are subject to change without notice.